Rebels with Applause

Broadway's Groundbreaking Musicals

Scott Miller

ON REFERENCE

HEINEMANN ■ Portsmouth, NH

Heinemann

A division of Reed Elsevier Inc.

361 Hanover Street

Portsmouth, NH 03801–3912

www.heinemanndrama.com

Offices and agents throughout the world

The author and publisher wish to thank those who have generously given permission to reprint borrowed material:

"The Miracle Song," "Simple," "Come Play Wiz Me," "I've Got You to Lean On," and "There's a Parade in Town" by Stephen Sondheim. Copyright © 1964 (Renewed) Stephen Sondheim (ASCAP). Burthen Music Company, Inc. (ASCAP) Owner of Publication and Allied Rights throughout the World. Chappell & Co. (ASCAP) Sole Selling Agent. All Rights Reserved. Used by Permission of Warner Bros. Publications U.S. Inc., Miami, FL 33014.

Lyrics from *Jacques Brel Is Alive and Well and Living in Paris* by Eric Blau. Reprinted by permission of Eric Blau. All Rights Reserved.

Lyrics from *The Ballad of Little Mikey* by Mark Savage. Reprinted by permission of Mark Savage. All Rights Reserved.

Lyrics from *Songs for a New World* by Jason Robert Brown. Reprinted by permission of Jason Robert Brown. All Rights Reserved.

"The Ballad of Floyd Collins," "It Moves," and "The Dream" words and music by Adam Guettel. Copyright © 1997 Matthew Music (ASCAP) (administered by Williamson Music throughout the World). International Copyright Secured. All Rights Reserved. Reprinted by Permission.

"The Riddle Song" words by Adam Guettel and Tina Landau, music by Adam Guettel. Copyright © 1997 Matthew Music (ASCAP) (administered by Williamson Music throughout the World). International Copyright Secured. All Rights Reserved. Reprinted by Permission.

Library of Congress Cataloging-in-Publication Data

Miller, Scott, 1964–

    Rebels with applause : Broadway's groundbreaking musicals / Scott Miller.

       p.   cm.

    Contents: The cradle will rock—Pal Joey—Oklahoma!—Anyone can whistle—Hair—Jacques Brel is alive and well and living in Paris—The ballad of Little Mikey—Songs for a new world—Floyd Collins—Rent.

      ISBN 0-325-00357-2 (pbk.)

      1. Musicals — History and criticism. 2. Musicals — Social aspects — United States. 3. Musicals — Political aspects — United States. I. Title.

ML2054 .M55 2001

782.1'4'097471—dc21

ON REFERENCE

2001016964

Editor: Lisa A. Barnett

Production: Vicki Kasabian

Cover design: Jenny Jensen Greenleaf

Manufacturing: Steve Bernier

Printed in the United States of America on acid-free paper

05   04   03   02   01   VP   1   2   3   4   5

This book is dedicated to my parents, Joan Zobel and Don Miller,
who ignited my love for musicals,
and to all my friends who put up with me
talking about this stuff all the time.

Also by Scott Miller

From Assassins to West Side Story:
The Director's Guide to Musical Theatre

Deconstructing Harold Hill:
An Insider's Guide to Musical Theatre

In the Blood
a novel

Contents

Acknowledgments

My deep thanks to my editor, Lisa A. Barnett, who keeps giving me the chance to do what I love most, think and talk about musicals, and share that passion with others. She was the first to give me an outlet for my ideas and that has opened so many other doors for me. My thanks to Steve Spiegel and Jim Merillat at Music Theatre International and to Bert Fink at the Rodgers and Hammerstein Organization, for their great generosity and help. A very big thank-you to all my friends on the Sondheim Internet discussion list (the smartest people in cyberspace) and my friends on the *Hair* Internet discussion list, whose information and inspiration have helped me immeasurably. Most of all, thanks to the people of the St. Louis area for supporting New Line Theatre, an alternative musical theatre company that couldn't survive in most cities, which has allowed me to do the work that informs everything I write.

verture

With my first two books on musical theatre, *From Assassins to West Side Story* and *Deconstructing Harold Hill,* I was occasionally criticized for allowing my social and political views to pop up here and there in my discussions of musicals. Well, I am guilty as charged. I freely admit it, and I have never figured out why that's a bad thing. Hallie Flanagan, who was the head of the Federal Theatre Project in the 1930s, once said, "Theatre, at its best, is always dangerous." And, I would add, it's always political.

How can I discuss *Assassins* or *Cabaret* without talking about politics? How can I discuss *Les Misérables* or *Carousel* or *Ragtime* without talking about social issues? And why would I want to? Any good musical—or play or movie or novel, for that matter—is about important issues, either on the surface or more subtextually, and there's no reason to pretend otherwise. Instead of shying away from this fact, we should celebrate it. Musical theatre isn't some ancient, dusty, irrelevant invalid; it's a thriving, vigorous art form that gives us an exciting forum in which to talk about our world and try to figure things out. After all, why bother doing *Carousel* or *Camelot* if its issues don't speak to our times as well as to its own?

Among other things, *Carousel* is about spousal abuse. *Camelot* is about the dangerous mixing of the personal and the political. *Chicago* is about corruption in the media and the justice system. *Assassins* is about political dissent. *Pippin* is about the lack of direction among young people. All of these things are just as vitally important today as they were when these shows were written. And the musicals discussed in this book are the same. *The Cradle Will Rock* is about corruption in government, religion, business, and art. *Oklahoma!* is about violence and sexual abuse. *Anyone Can Whistle* is about government-imposed conformity and political corruption. *Floyd Collins* is about family and God. *Jacques Brel* is about war, social issues, and politics. *Hair* is about racism, violence, sexuality, religion, politics, and consumerism.

Unfortunately, there are a lot of people who think musical theatre *is* an ancient, dusty invalid—even people who love musicals. Even Stephen Sondheim, the most brilliant musical theatre artist alive today, said in a recent *New York Times* interview that musical theatre is dead. But I think he's wrong. And this book is proof. Not only does it include chapters on brilliant musicals of the past—*The Cradle Will Rock* (1937), *Pal Joey* (1940), and *Oklahoma!* (1943)—but it also includes chapters about brilliant musicals from the last few years—*Songs for a New World* (1995), *Floyd Collins* (1996), and *Rent* (1996).

Perhaps part of the reason Sondheim thinks musical theatre is dead is because both Broadway and off Broadway, where he works, have become so commercialized that it's nearly impossible for innovative new work to get produced there. But dozens of brilliant new musicals are being produced around the country in regional theatres every year and one of those is included here too—*The Ballad of Little Mikey*, a show that has had great success in Los Angeles, Chicago, St. Louis, San Francisco, and across the United States, even though it's too edgy for Broadway.

As a result, we mostly see revivals of older shows on Broadway, many of them the brainless, excuse-for-a-big-dance-number kind of musicals in which the characters serve the songs instead of the other way around, in which the choreography is there to dazzle rather than to tell the story or reveal character.

But despite Broadway's current cowardice, live theatre is still among the most powerful tools for social and political change in the world today, partly because it's sneaky; it does its job without its audience noticing. But it's also partly because it's nonthreatening. People go to see *Carousel*, an "old-fashioned musical," and come out having unknowingly participated in a discussion of the lasting effects of spousal abuse. People see *Camelot* and come out thinking about Bill Clinton and Monica Lewinsky. People see *Ragtime* and come out thinking about race relations in America.

Admittedly, there are still a lot of people who just don't think serious issues have any place in musicals because they think musical theatre is a silly and trivial art form. After all, they tell me, real people don't just break into song in everyday life. (They don't know some of my friends.) And this antinaturalism is more than they can handle, so they just stay away from the ridiculous conventions of musicals altogether.

I wonder if those people went to see any of the *Star Wars* movies. After all, I don't know any real people in everyday life who have a light saber or a wookie. I wonder if those people watch sitcoms. I don't know any real people in everyday life—aside from some of my friends—who have a live studio audience or, worse yet, a laugh track. Tom Hanks was once on David Letterman's show declaring that he doesn't like musicals because it's so silly the way characters break into song. Yet falling in love with a mermaid or suddenly turning from twelve years old to thirty years old isn't silly at all, right?

What all these simpleminded complainers don't seem to understand is that *all* art is artificial. God makes lousy theatre, as the saying goes. Art makes order out of the chaos of the real world. Art arranges real life so that it's easier to see and understand certain things. Singing is just the language of musical theatre the way the soliloquy is the language of Shakespeare, the way special effects are the language of sci-fi, fantasy, and horror films, the way paint is the language of da Vinci, Monet, and Picasso.

Why is one pretense better than another? Why is one language better than another? What's important is how that language is *used* to explore—not re-create—the real world, the issues that we care about, our fears and joys and triumphs. Musicals can do that every bit as effectively as nonmusicals. Some people would even argue that musicals do that *more* effectively because music can better explore the abstract emotional terrain of the human heart, because music can communicate extreme emotion better than mere words (which is why I still think *West Side Story* is better theatre than *Romeo and Juliet*). What's important is that art in any form communicates with its audience. What's important is that people come out *thinking*—about themselves, their lives, the world around them.

Also important is that the artists creating the show are thinking. And that's what this book is about. As with my first two books, I'm not asking you to agree with everything I say—after all, art is by its nature subjective—but I am challenging you to think about musicals more seriously and more fully than you ever have before. And I'm also challenging you, whether you're a theatre artist or an audience member, to demand intelligence, innovation, and adventurousness from our musical theatre, this most American of all art forms, wherever you encounter it, in high schools, in community centers, in small professional companies, in regional theatres, and on Broadway. We owe it to the art form, to ourselves, and to one another.

This book is like my first two books in that it analyzes and discusses a group of really good, really interesting musicals. But it's different in one important way: every musical discussed in this book is a groundbreaker, a show that changed the rules, that took big risks, that made people look at musicals differently. And though my first two books were arranged alphabetically, this book is arranged chronologically, which makes it a kind of guided walking tour of the history of innovation in musical theatre, and therefore, a history of the art form itself.

We start with the very political *The Cradle Will Rock*, a show that elevated musical theatre into the realm of the socially conscious theatre of the 1930s; then move on to *Pal Joey*, which forced musical comedy to grow up and bridged the gap between musical comedy and serious musicals; then *Oklahoma!*, which began the Rodgers and Hammerstein revolution that changed everything that came after; *Anyone Can Whistle*, the first of the Sondheim musicals that was truly "Sondheim" in its innovation and its focus on social issues; *Hair*, the show that brought real rock music and devices of the 1960s experimental theatre movement to Broadway for the first time; *Jacques Brel*, the first fully plotless, nonlinear concept musical; *The Ballad of Little Mikey*, a gay musical that bridged the gap between old-fashioned "gay-angst" plays and the new generation of gay work; *Songs for a New World*, a concept musical for the 1990s from one of the most important voices of Broadway's future, Jason Robert Brown; *Floyd Collins*, an important work that took huge leaps in subject matter and presentation style, from another of the most important voices of Broadway's future, Adam Guettel; and *Rent*, which brought real rock music back to Broadway after a long absence, making the Broadway musical truly populist again, a show that has already changed the face of Broadway in many ways.

There are so many people who don't respect musical theatre, directors who butcher scripts and scores, who add schtick, cut songs, rewrite dialogue, things they'd *never* do to a play, and all because they don't think musicals are "real" or "serious" theatre, because they think they know better than Stephen Sondheim, Hal Prince, or Lerner and Loewe how to make a musical. I hope that this book, in concert with my other two, will reverse that trend, will demonstrate to people how magnificent, how complex, how sophisticated, and how worthy of respect most musicals are. Musical theatre is one of America's only indigenous art forms, perhaps our country's greatest cultural gift to the world, and it deserves nothing less than our greatest respect and our greatest love.

1   The Cradle Will Rock

Book, music, and lyrics by Marc Blitzstein
Originally directed on Broadway by Orson Welles
Licensed by Tams-Witmark Music Library

I n 1947, the *New York Times* said that *The Cradle Will Rock* "has quali-
ties of genius . . . It catches fire, it blazes, it amuses and grips the
listener." It's both a wonderful musical and a remarkable piece of
theatre history. If someone didn't already know the work of its composer, Marc Blitzstein, he might say the score sounds like Kurt Weill
mixed with Stephen Sondheim, maybe with a little Kander and Ebb
sprinkled on top. Of course, *Cradle* came twenty years before Sondheim's first musical and nearly thirty years before Kander and Ebb's
first big hit. Blitzstein called his show "a labor opera composed in a
style that falls somewhere between realism, romance, vaudeville,
comic strip, Gilbert and Sullivan, Brecht, and agitprop." It was the
first American musical from a working-class perspective. It laid the
groundwork, in its politics and its episodic construction, for later
shows as varied as *Cabaret, Hair, Pippin, Chicago, Assassins,* and *Rent.*
And like *Chicago,* it is thoroughly of its time and yet it doesn't feel
dated. There are just as many whores in politics, religion, academia,
and the arts today as there were in the 1930s. As televangelists continue to make millions and live in gilded mansions, as politicians
continue to receive gifts and campaign contributions from giant cor-
porations, foreign powers, and other special interests, *The Cradle Will
Rock* will always seem as if it could have been written last year.

It was the first musical comedy Marc Blitzstein ever wrote, even
though he was already, at age thirty-two, an internationally respected
classical composer and music commentator. Completed in only five
weeks, its subject matter is very serious and yet it lives in a world of

cartoon characters and melodrama. It's one of the funniest musicals of the 1930s, but even though the audience laughs at all the characters, Blitzstein somehow manages to create an emotional investment that pays off in the show's very passionate, very dramatic ending. Its politics are communist and unionist, yet it is unmistakably an American musical comedy and it still today holds a place of honor in musical theatre history. It's the kind of theatre for which the term *agitprop* (condensed from "agitational propaganda theatre") was invented, and yet, even though it is heavy-handed and didactic, and even though its motives are altogether transparent, it is still a funny, thoroughly entertaining musical, appealing precisely because of the honesty about its intentions.

Despite the fact that most people have never seen *The Cradle Will Rock*—or even heard of it—there are, remarkably, five cast recordings: the original 1937 cast, the 1964 off-Broadway cast, the 1983 off-Broadway (and London) cast, the 1994 Los Angeles cast, and the 1999 movie soundtrack. The only other musicals that have that many cast recordings are the big hits like *The Sound of Music* that everybody knows. That *Cradle* has been recorded so many times is a testament to the love so many people feel for the show and to its flexibility, which lends itself so easily to so many interpretations of its hilarious, blistering, angry story.

False Starts

In the fall of 1936, the Actors' Repertory Company in New York agreed to produce Marc Blitzstein's new leftist, unionist musical satire *The Cradle Will Rock*, with John Houseman producing and the twenty-one-year-old wunderkind Orson Welles directing. Blitzstein had been writing serious music for years and was considered one of America's preeminent composers, but this was his first foray into musical comedy. It was an example of the socially conscious work that had taken the theatre world by storm in the middle 1930s, a kind of theatre that the American musical theatre had not yet explored. In the aftermath of the Depression and the subsequent national disillusionment, many theatre artists and some of the theatregoing public had become members of the Communist party. Blitzstein himself was a member of the Communist party and there are indications that *Cradle* had been percolating for a long time. As far back as 1928, he had written a small cantata based on Walt Whitman's lines "Out of the cradle, gently rocking." In 1935, Clifford Odets' pro-union Broadway play *Waiting for Lefty*—with a structure later imitated by *Cradle*—had been successful and had paved the way for more work like it. But only two months after the agreement had been made between Blitzstein and Actors' Repertory Company, the company decided not to produce *Cradle* after all, because of its incendiary politics.

Its politics were incendiary precisely because the issues were so real. In December 1936, autoworkers at the Flint, Michigan, General Motors plant staged a forty-four-day sit-down strike at the urging of the mostly communist union leadership. General Motors finally gave in and recognized the union in February, but Henry Ford hired six hundred armed guards to prevent unionization at the Ford Motor Company. In March 1937, the larger steel companies, known as Big Steel, agreed to their first union contracts. But the smaller steel companies—Little Steel—refused to bargain and recruited the clergy, police, and others to support their fight against the unions. Blitzstein's musical, set in fictional Steeltown, USA, was coming to dangerous life across America, and his fiction was becoming less and less fictional.

Houseman and Welles were now working for Project 891 of the Federal Theatre Project, part of Franklin Roosevelt's Works Progress Administration, and they decided to pick *Cradle* back up. Rehearsals began in March, with two actors in the cast who would later be blacklisted by the House Un-American Activities Committee in Washington, D.C.: Howard Da Silva, who went on to star on Broadway after the blacklists had disappeared, and Will Geer, who would later play Grandpa Walton on TV. The actors were each paid $23.86 a week and the show was scheduled to open May 1, but because of Welles' other commitments, progress was delayed and a new opening was set for June 16. Meanwhile, on May 30, Republic Steel, one of the Little Steels, arranged for the Chicago police to attack union picketers, their wives, and their children, killing three and injuring eighty-four. *Cradle* was getting too close to the truth, or, perhaps, the truth was getting too close to *Cradle*. People in high places were getting nervous.

On June 10, the Federal Theatre Project budget was slashed. Seventeen hundred workers were fired, pickets popped up everywhere, and all openings of new shows were put on hold until July 1, including *The Cradle Will Rock*. Interestingly, though three shows were slated to open before July 1 and should have been shut down, the other two were allowed to open anyway. Only *Cradle* was shut down. Rehearsals continued anyway as Welles and Houseman kept fighting to be allowed to open. The final dress rehearsal on June 15 was a logistical nightmare, with set trouble, missed cues, and other random disasters.

Oh What a Night

On the morning of June 16, opening night, the Federal Theatre Project began calling the press, announcing the cancellation of *The Cradle Will Rock*. Armed guards (Houseman referred to them as Cossacks) were posted at the theatre to make sure no one removed sets, costumes, props, or anything else paid for by the Federal Theatre Project, including actor Howard Da Silva's toupee. Houseman spent the day calling members of the press, telling them the show would indeed open in another theatre, which he still had not found. Actors' Equity, the actors union, informed Welles that as long as the actors in *Cradle* were employees of the Federal Theatre Project, they could not appear on any stage that wasn't officially sanctioned by the project. The musicians union then told Welles that if they moved to another theatre, they could no longer pay their musicians the reduced pay rate allowed for the Federal Theatre Project. Welles and Houseman would have to pay the musicians full union scale, as well as back pay for rehearsals, and they would have to hire more musicians in accordance with the standard Broadway contract. There was no way Welles and Houseman could afford this.

So Welles came up with a plan: the actors would come to the new theatre, wherever it might be, sit in the audience, and when the time came, perform their roles from the house. Of course, many of the actors were not comfortable with this plan, fearing that they might lose their jobs with the Federal Theatre Project.

Still, Welles and Houseman insisted the show could go on, without sets, without lights, without an orchestra, perhaps even without some of the cast. They planned to put Blitzstein onstage at a piano (he was not a member of the musicians union) to play the whole score and even sing some of the parts if necessary. They sent an assistant, Jean Rosenthal, to go find a piano and a truck and just keep driving around Manhattan until they could book another theatre.

By late afternoon, the press and hundreds of ticket holders began gathering outside the theatre. Some of the cast came outside and performed for them to keep them occupied. A few minutes before eight o'clock, a theatre was found—the Venice—twenty-one blocks uptown, for a rental fee of one hundred dollars. They sent the assistant up there with the piano, and they led the crowd, now swelling to even greater numbers, on a twenty-one-block march uptown to the Venice, picking up hundreds more along the way. The show began at 8:50 P.M., with Blitzstein alone onstage and a single follow spot focused on him.

As Blitzstein began singing the first song, he heard a small voice begin to sing along out in the house, and the follow spot swung out in the audience to illuminate Olive Stanton, a novice actress in her first show, who was playing the role of Moll. Slowly, one by one, the actors stood when their cues came and ended up playing the whole show in and among the audience, never venturing onstage. Though most of the cast had come to the Venice, Blitzstein sang eight of the roles that night, while some of the actors doubled up on other roles. Occasionally during the evening, the one musician who had come along, an accordion player, would stand up at his seat and play along with the solo piano. When the finale of the show ended, the audience went wild, cheering and screaming for what seemed like forever. Not only had New York seen the premiere of an exciting new musical by a gifted writer and composer; these lucky people had witnessed the birth of a theatrical legend.

The Cradle Will Rock ran for nineteen performances like that at the Venice Theatre, although the Federal Theatre Project kept telling callers that the show was not running anywhere, and all of the performances were done with the actors out in the audience. The *New York Times* said the show was "written with extraordinary versatility and played with enormous gusto, the best thing militant labor has put into the theatre yet." Brooks Atkinson wrote in the *Times* that the show "raises a theatregoer's metabolism and blows him out of the theatre on the thunder of the grand finale." The *Herald Tribune* called it "a savagely humorous social cartoon with music that hits hard and sardonically." The *New York Post* called it "a propagandistic tour de force." Hallie Flanagan, head of the Federal Theatre Project, defended this controversial show by saying, "The theatre, when it's good, is always dangerous."

Welles resigned from the Federal Theatre Project over the attempted closing of *Cradle* and Houseman was fired for insubordination. Unfazed, they formed the Mercury Theatre and went back to work. During the summer of 1937, they produced *Cradle* all over New York, in outdoor auditoriums, amusement parks, and other unlikely locations, as well as touring to the steel districts of Pennsylvania, Ohio, and elsewhere. In the fall of 1937, Welles and Houseman put together a series of Sunday night performances to enable original cast members now in other shows to participate. This time, Welles put the actors onstage, sitting in three rows of chairs. With the solo piano still onstage, they used the piano as a prop, as a drugstore counter or a judge's bench. Of these performances, *Stage* magazine said, "Remarkable how, in an entertainment world drugged with manufactured glamour, they conjure Steeltown out of thin air, set it raw and terrible before your eyes." The critics again praised it, even those who had hated it just a few months before. Still, some held out. George Jean Nathan wrote that it was "little more than the kind of thing Cole Porter might have written if, God forbid, he had gone to Columbia instead of Yale."

In December, Welles presented a radio production of the show. The show opened for a proper Broadway run on January 3, 1938, and ran 108 performances. Although still using only solo piano, the producers were forced by the musicians union to pay ten musicians *not* to play each night. Blitzstein chose ten of his neediest friends for the job. Though *The Band Wagon* had been the first musical to record a cast album, *Cradle* was actually the first cast album to be released.

In June of 1938, amateur rights were released and radical groups around the country began producing *Cradle*. It was the first racially integrated show ever to play the South. The Chicago production featured journalist Studs Terkel as Editor Daily. In May 1939, Harvard senior Leonard Bernstein directed and accompanied a performance of *Cradle* on the Harvard campus, with his fifteen-year-old sister, Shirley, as the prostitute Moll. A local city council member called for the chief of police to investigate the "Reds" at Harvard who had put on this "indecent" show. The show was revived in New York in 1947 in a concert presentation at City Center—the first time the orchestrations were used—conducted by Bernstein with several of the original leads. It was then produced later that year on Broadway, starring Alfred Drake as Larry Foreman and Vivian Vance as Mrs. Mister, running a mere thirty-four performances. It was revived again by the New York City Opera in February 1960, staged by Howard Da Silva, who had created the role of Larry Foreman. In November 1964, it was revived off Broadway in a production starring Jerry Orbach and directed again by Da Silva. It was revived again off Broadway in 1983, this time with Patti LuPone as Moll and directed by John Houseman. This production toured the United States, played the Old Vic in London, and was videotaped for PBS.

Politics and Poker

The political atmosphere in America in 1937 was ripe for a show like *The Cradle Will Rock*. In 1936 there was no hint of unionism at U.S. Steel, but by February 1937, just five months before *Cradle*'s premiere, the steelworkers had unionized and U.S. Steel had signed a collective bargaining agreement. In response to this new movement, antilabor organizations were springing up all over America, with patriotic names that hid their real agendas, names like the Liberty League, the Citizen's Alliances, and others in the same vein. In early drafts of *Cradle*, Blitzstein had injected more reality into his story, giving characters real names rather than the morality play labels that he used in the final draft. Mr. Mister was originally named Mr. Morgan, after millionaire J. P. Morgan, and Larry Foreman was named John L. Lewis, after the head of the CIO.

Labor strikes were becoming an everyday occurrence in America, many of them violent and bloody. In a confrontation over a strike at Standard Oil, nineteen men, women, and children were murdered by company guards. The thirties was a decade of incomparable battles between the new unions and company owners. In 1932, the California pea pickers, the airline pilots, the autoworkers, and the coal workers all organized into unions. In 1933, California farm workers, New Mexican miners, and workers at Detroit Tool and Die and Hormel Meat Packing Company organized. In 1934, textile workers, farm workers, rubber workers, and longshoremen organized. In 1935 and 1936, American saw the organization of metalworkers in the Midwest, lumberjacks in the Pacific Northwest, southern sharecroppers and farm workers, and seamen, as well as the first sit-down strikes at Bendix, General Motors, and Firestone Rubber. The *Detroit News* declared that sit-down strikes had replaced baseball as the national pastime. In 1934, the U.S. Supreme Court ruled that Roosevelt's National Industrial Recovery Act was unconstitutional, taking away from American workers the right they had been given to organize and bargain collectively. But Congress passed the new National Labor Relations Act to re-create the right to collectively bargain.

From Russia with Love

In addition to all this, thousands of Americans were joining the Communist party in the 1930s and it's not hard to see why. One day, everything's fine, everybody loves democracy, and all's right with the world. The next day, the stock market crashes, people lose their life savings, and unemployment skyrockets from less than half a million to about four million in two months, eventually reaching a whopping sixteen million within a few years. So many people lost everything they had— money, businesses, families. The suicide rate leapt. Many people stopped believing in democracy. It had failed them. The promises of communism—the redistribution of wealth, expansive rights for workers—were very seductive. Some historians believe that if it hadn't been for Roosevelt's New Deal programs like the Federal Theatre, the American Communist party would have grown even stronger than it did. Many famous artists, actors, directors, writers, composers, and poets were members of the party and began to create aggressively leftist art. Years later, both Howard Da Sliva (who played Larry Foreman) and Will Geer (Mr. Mister) would be called by Senator Joseph McCarthy before the House Un-American Activities Committee and because they would refuse to cooperate by naming names, they would be blacklisted in Hollywood for many years. It was in this atmosphere, in which democracy was suffering a severe PR problem, that Blitzstein wrote *The Cradle Will Rock*.

Hallie's Comet

Into the mix came Hallie Flanagan. Under the leadership of Flanagan, the groundbreaking, history-making Federal Theatre Project hit the ground running. The Federal Theatre was part of the vast U.S. government emergency relief program during the Depression called the Works Progress Administration (WPA). The purpose of the WPA and the Federal Theatre Project—as far as the government was concerned—was to create jobs to put unemployed Americans back to work. WPA projects included dams, highways, thousands of buildings, and lots of other construction. The Federal Theatre Project was one of the arts programs in the WPA, along with the Federal Music Project, the Federal Art Project, and the Federal Writers Project, all putting artists to work. In fact, during its short four-year existence, the Federal Theatre, with a budget of $6.7 million, gave work to 40,000 theatre artists, including directors Elia Kazan, Sidney Lumet, and Orson Welles; actors Burt Lancaster, E. G. Marshal, Gene Kelly, Joseph Cotton, and Arlene Francis; and dozens of designers, stage managers, stagehands, and so many others.

But the project's director, Hallie Flanagan, had two other goals as well. She wanted to create theatre that was closer to the real lives of ordinary Americans, theatre that dealt with real-world issues and presented realistic portrayals of everyday Americans. She also wanted to create a "national theatre" that would reach millions of people across the country who had never seen live theatre before. The Federal Theatre was the incubator for lots of very brave, very political, and experimental work, as well as reinvented classics, puppet theatre, children's theatre, black theatre, soviet theatre, touring theatre, vaudeville, radio theatre, dance, and much more. The Federal Theatre reached twenty-five million Americans during its four years, about 25 percent of the American public, most of whom had never before seen live theatre. It was one of the largest, most influential theatre projects in the history of the world. It was also the only time the U.S. government was directly responsible for producing theatre. The Federal Theatre was specifically designed to create theatre so vital to community life in towns across America that theatre projects and companies would continue after the Federal Theatre had ended.

Many of the Federal Theatre projects were like nothing anyone had seen before. For instance, Orson Welles, at this point only twenty-one years old, directed a Federal Theatre production of *Macbeth* set in Haiti with an all-black cast, known as the "voodoo *Macbeth*," at a theatre in Harlem. Like many of the Federal Theatre productions, it was an enormous hit, bringing Broadway critics and audiences to Harlem to see the remarkable show. After a seven-month New York run, it went on a nationwide tour. One Federal Theatre play, *It Can't Happen Here*, opened in twenty-four cities in seventeen states, all on the same night, creating for the first time a genuine national theatre. But the works created by the Federal Theatre were often political lightning rods. One children's theatre piece, *Revolt of the Beavers*, about a group of beavers plotting to overthrow a ruthless beaver king to achieve equality for all, was so controversial (it was called communistic) that it was shut down after one month. Brooks Atkinson wrote in the *New York Times*, "Mother Goose is no longer a rhymed escapist. She has been studying Marx; Jack and Jill lead the class revolution." The play was directed by Elia Kazan, who would go on to direct *A Streetcar Named Desire, Cat on a Hot Tin Roof, Death of a Salesman*, and other great American plays. Kazan would also go on to name names in front of the House Un-American Activities Committee and ruin the careers of many of his colleagues.

Give My Regards to Broadway

Except for the anomaly of the socially conscious *Show Boat* in 1927, Broadway musicals had not yet matured. Unlike the very serious, socially conscious theatre going on around them, musicals were still silly, inconsequential, largely nonsensical stories constructed around (hopefully) hit songs. There were two trajectories Broadway musicals were on at the turn of the century, one toward operettas with exotic locales, royalty, and fantasy, and the second toward very American, lightweight, romantic comedies. George M. Cohan had set Broadway on the second path and set the stage for most of what was to come in American musical theatre. The First World War generated enough anti-German sentiment that it effectively killed the first path toward operetta.

In the decade before *The Cradle Will Rock*, the standard fare on Broadway was shows like *Hit the Deck!, Good News!, Whoopee, Girl Crazy, Anything Goes,* and *Babes in Arms*. There were exceptions, of course, including the racially charged *Show Boat*, the Gershwins' savagely funny political satire *Of Thee I Sing*, and the "folk opera" *Porgy and Bess*. The prolabor revue *Pins and Needles* opened a few months after *Cradle* and included one sketch by Blitzstein. But it would be several years before musical comedy would take a giant step forward with *Oklahoma!* in 1943. What makes *Cradle* a little less surprising than it would have been otherwise is that Blitzstein was not a musical comedy composer. He was a serious concert and opera composer with a clear social and political agenda, a composer who was already working in a different tradition, and he was already at the center of the political, socially conscious, groundbreaking, rule-busting art of the 1930s. That he would write a musical like *Cradle* makes perfect sense in retrospect.

Mister Family

The characters in *The Cradle Will Rock* are archetypes, universal personalities, but they are also very specific, very carefully drawn individuals. Blitzstein gives them real, compelling lives and that's what gives the audience an emotional stake in the action, lending the finale a much more powerful wallop than it would have otherwise had.

Just as Moll is the audience's stand-in, the newcomer who knows nothing, Harry Druggist is our guide through the social minefield of Steeltown. He is also Steeltown's own King Lear, his son dead, his life in ashes, on the edge of insanity, only now able to see with clarity what's going on around him. A druggists union was being formed as Blitzstein wrote the show, and labor organizer Tom Mooney had been imprisoned since 1916 on a frame-up over an explosion, much like the drugstore scene in the show.

The Reverend Salvation is reminiscent of the popular evangelist Billy Sunday, who had entered politics by preaching that Christians should hate the Germans during World War I. Like more contemporary evangelists Pat Robertson and Jerry Falwell, the Reverend Salvation leaves God behind when politics and religion come into conflict. Here again, *Cradle*'s relevance to modern-day America is both amazing and disturbing.

Of the hero, Larry Foreman, Blitzstein wrote, "He's not very good-looking—a humorous face and an engaging manner. Confidence is there, too; not self-confidence; a kind of knowledge about the way things probably have to work out. It gives him a surprising modesty and a young poise." The leaflet scene in *Cradle* echoed similar scenes in Brecht's play *Mother* and a 1934 Soviet film called *Maxim's Youth*, which also had a scene in which a worker is mashed by a machine, like Blitzstein's unseen character Joe Worker. Ella Hammer, Joe Worker's sister, was originally to be paired with a pro-union farmer named Sickle, as symbols (hammer and sickle) of what Blitzstein thought was the superior social system in the Soviet Union.

Dauber and Yasha, the two sycophantic artists, are particularly funny when you know Blitzstein's early career. Their philosophy of "Art for Art's Sake" was, in fact, Blitzstein's philosophy when he was younger, though he later discarded it. Was he making fun of himself or did he not see the connection? Was he commenting on his own prostitution? He was certainly aware of the problem in 1936, when he wrote, "We composers are the tools of a vicious economic setup.

The unconscious (sometimes not so unconscious) prostitution in today's world is one of the sorry sights to see." In some productions of *Cradle* during his lifetime, Blitzstein explicitly called for these characters to be played as gay, which may also be some indication that they were meant to represent a younger Blitzstein. Also, the characters of Mr. Mister and his family are particularly funny when you consider that Blitzstein's own family was made up of bankers, that, in fact, Blitzstein himself grew up in a life of relative privilege.

Rock Music

The Cradle Will Rock departed greatly from both operetta and musical comedy. It departed from opera and operetta by dramatizing ordinary people in ordinary situations and it departed from musical comedy in treating those ordinary people and their lives seriously. But Blitzstein wasn't just writing about unions and the prostitution of the professional classes; he was also commenting on American music itself and the ways in which it can be used and prostituted.

The show was meant to be a workers story, a new kind of theatre—and music—for the people. Blitzstein sought out untrained singers—just listen to the awful singing on much of the 1937 cast album—to avoid the falseness of an operatic sound. He wanted these characters to sound like real people. Brecht called his style of singing *misuk*. Because of that first performance at the Venice theatre, the show was almost always performed with only solo piano, often with the actors out in the house, forever annihilating the separation of actor and audience, forever discarding the suspension of disbelief that most theatre asks for. This was a show that admitted its artifice. Following in the philosophical footsteps of Brecht, though perhaps accidentally, the show denied the audience members the comfort of escapism, never allowing them to get lost in the "reality" of the story. Instead, the show constantly reminded the audience that this was a show, that these were actors, forcing the audience to react intellectually as well as emotionally. *Cradle* became what Brecht called a *Lehrstück*, a piece of music that teaches its audience.

Blitzstein's score uses American pop music but elevates it, complicates it, twists it, and adds dissonance and chromaticism to suggest that things aren't as simple or happy as pop songs paint them. There's always something "wrong" with this pop music, this moment, this sentiment, as demonstrated in the song "Croon Spoon," in which the melody keeps hitting "wrong" notes. Even the title makes fun of the simplicity and vocabulary of pop songs. This is a song that ridicules itself and the characters who sing it. And giving this song to the lazy, spoiled Mister siblings, Blitzstein suggests that mindless pop music has no legitimate purpose in society. Likewise, the song "Honolulu" is a parody of the dozens of South Seas songs emerging at this time, as the United States was taking over Hawaii, songs that tried to make it all seem romantic and exotic instead of imperialistic.

Blitzstein uses a number of musical quotations, usually as subtle jokes, throughout the score. He quotes the "Star-Spangled Banner" ("by the dawn's early light") in the middle of the instrumental night court theme that recurs many times throughout the show. He quotes Bach in the Reverend Salvation's sermons. And Mrs. Mister's Pierce Arrow horn is a quote from Beethoven's overture to Goethe's play *Egmont*. Blitzstein is showing us with this musical quote how rich people can debase art by throwing money at it without any genuine appreciation for it, a significant theme in the movie version of *Cradle*.

The Reel Story

Tim Robbins' magnificent 1999 film *Cradle Will Rock* tells the story of Blitzstein's musical (interestingly, before he died, Orson Welles was trying to raise financing for a film about *Cradle*'s historic first performance) and the movie places the musical in a social and political context, but like Stephen Sondheim's experimental musical *Assassins*, Robbins' movie aims for thematic and psychological truth more than historical accuracy. In fact, the film begins with the words "A (mostly) true story." Robbins plays fast and loose with a number of historical facts and brings together events that actually happened years apart to reveal a larger context for Blitzstein's remarkable musical. Robbins is not making a documentary. Not only is he not interested in the accuracy of minor facts, but he is very much interested in making an entertaining movie. And he uses the conventions of the time to paint his pictures, using the devices of the screwball comedies of the 1930s and classic films by Frank Capra, Preston Sturges, and their contemporaries.

Tim Robbins uses the ghosts of German director/playwright Bertolt Brecht and Blitzstein's wife, Eva. In Robbins' movie, Brecht and Eva appear to Blitzstein, talk to him, make suggestions, and offer criticisms of his musical. Again, Robbins is not suggesting that Blitzstein saw ghosts; this is a dramatic device to show the influence of these two people on Blitzstein and his work. In real life, Eva read almost everything Blitzstein wrote. Though he was gay and their marriage was largely nonphysical, she was his muse and his most strident critic. Even though she had died by the time he wrote *Cradle*, her influence over him and his work no doubt continued.

Similarly, though Blitzstein had harshly criticized the work of Brecht and composer Kurt Weill early in his career, he later came to admire their work and even emulate it. In fact, *The Cradle Will Rock* owes a great debt to Brecht and Weill, especially in its eventual bare-bones presentation style. Blitzstein actually met Brecht in 1936 and played for him the prostitute's song, "Nickel Under the Foot," before any plans were made for the musical into which the song was eventually put. Brecht was quite impressed with the song and told Blitzstein that he should write a piece about *all* kinds of prostitution, not just the literal kind—the prostitution of the press, the church, the courts, the arts, government, and money. The idea would percolate in Blitzstein's brain for months before Brecht's suggestion would inspire the creation of *The Cradle Will Rock*. Soon after, Blitzstein heard Brecht and Weill's song "Pirate Jenny" from *The Threepenny Opera* and he loved it. When Blitzstein wrote *Cradle*, he dedicated it to Brecht. So it makes good dramatic sense in Robbins' film to dramatize Brecht's influence by having his ghost hanging over Blitzstein's shoulder, making suggestions, challenging him, ridiculing the cheap, easy moment, and pushing Blitzstein to be the best he can be.

Robbins also ties his movie to the stage musical thematically. The musical is about prostitution in various professions, the prostitution of the clergy, the press, artists, doctors, merchants, educators, and others, all set against the one *actual* prostitute, Moll, who is drawn with more integrity than any of the "respectable" characters. Robbins riffs on this theme by zooming in and focusing even more specifically on the prostitution of various kinds of artists. In the film, the painter Diego Rivera prostitutes himself to Nelson Rockefeller, the ventriloquist Tommy Crickshaw prostitutes himself by agreeing to tutor no-talent kids in exchange for a performing job, and the Italian Margherita Sarfatti prostitutes her national art treasures by selling masterpieces by da Vinci and Michelangelo to rich Americans in order to finance Mussolini's war machine. Just as famous artists of the past prostituted themselves (though some might call that too harsh) by securing royal patrons and dedicating their works to these moneyed folks, the same thing happens in the *Cradle Will Rock* film. To underline that point in one scene, Robbins presents the rich characters costumed as royalty of the past at a costume ball to benefit the Metropolitan Museum of Art. These rich men discuss how they can control and shape with their money the kind of art that is created in America. It's both a funny juxtaposition and a chilling moment because, to an extent, it's true. They do have the power to shape what is seen and, therefore, what is created.

The other parallel in the movie is the use of one label-name like those Blitzstein uses in the musical. In the stage show, Blitzstein calls his characters names like Mr. Mister, Harry Druggist, Reverend Salvation, Editor Daily, Dr. Specialist, the immigrants Gus and Sadie Polock, the oppressed worker Ella Hammer, and the union organizer Larry Foreman. He even names the painter Dauber, a label referring to an amateurish painter, and he names the musician Yasha, after the famous violinist Jascha Heifetz. Similarly, Robbins sneaks one label-name into his movie, so subtly that most people probably don't even notice. He calls one of his few fictional characters in the film, a rich businessman, Gray Mathers, a pun on *gray matter*, a hint that Mathers is a very smart, very successful businessman but has no aesthetic sense, no heart. He clearly couldn't care less about the da Vinci painting he buys from Margherita Sarfatti. His world is a cultural wasteland and the matters he deals with are gray and colorless.

One of Tim Robbins' most brilliant moves during filming of the movie was to save the shooting of the history-making, opening night renegade *Cradle* performance until the end of the shooting schedule. Before starting, he explained to the audience of extras the background of the event but did not tell them about the actors performing the show out in the house. Instead, he let the surprise of Olive Stanton rising to sing the first song register naturally on the audience. As the show proceeded, he just let the audience members react naturally to each surprise and found that they laughed and cheered and applauded just as their 1937 counterparts did, sometimes in completely unexpected places. The incredible excitement of the evening built realistically and actor Hank Azaria, who played Blitzstein, said it was a night he will never forget.

Of course, the strangest things in the movie are all real. There really was a children's musical called *Revolt of the Beavers*, and it really did cause an uproar and get the hostile reviews quoted in the movie. Hazel

Huffman, the disgruntled Federal Theatre worker, was also real. In real life, she was fired from the Federal Theatre for opening and reading Hallie Flanagan's mail, after which she testified before the House Un-American Activities Committee with no real evidence but plenty of allegations against Flanagan of "communist sympathies." The testimony by other witnesses of "racial mixing" in the Federal Theatre was also real and caused great upset among Southern congressmen.

The funeral procession for Crickshaw's ventriloquist dummy at the end of the film really happened but in another context. In real life, it happened at the end of the last performance of Yasha Frank's *Pinocchio* in Los Angeles (the show that inspired Walt Disney to make the animated feature), and it didn't really happen until June 1939, when the announcement was made that the Federal Theatre Project was being shut down.

Other Resources

There are five cast recordings of *The Cradle Will Rock*. The most dramatic and funniest of them is the 1994 Los Angeles cast album. It conveys the biting satire and wacky humor of the show better than any other recording. The original 1937 cast album is almost too painful to listen to. Many members of the original cast were terrible singers and the sound quality is poor, even though it's been put on CD. It's interesting to hear for historical purposes but isn't easy on the ears. Both the 1964 and the 1983 off-Broadway cast albums are strong but not as much fun as the 1994 recording. The 1999 movie soundtrack contains only part of the score, but it has some excellent performances, most notably Audra McDonald's rendition of "Joe Worker." The videotape of the film *Cradle Will Rock* is commercially available and beautifully portrays the incredible excitement of that first night, as well as the political and social forces in which the show was written and performed. They've also published a nice coffee-table book with the film script and articles on the pertinent historical events, but be careful; some of the historical material contains factual errors.

Some collectors may have a videotape of the PBS broadcast of the 1983 production with Patti LuPone, which is interesting because it was directed by Houseman and apparently re-created the second 1937 production. It also includes Houseman telling the story of that first night. Creative Arts Television in Kent, Connecticut, sells videotapes of various arts-related television programs and it sells one video with three programs about *Cradle*. The first of the three programs features the 1964 cast performing excerpts from the show and an interview with Howard Da Silva, the original Larry Foreman. The other two programs feature interviews with composer Aaron Copland and composer/conductor Leonard Bernstein, both close friends of Blitzstein's; Howard Da Silva; and others, as well as Da Silva performing the title song from *The Cradle Will Rock* and others performing other Blitzstein songs. Eric Gordon's book *Mark the Music: The Life and Work of Marc Blitzstein* is a magnificent biography with tons of detail on *Cradle*. It's out of print at this writing but still pretty easy to find. Also out of print is Hallie Flanagan's book about the Federal Theatre Project, *Arena*, and it's much more difficult to find.

2 Pal Joey

Book by John O'Hara, based on his stories
Music by Richard Rodgers
Lyrics by Lorenz Hart
Originally directed on Broadway by George Abbott
Licensed by Rodgers and Hammerstein Theatre Library

In 1940, musical comedy was about escapism. There had been a few exceptions—*Show Boat* and *The Cradle Will Rock*—but the majority of musicals on Broadway were silly, lightweight comedies about young love, unmotivated dancing, catchy tunes, and fantasy. Looking back, musical theatre historian Ethan Mordden wrote, "With *Pal Joey* . . . we find something even more unlikely than fantasy: real life."

Pal Joey was about casual sex, predatory men, and promiscuous women. Sex had been lurking in musical comedy for a long time, especially in the bawdy songs of Cole Porter, but never before had a musical tackled real sex, recreational sex, cheerfully adulterous sex. This was something new. And though most musical comedy was about romance, never before had a musical been so clearly and exclusively about copulation. Both leading characters wanted very little besides sexual intercourse. It might be fair to say that musical comedy hit puberty with *Pal Joey*, and it would hit maturity three years later with *Oklahoma!*.

Still, it's important to remember that Joey Evans wasn't the first nontraditional leading man. Other musicals had already featured less than heroic heroes, such as Gaylord Ravenal in *Show Boat*, but Ravenal wasn't *Show Boat*'s central character. Until *Pal Joey*, no musical comedy had centered on a genuine scoundrel, and it wouldn't be the last time. Joey's descendants include Billy Bigelow (*Carousel*), J. Pierpont Finch (*How to Succeed*), Harold Hill (*The Music Man*), Franklin Shepard (*Merrily We Roll Along*), Henry Higgins (*My Fair Lady*), Marvin (*March of the Falsettos*), Guido Contini (*Nine*), and others. And it's not only a male phenomenon; there's also Eva Peron (*Evita*) and Norma Desmond (*Sunset Blvd.*). And it all began with Joey.

I Could Write a Book Musical

John O'Hara originally wrote his "Pal Joey" stories for the *New Yorker*, as a series of short pieces in the form of letters written to Pal Ted, a fictional New York bandleader, from Pal Joey, a cheap, usually down-on-his-luck singer. O'Hara approached Rodgers and Hart about turning his stories into a musical. Luckily, O'Hara knew virtually nothing about musicals and he had no idea how utterly wrong his stories were for a musical comedy. Joey was a heel, a cad, a user, and a loser, not the kind of guy that populated musicals. Also luckily, Rodgers and Hart were very interested in O'Hara's idea. Years later, Rodgers wrote, "Not only would the show be different from anything we had ever done before, it would be different from anything anyone else had ever tried. This alone was reason enough for us to want to do it . . . It seemed time to us that musical comedy get out of its cradle and start standing on its own feet. Looking at the facts of life."

So O'Hara wrote an all-new story about Joey, using the *New Yorker* pieces only as background, as a prelude to the action of the musical. A few details remain in the show that refer back to O'Hara's *New Yorker* stories, such as the banker's daughter in Columbus, and this gives Joey a full, real life; he has a detailed past that most musical comedy characters didn't have at the time. And there are two incidents in the show that are from the stories: the scene in front of the pet store window and the interview between Melba and Joey. Aside from that, the material was all new. Most importantly, O'Hara created the rich, bored, oversexed Vera Simpson as Joey's lover and sparring partner.

Pal Joey first opened in 1940, starring Gene Kelly and Vivienne Segal, running a respectable 374 performances. It ran the season, closed for the summer—as shows usually did before air-conditioning—ran three more months, then went on tour until 1942. Richard Watts, of the *New York Herald-Tribune*, called the show "Brilliant, sardonic, strikingly original . . . a hard-boiled delight." But many of the reviews were very negative. Broadway was not ready for Joey yet.

Ten years later, the song "Bewitched" was rediscovered by dance bands and seven different versions of the song made it to the top of the charts. Also, perhaps because of the song's newfound popularity,

Columbia Records producer Goddard Lierberson decided in 1950 to record the whole score for the first time, with Vivienne Segal and Harold Lang. In 1951, composer Jule Styne saw future choreographer Bob Fosse play Joey in a summer stock production and decided to produce a revival of the show. The next year, *Pal Joey* opened again on Broadway with Harold Lang (and Fosse as his understudy) and Vivienne Segal, this time running 540 performances, beating out the original production. By now, audiences were definitely more sophisticated; four Rodgers and Hammerstein shows had opened, and two were still running: *South Pacific* and *The King and I*. Walter Kerr wrote in the *New York Herald-Tribune* that *Pal Joey* was "one of the shrewdest, toughest, and in a way most literate books ever written for musical comedy." In the *New York Post*, Richard Watts said, "*Pal Joey* is definitely an authentic work of art. But it is also great fun, in its strangely savage and sardonic fashion." Watts said the show was "revolutionary in its toughness and scorn for musical comedy sentimentality. To tell the truth, it shocked people because it took as its central figures a kept man and [the] rich woman who kept him, and it didn't molest him with moral disapproval." This lack of moral judgment from the authors is what made so many people uncomfortable with the equally shocking musical *Assassins* in 1991.

After a 1954 London production, a film was made in 1957 with Frank Sinatra, Kim Novak, and Rita Hayworth; both women were dubbed. They rewrote the show a great deal, cut eight of the score's fourteen songs, and added four other Rodgers and Hart songs. A few years later, Bob Fosse twice re-created the role at New York's City Center, first in 1961 and again in 1963. Robert Coleman wrote in the *New York Mirror*, "It's a tuneful, flavorsome, satiric lullaby for the stay-up lates who used to make it easy and blow it fast. It's a cutting gem, a classic of its kind."

In 1995, New York's *Encore!* series presented the show in concert and made a new recording with Patti LuPone, Peter Gallagher, and Bebe Neuwirth. In 1999, playwright Terrence McNally did a revision of the script for a proposed Broadway revival and submitted it to the producing organization Livent right before it went out of business.

Today, *Pal Joey* may seem old-fashioned in some respects, but we have to see it in its original context: a musical comedy—*before* the Rodgers and Hammerstein revolution—that dealt with a hustler and thief, adultery, premarital sex, blackmail, and other fun things. A musical comedy centered on an antihero is something we're used to now, but it was utterly subversive in 1940.

Why It Shouldn't Have Worked

As with most groundbreaking shows, the main reason *Pal Joey* shouldn't have worked is that nothing like it had ever been done before. In the first five minutes of the show, Mike, the owner of the club, asks Joey if he does cocaine and if he's into young boys, quite a plateful for a 1940s musical comedy audience. In fact, there are several references to homosexuality in the show, something no one else would have dreamed of doing at that time. And these weren't sideways snickerings at effeminacy, as in *Anything Goes* and *Girl Crazy*; these were clear, pointed references to men having sexual relationships with other men. It's a risky way to start a musical comedy, but it proves the ten-minute rule, which says that you can do anything you want in a musical (or play or movie) if you do it within the first ten minutes, to establish the ground rules and clue the audience in to exactly what to expect for the rest of the evening. Audiences seeing *Pal Joey* for the first time knew in the first ten minutes what they were in for.

But the main reason the show shouldn't have worked is Joey himself. He's a two-bit crooner who has worked only in cheap nightclubs, who will clearly never be a success, who obviously doesn't respect women, who cheats and cons every chance he gets because if he didn't, he'd never get anywhere. And unlike almost all other leads in plays, musicals, movies, and books, Joey does not change over the course of the show. He doesn't learn anything. He ends the show right back where he started, whether that's with the show's original final song, "I'm Talkin' to My Pal," or with the revised ending, a reprise of "I Could Write a Book." Either way, Joey is alone again and on the prowl, having grown not at all, having matured not at all. His lack of growth breaks one of the cardinal rules of dramatic construction.

And yet Joey is a very complex man. Richard Rodgers wrote in the *New York Times*, "Joey is a disreputable character, and Larry [Hart] understood and liked disreputable characters. He knew what John O'Hara knew—that Joey was not disreputable because he was mean, but because he had too much imagination to behave himself, and because he was a little weak. If you don't understand this about Joey, you'll probably find him hard to take. If you do understand it, you'll

be able to chuckle at him and understand him in more than a superficial sense." But in 1940, musical comedy audiences weren't used to
having to understand complex leading characters in their musicals.
They were used to gags, great songs, and great dancing.

Joey isn't the only disreputable leading character; so is Vera. Who
else would have written so unsavory, so sexual a woman's role in a
1940 musical comedy? Vera's presence creates a fascinating role reversal. She studies and uses men the way Joey usually studies and
uses women. In fact, Vera is far more the predator than Joey is. She is
overtly sexual, in a way only men are supposed to be. The lyrics to
her song "Bewitched" were so sexual that Hart had to rewrite them
before they could be sung on the radio. Joey tries to use his usual routine on Vera, but it doesn't work because his routine is designed for
women and Vera has taken on the role of the man in their relationship.
In the song "What Is a Man?" Vera asks if a man is a wolf or a mouse;
this is significant because *mouse* is the term Joey uses for girls he targets; he has become the hunted instead of the hunter. Vera goes after
Joey because he's easy to conquer, because he's different, nothing
more—not because there's anything particularly exciting or attractive about him, although she does comment on his sexual prowess.
Also in the same song, Vera considers that men may be of no use other
than to look good and provide sex, an attitude usually reserved for
men at that time. What were Rodgers and Hart thinking? Everything
about this show was subversive.

Joey also presents a nearly insurmountable casting problem. Like
Sally Bowles in *Cabaret*, Joey can't be *too* good an entertainer. If he's
too talented, he would be doing better than working in seedy, two-
bit clubs. And as with *Cabaret*, the movie version of *Pal Joey* made a
big mistake in casting a lead who was too good; Sinatra would not
have been trapped in second-rate clubs any more than Liza Minnelli
would have. But how do you cast a Broadway musical in which the
lead can't appear to be too talented? In the original production of
Cabaret, director Hal Prince cast Jill Haworth as Sally, specifically because she wasn't a very good singer, and many of the critics blasted
her for it. On stage, the first two Joeys, Gene Kelly and Bob Fosse,
were right for the role because neither one was primarily a singer.

Rodgers, Hart, and O'Hara seemed to get a perverse kick out of
breaking the rules at every turn in *Pal Joey*, putting gigantic hurdles
in front of themselves over and over again, as if their Act II song "Do

It the Hard Way" was a theme song for the creation of the show. Instead of opening with a big chorus number, as most musicals did, *Pal Joey* opens with Joey alone onstage, auditioning for a bored club owner with a mediocre song. And the club owner doesn't even let him finish the song. O'Hara wanted to open the show with Rodgers and Hart's hit "Blue Moon," but the songwriters wanted something more mundane and more artificial to better characterize Joey in those first few moments. Joey would have hated "Blue Moon." So Rodgers and Hart wrote "A Great Big Town," refusing even to give the audience a good opening number. Today, their choice seems right because it makes dramatic sense—content dictates form, as Stephen Sondheim says— but this wasn't a choice anyone else had ever made in 1940. Rodgers fought against the conventional rules of writing opening numbers through much of his career.

Also, surprisingly, there is no comic secondary couple in *Pal Joey* and the relationship between the primary couple, Joey and Vera, is decidedly unromantic. Gladys and Ludlow Lowell don't count as a secondary couple because Lowell doesn't show up until halfway through Act II, and they don't have their own plot line, the way Ado Annie and Will Parker do in *Oklahoma!* and the way Reno Sweeney and Sir Evelyn Oakleigh do in *Anything Goes*. O'Hara constructed his script according to the rules of nonmusical plays and film, not the rules of musicals; it's a safe bet he didn't even *know* the rules of musical comedy structure. Perhaps the success of this experiment pointed Rodgers in the direction he would follow from then on, treating musicals less like musicals and more like plays.

Once again contrary to convention, the love songs in *Pal Joey* are never sincere love songs. "Bewitched" is extremely raunchy and its reprise pokes fun at itself and at the conventions of musical comedy love. It was almost as if Larry Hart and, to a lesser extent, Richard Rodgers had grown bored with musical comedy. They had taken it as far as they could. They had conquered it. Its conventions were no longer challenging or interesting for them. Even though they couldn't have known it, it's almost as if they had to tear old-fashioned musical comedy apart with *Pal Joey* in order to make room for the new form of *Oklahoma!* three years later.

But the innovations of *Pal Joey* were almost lost to the ages. If not for the 1952 revival, *Pal Joey* might well be only a footnote in musical theatre history instead of a milestone. The truly innovative shows are only influential if they're hits. Nobody remembers Kurt Weill and Alan Jay Lerner's groundbreaking 1948 concept musical *Love Life*, which ran about as long as the first production of *Pal Joey*, but we all know *Oklahoma!*, which ran nearly ten times as long.

Songs for a New World

Like everything else in the show, the orchestrations were way ahead of their time, with the sound of swing, which had not yet been used on Broadway in 1940. Hans Spialek's very modern-sounding orchestrations were revised for the 1952 revival and the originals were subsequently lost. But in 1995, the day before a new studio recording of the score was to be made, boxes of original orchestra parts from the show were discovered in a warehouse and an authentic reconstruction of the score could at last be undertaken. As a result we can hear on the 1995 recording almost exactly what Broadway audiences heard in 1940, proving once again that orchestrations can be nearly as important as the songs themselves.

Hans Spialek worked wonders with the *Pal Joey* orchestrations. He separated the club songs from the other songs by giving them different sounds and textures. The songs performed in the club are all brassy and bluesy, while the book songs are all built on smooth, legato strings. And when a song crossed that boundary, when a song like "Plant You Now, Dig You Later," was a book song that morphed into a club number, Spialek set the introduction to strings, and gave the verse more brass. He further played with this exchange in Joey's dream sequence at the end of Act I, sometimes shifting abruptly, and sometimes comically, between these two sounds, as Joey's thoughts shifted back and forth between life inside and outside the club. This separation of sound isn't even something the audience is apt to notice consciously, but it makes the two kinds of numbers *feel* different, and it separates the two worlds from each other, giving the book numbers a more old-fashioned Broadway sound and the club numbers a more modern, less Broadway, swing sound.

The two kinds of songs in *Pal Joey* not only sound different but also function differently. The songs performed in the club are diegetic songs, a kind of musical theatre song in which the characters are aware they're singing. For instance, in the opening song, "A Great Big Town," Joey knows he's singing; he's auditioning for a singing job. But with

"Bewitched," Vera isn't aware that she's singing; here, singing is just the language the writers chose to communicate her thoughts. "A Great Big Town" is a diegetic song, a song that functions within the world of the plot; "Bewitched" is a book song, the kind of song that tells the story in the same way the book (the script) does.

There are other shows that use these two kinds of songs this way, but *Pal Joey* was the first to do it. Later examples include *Cabaret, Kiss Me Kate, Gypsy, Dreamgirls, 42nd Street, Merrily We Roll Along*, and *Follies*. Some shows had isolated examples of diegetic songs before *Pal Joey*, and many have since then, such as "Your Eyes" in *Rent*, the "Parlor Songs" in *Sweeney Todd*, and "The Ballad of Floyd Collins" in *Floyd Collins*, but *Pal Joey* was the first show to use diegetic songs dramatically, to exist within the world of the action and to characterize at the same time. Like the songs in *Pal Joey*, good diegetic songs have a double function; they operate as entertainment inside the action of the show, but they also comment on the action from outside that world. In *Pal Joey*, Joey is the link between these two kinds of songs.

In creating the sound of Joey's world, Hart wrote better and more subtle lyrics than he had ever written before, fashioning subversively and deceptively mediocre lyrics for the diegetic club songs, using cliches where he would have never used them before, restraining himself from being his most literate and sophisticated, and creating songs that lived fully in the world of cheesy nightclubs. Making the club songs purposefully insipid was a serious gamble; no songwriter had ever intentionally written mediocre or insipid material for a Broadway musical before, but that was what the dramatic situation called for, and Hart was too good a writer and too enthusiastic a risk taker not to comply. Were 1940 audiences sophisticated enough to understand what he was doing? Apparently not. But by 1952, well after the Rodgers and Hammerstein revolution had begun, audiences were ready for what Hart had wrought.

Anti-Love Songs

In real life, lyricist Larry Hart couldn't find love. He was gay, extremely short, an alcoholic, prone to depression, and he usually resorted to male prostitutes for affection. He ended up drinking himself to death. Not surprisingly, many of his love songs are about impossible and/or unrequited love. Even his more straightforward love

songs can be ironic, as if Hart had decided that if he couldn't participate in love, he'd laugh at it instead.

"I Could Write a Book" is the first love song in *Pal Joey*, but it's an
insincere love song. Joey has no feelings for Linda; he's just trying to
seduce this innocent girl. He doesn't mean any of what he's singing.
Joey (and Hart) is taking the form of the old-fashioned love song and
turning it on its ear, using it only for sexual conquest. We see this con-
firmed when he uses the exact same song—the same pickup line—
on another girl as the show ends. This could have been the kind of
song theatre songwriters had been writing for years, but here Rodgers
and Hart injected dark irony into a song form they helped develop.
They were growing as dramatists. They were heading for the kind of
dramatic songwriting Rodgers would finally achieve with Oscar Hammerstein II in *Oklahoma!*.

"What Is a Man?" is the next love song, but again it's twisted. Vera
knows Joey is an animal, a scumbag, and she loves that. That's why
she's going after him. This song is a catalog of what's *not* loveable about
Joey. "Bewitched" is next, another odd love song, so very frank and
very sexual. Rodgers thought the lyrics for this song and "Den of Iniquity" were offensive and wanted them rewritten, but Hart refused,
until after the show opened and he realized rewriting "Bewitched"
was the only way to get it recorded by pop singers and, therefore, the
only way to make real money off the song. In one of orchestrator Spialek's many experiments, he used the eerie sound of extremely high
violins playing a sound known as harmonics in the second half of
each verse of "Bewitched" to give the song an uneasy feeling. The lyric
and the orchestration point in the same direction: this is not love and
it's not going to end well. Later in the show, the Act II reprise of "Bewitched" deconstructs itself, making fun of love songs and musical
comedy love, making fun of the first "Bewitched," even making fun
of Hart's acrobatic rhymes in the first "Bewitched," playfully throwing in the words *dyspeptic* and *antiseptic*, two words utterly wrong for
a love song. It was essentially a big screw-you to old-fashioned musical comedies and to the audiences who loved them. No musical comedy song had ever done anything like this before. In retrospect, it's
easy to see that Hart was growing weary of musical comedy and that
his career would soon be over.

The final love song in the show, "Den of Iniquity," is the only
number even close to being a sincere love song and yet it's all about
copulation and the joys of adultery.

The Club Numbers

The numbers performed in the club also make fun of old-fashioned show tunes, although more good-naturedly. These songs parody the very stuff Rodgers and Hart had been writing for fifteen years. "A Great Big Town" makes fun of empty city-songs like "San Francisco" and Rodgers and Hart's first big hit, "Manhattan," and to that end, it's full of intentionally tired cliches. The stage direction in the script describes this song as "a real cheesy, razzmatazz chorus line affair with plenty of bumps and grinds." The song "You Mustn't Kick It Around" is a standard chorus girl club number, but this time one about the end of an affair, providing foreshadowing for the doomed affair between Joey and Vera. The stage direction for this one calls it "a standard musical comedy night club number." The song "That Terrific Rainbow" is a parody of gimmicky vamp songs, like "Hard-Hearted Hannah."

"Happy Hunting Horn" and "Zip" are two songs that fall in the crack between diegetic songs and book songs. Do the characters know they're singing in these songs? In an older show, we'd assume these are book numbers, that the characters don't know they're singing, and that the big dance break after "Happy Hunting Horn" is just part of the language of the show. And in fact, both "Happy Hunting Horn" and "Zip" do grow directly out of dialogue, the way book songs usually do. But both numbers are also set in the club, and *Pal Joey* is not an old-fashioned show. Also, the script says that there is applause from the other characters after "Zip," so everyone onstage must be aware that Melba was singing if they're applauding her. It's a tough call, and ultimately, one the director and choreographer of each production have to answer. Like the other songs in the club, "Zip" is also a parody—of strip numbers, of celebrity interviews, of the stereotype of strippers as dummies—and that's another indication that it's a diegetic number.

The Act II opener, "Flower Garden of My Heart" is a wicked parody of expensive, overproduced revues like the Ziegfeld Follies and George White's Scandals, and it even has a couple of comic Gershwin musical quotes in the dance break, a reference to the fact that Gershwin wrote music for six editions of the Scandals. According to the script, the lead singer in this song is supposed to be slightly off-key, and the song's lyric is peppered with intentionally bad grammar to make it clear that this number is Joey's failed attempt to bring some class to his new club. The stage direction says, "Although lavish, there is still something pretentious about it, like a cheap Ziegfeld number." As before, this use of parody was not usual musical comedy fare. Who else would start the second act of a musical with an intentionally mediocre song?

Dream a Little Dream

At the end of Act I, there is a dream sequence, a kind of precursor to the dream ballet that would end the first act of *Oklahoma!* three years later. And like the dream ballets that would follow it, this sequence explores Joey's state of mind through the use of dance and music. It's interesting that in 1943, when everyone was raving about how groundbreaking *Oklahoma!*'s dream ballet was, no one remembered *Pal Joey*'s dream ballet from only three years before. Perhaps the reason is that in 1940, *Pal Joey* was largely dismissed as unpleasant, foul, and not very good musical comedy; and innovations are rarely remembered if they're not in hit shows. It wasn't until 1952, after *Oklahoma!*, that *Pal Joey* became the classic that we now know it to be, and by that time, conventional wisdom had already declared that *Oklahoma!* was the show that perfected the psychological dream ballet. Everyone forgot that *Pal Joey* had beaten *Oklahoma!* to the punch.

As in *Oklahoma!*, the dream sequence in *Pal Joey* starts with a song, nothing more than a throwaway song, really, called "What Do I Care for a Dame?" The song itself is ordinary, nothing much to the melody or lyric, acting as an introduction to the instrumental dream sequence. Like the dream ballets that would follow it in later years, the music of this sequence is based on melodies from the rest of the score.

The two main melodies used are "A Great Big Town," which represents Joey's ideal of nightclub music (remember this is the music he chose to audition with, so he must think pretty highly of this song), and "Bewitched," the song representing Vera, who will provide the money to open the nightclub Joey dreams of owning. In fact, there are a few very abrupt, very funny switches back and forth between the lush romanticism of "Bewitched" and the brash jazziness of Joey's club music. To make the joke really clear, at one point the music is playing "Bewitched" when all of a sudden, it's interrupted by a loud, raucous musical quote of "Frankie and Johnny" for only four brief measures; then it goes right back to "Bewitched." It's funny because the two songs are so different, and because the interruption is so unexpected. It's also funny because there's a comic parallel between the central relationship in *Pal Joey* and the murderous-adulterous relationship in "Frankie and Johnny."

But in addition to financial backing, "Bewitched" also represents Joey's loveless relationship with Vera, and it is also contrasted with occasional musical quotes of "I Could Write a Book," that melody reminding Joey of Linda, the "nice girl" who actually has feelings for him. Joey has conflicted feelings about whether to stay with Vera, who doesn't care about him but who can give him the money to realize his dream, or to pursue Linda instead and possibly end up with a real relationship. Yet despite his conflicts, his choice is pretty clear; love is low on his list of priorities. The other melody we hear in the dream sequence is from the song "I'm Talkin' to My Pal," the show's original final song, which was cut—a song about how much Joey treasures his independence. But this song is soon pushed aside again by "Bewitched," reminding Joey that he's not independent in the least.

It's a great sequence, both musically and dramatically, and it tells us as much about Joey's mindset as *Oklahoma!*'s dream ballet tells us about Laurey; maybe even more, since Laurey doesn't hide much during the rest of the show, but Joey hides everything.

This dream sequence is just further proof that *Pal Joey* was unlike anything that had ever come before, in dozens of different ways. But because its first production wasn't embraced the way its 1952 revival was, *Pal Joey* is almost always overlooked for its innovations—innovations that were unbelievable in 1940 but business as usual in 1952. Still, even today, *Pal Joey* is awfully hard-boiled, and it can easily stand up against modern musicals in terms of content. Even today, few musicals would mention cocaine, homosexuality, and pedophilia at all, much less in the first five minutes. Even today, few musicals deal with casual sex as bluntly, as darkly, and as playfully as *Pal Joey* does. Rodgers, Hart, and O'Hara opened so many doors for those who would come after them. They prepared the way for so many other innovations. And for that, we all owe them a great debt of gratitude. At the very least, we owe them the recognition of all they accomplished.

Other Resources

The *Pal Joey* script is not available commercially, but the score and vocal selections are. The script is available only through the Rodgers and Hammerstein Theatre Library. The 1950 recording that brought the show back from the dead is available on CD, as is the 1995 recording, which includes the only commercial recording of "I'm Talkin' to My Pal." O'Hara's *New Yorker* stories were collected in a book after the show opened, and though that book is out of print now, it's not hard to find through used-book stores or on the Internet. If you're working on the show, or if you just really love *Pal Joey*, the stories are a real treat.

3 Oklahoma!

Book and lyrics by Oscar Hammerstein II
Music by Richard Rodgers
Originally directed on Broadway by Rouben Mamoulian
Originally choreographed by Agnes de Mille
Licensed by Rodgers and Hammerstein Theatre Library

Oklahoma! is the most important accident to happen in the history of musical theatre. No one could have foreseen the impact this unimposing, seemingly unsophisticated little show would have on the future of the art form. No one could have guessed that for decades to come almost all musicals would be written in the Rodgers and Hammerstein style, that *Oklahoma!* was not only breaking the old rules but also making all-new ones, that silly, frothy musicals would forever more be considered old-fashioned.

In 1998, the *London Daily Mail* said of a revival of *Oklahoma!*, "It's not just a classic American musical but—and this is the real surprise—a truthful, touching and gripping drama about growing up and falling in love, about dreams and nightmares." In 1999 the *New York Post* said, "Rogers and Hammerstein are truly up there with Eugene O'Neill as the great American theatre creators." As the twentieth century came to a close, the New York Drama League voted *Oklahoma!* the Best Musical of the Century. With twenty-twenty hindsight, we can see now that *Oklahoma!* presaged musicals as diverse as *West Side Story*, *Sweeney Todd*, *Rent*, and *Ragtime*.

In the early 1940s, composer Richard Rodgers, famous for his jazzy, urbane, sophisticated Broadway scores, had been enjoying a string of hit musical comedies with his partner, Larry Hart (*Babes in Arms*, *On Your Toes*, and many others), but Hart was becoming harder and harder to work with as his alcoholism and self-loathing over his looks and his homosexuality began more and more to get in the way of work.

Broadway lyricist Oscar Hammerstein II, famous for his sentimental, romantic lyrics, had written with various partners some of the theatre's greatest musicals and operettas, including the groundbreaking *Show Boat* with Jerome Kern. But as the '40s began, Hammerstein was suffering a ten-year slump.

Theresa Helburn, one of the directors of the highly respected Theatre Guild, saw a summer stock theatre production of Lynn Riggs' cowboy play *Green Grow the Lilacs*, a play the Theatre Guild had produced on Broadway in 1931. The show had been a big flop originally, but after seeing this new production ten years later with even more folk songs than the original had included, Helburn realized the more music the play had, the better it became. She brought composer Richard Rodgers to see it and he agreed that what it needed was an original score to make it into a true musical.

When Larry Hart declined to work on *Oklahoma!*, Rodgers asked Hammerstein, who agreed only after making sure he wasn't coming between Rodgers and Hart. As the new partners proceeded to work together for the first time, Hammerstein began writing some of the best lyrics of his career and he brought out a new side of Rodgers, a lush, romantic, deeply emotional side that Rodgers had rarely explored before. Their partnership would become a turning point in American musical theatre, changing everything that came after, and they would go on to write several masterpieces, such as *Carousel, South Pacific,* and *The King and I*, among other shows, which would change forever the way people wrote musicals.

Putting It Together

Many years later, Hammerstein's protégé Stephen Sondheim would comment, only half-jokingly, that *Carousel* is about life and death while *Oklahoma!* is about a picnic. But really, that's not far from the truth. *Oklahoma!* is mostly about the mundane, everyday lives of territory folk in 1906 Oklahoma, just before it became a state. So how did it start a major revolution in the American musical theatre? Why did it change everything, after the more substantial *Show Boat* couldn't do it sixteen years earlier?

There are a lot of reasons. First, it's true that the main action of *Oklahoma!* is centered on the seemingly trivial tension over which guy Laurey will choose to take her to the box social and which of them will win her basket in the auction. But it's also about attempted murder and the threat of rape. Jud is a murderer. Whether or not Laurey goes to the social with him *is* a big deal. It is genuinely dangerous for Laurey to be alone with Jud, to be his date; his advances on the way to the social were probably leading to rape, and he might be waiting to finish the job after the auction, which is why it's so important that Curly win Laurey's basket. And underneath all this, the show is also about responsibility to the community, a serious theme Sondheim would explore more thoroughly forty-four years later in his musical *Into the Woods*. Though it may not have been a conscious statement, the overture of *Oklahoma!* even starts with "The Farmer and the Cowman," the show's one song specifically about responsibility to the community, underlining the importance of that theme.

The second reason the show was so revolutionary is that, though dance had been successfully integrated into the plot in Rodgers and Hart's musical comedies *On Your Toes* (1936) and *Pal Joey* (1940), *Oklahoma!* was the first hit show in which dance was used to explore character and plot, as a language instead of merely a plot device, a practice that would be used again later in *Carousel, The King and I, West Side Story, Ragtime*, and a few other shows. *Pal Joey* had done this, but *Pal Joey* hadn't been a hit, so no one seemed to notice. As with *Pal Joey*, the dance in *Oklahoma!* was used the same way as music and words were, as a language that told the story, that conveyed important information. Without words, Agnes de Mille's dream ballet gave us deep, clear insight into Laurey's feelings, hopes, and fears. And because the show was such a hit, for years after *Oklahoma!*, every new serious musical had to have a dream ballet, even if there were no real need for it. Even *West Side Story* in 1957 and *Contact* in 2000 used the same kind of dream ballet.

The third reason is that, though *Oklahoma!* retained a few old-fashioned devices, it also broke lots of rules. While other shows opened with big chorus numbers and pretty girls, *Oklahoma!* opened with an old woman sitting alone onstage, churning butter as a solo male voice sang a cappella offstage. The audience didn't see girls until forty-five minutes into the first act! While most hit musicals were set in contemporary New York, *Oklahoma!* was set in turn-of-the-century Oklahoma territory. While most musicals had a secondary comic couple, *Oklahoma!* had a secondary comic *triangle*, which balanced and foreshadowed the more dangerous primary love triangle. While most hit musicals lined up the stars—Ethel Merman, Al Jolson, Eddie Cantor—before a single note was written, *Oklahoma!* did not have one big name in the cast.

It shouldn't have had a prayer.

Perhaps what *Oklahoma!* did that no other show had done before was to take all the innovations, experiments, and surprises that had shown up in numerous separate musicals over the previous twenty years, put them all together in one show, and integrate them seamlessly and thoughtfully into the drama of the story, much the way *Rent* did more than fifty years later. *Oklahoma!* took the social issues of *Show Boat*, the long-form musical scenes of *Show Boat* and *Love Me Tonight*, the ordinary people of *Porgy and Bess*, a murder over love from *Rose Marie* (and *Porgy and Bess*), the dramatic use of dance from *On Your Toes*, the psychological content of *Lady in the Dark*, a dark, frank view of sexuality and a psychological dream ballet from *Pal Joey*, and a cast of talented unknowns, as in *The Boys from Syracuse*. It took all these previous innovations and it made them all work together for the very first time. Not surprisingly, most of the shows just mentioned were written by either Rodgers or Hammerstein with other partners, so these two were the perfect team to bring it all together in a unified whole, maybe the only two people who could. Just as *Oklahoma!* brought together many past innovations to move musical theatre toward more serious drama, *Rent* did the same thing in 1996 to move musical theatre away from the elitism that had plagued it.

Most surprising of all—especially to its creators—was that the unusual, rule-busting *Oklahoma!* became a monster hit, running more than five years and 2,212 performances on Broadway, becoming the longest-running show of all time. This was unheard of; Broadway shows just didn't run that long. The next longest-running show at that time was the 1919 musical *Irene,* which had run only 670 performances, less than one-third as long. *Oklahoma!* was definitely a new phenomenon. The national touring company of *Oklahoma!* ran, uninterrupted, for almost ten years. The *New York Herald Tribune* said of the original production, "Songs, dances, and a story have been triumphantly blended . . . a striking piece of theatrical Americana." The *Daily News* said, "*Oklahoma!* really is different—beautifully different."

The U.S. Army and Navy requested a USO tour of the show to play for more than a million and a half troops in the Pacific. At one point, sheet music sales for "People Will Say We're in Love" topped nine thousand copies a day and sales for "Oh, What a Beautiful Mornin'" topped four thousand a day. It took less than a year to sell more than a million pieces of *Oklahoma!* sheet music. The original cast album sold eight hundred thousand copies during the Broadway run. The show won a Special Pulitzer Prize for Drama, two Oscars (the Tony Awards weren't around yet), then a Special Tony Award in 1993, a London Evening Standard Award in 1998, an International Emmy Award in 1999, and four Olivier Awards (the British Tony Award) in 1999. Today, the show is done in six hundred theatres a year.

Rodgers said in his autobiography, "The chief influence of *Oklahoma!* was simply to serve notice that when writers come up with something different and it has merit, there would be a large and receptive audience waiting for it. From *Oklahoma!* on, with only rare exceptions, the memorable productions have been those daring to break free from the conventional mode."

The Show They Love to Hate

So why do so many people hate *Oklahoma!*? Why do so many people underestimate its gifts? It's true that it isn't as complex or as well-crafted as *Carousel, South Pacific,* or *The King and I,* but it is far more exciting and has far more depth than most people give it credit for. As with the rest of Rodgers and Hammerstein's musicals, we're too used to *Oklahoma!*. We've seen it too many times, and perhaps we've seen it done poorly. Too many directors don't respect the material and don't give it the same effort they would give to *Death of a Salesman* or *A Streetcar Named Desire,* so they end up with anemic, bland, simpleminded productions of this richly textured musical.

We've lost the ability to look at the show with fresh eyes and see it the way the audiences saw it in 1943. Americans operate under a handicap with most of the serious musicals written before 1960. When shows like *Oklahoma!* and *Carousel* were written, the actors in Broadway musicals were not generally up to the dramatic demands of the material. They weren't equipped the way actors are today to explore character and subtext, to approach a musical with the same seriousness of purpose with which they would approach work by Eugene O'Neill or Tennessee Williams. In 1943, musical theatre actors were trained only to sing well and project—after all, this was before actors had microphones, and they had to be heard over the orchestra. The result is that the characters were often played somewhat superficially in the original productions and those portrayals became the blueprints for subsequent productions. Fortunately, the acting in the Rodgers and Hammerstein films is much better—especially Gordon MacRae's in *Oklahoma!* and *Carousel*—since those are the permanent records of the shows.

It took decades and foreign directors to breathe new life into *Carousel, The King and I,* and *Cabaret,* allowing us to see again how truly magnificent those shows are, how rich and dark and subtle they are, and the same is true of *Oklahoma!,* which was directed brilliantly by Trevor Nunn in 1998 for London's Royal National Theatre, finally giving it a new life and giving audiences another chance to see how amazing it is.

Do Re Mi

There was so much new about *Oklahoma!*. Hammerstein's lyrics were certainly unusual on Broadway in 1943. They weren't about virtuoso rhymes, sexy double entendres, streetwise slang, or the witty turns of phrase common to musical comedy. They also weren't about the lush, romantic, purple language and exotic metaphors common to operetta. His lyrics were about truth, above all, in language natural to the characters and setting, expressing real, simple emotions, fears, and hopes, language that seemed utterly natural and never called attention to itself as art. Hammerstein approached lyric writing as a serious dramatist, not as an entertainer. His lyrics grew organically out of the dialogue, continuing seamlessly from spoken word to song. Instead of formally announcing a topic with the first line of a song, Hammerstein's lyrics picked up the conversation where it left off and carried it forward. Perhaps this is why he hadn't had a success on Broadway for ten years before *Oklahoma!*. His philosophy was not what audiences wanted, even though it's standard practice in musical theatre today.

Perhaps what contributed to the surprising newness of Hammerstein's work for *Oklahoma!* is the change he made in his process. He was used to letting his composers write the music first, to which Hammerstein would fit lyrics. Rodgers was certainly used to writing music first and letting Larry Hart fit his words to Rodgers' tunes. But when Hammerstein and Rodgers set to work for the first time, Hammerstein asked that he be allowed to write the lyrics first. Because they were both more intent this time on creating serious drama than they had been before, Rodgers agreed. Lyrics were no longer just along for the ride; now they were as important, if not more important, than the music. Hammerstein's lyrics before this time were certainly first-rate, but his lyrics with Rodgers were clearly the best of his career up to that point, and this reversing of the work process might be part of the reason.

During his time with Rodgers, Hammerstein was famous for writing some of the freshest love songs musical theatre ever heard. One of the reasons they were so interesting is that he always found a way around saying "I love you" directly. In *Oklahoma!* he wrote a lyric in which the two lovers deny their love even though we know the truth in "People Will Say We're in Love." Likewise, *Carousel* had "If I Loved You," *Flower Drum Song* had "Don't Marry Me" and "Love Look Away," *Allegro* had "The Gentleman Is a Dope," *The Sound of Music* had "How Can Love Survive?" and *The King and I* had "Shall We Dance?"

Hammerstein was truly a wordsmith. The details he included in his lyrics for "Oh What a Beautiful Mornin'" are remarkable, putting the audience right in the middle of the Oklahoma territory—the haze on the meadow, the corn thriving in the sun-drenched country air, the statue-still cattle, the subtle music of the breeze, the rustle of the willow. Not only does Curly notice all these things but he revels in them, he loves them, and he loves his life. Hammerstein tells us a lot about Curly, his life, his deep connection to the earth, and his philosophy of life, all indirectly through this seemingly simple song. He gives us in this first lyric information that tells us Curly will be a great farmer, a decision Curly doesn't even know he'll make yet. And Hammerstein rejects high poetic language because this is a cowboy singing these words, not a poet. It has to sound like it's coming spontaneously from Curly's mind and mouth, not Hammerstein's pen, something virtuoso lyricists like Cole Porter, Larry Hart, and Ira Gershwin never bothered about.

Likewise, Rodgers left behind his Tin Pan Alley jazziness when he wrote *Oklahoma!* and he turned instead to music that dramatized, that helped tell the story through its rhythms, its style, and its tone. Rodgers' music was no longer about toe tapping and sheet music sales, even though they happened anyway. Now it was about telling the story, about establishing the cultural context, about allowing the characters' emotions to soar when they needed to soar or turn inward and personal when they needed to do that. Rodgers wisely chose to write songs that sounded like folk music for *Oklahoma!*, simple and direct, instead of songs that sounded like 1940s Hit Parade tunes. He would maintain this musical integrity throughout his partnership with Hammerstein; in fact, in later years, he was always amused at how many people told him they grew up singing that old German folk song "Edelweiss," a song Rodgers wrote entirely from scratch. The only songs in *Oklahoma!* that weren't in the folk song idiom were "Lonely Room" and "It's a Scandal! It's an Outrage!"—the two songs sung by the outsiders in the story.

Both Rodgers and Hammerstein were fiercely intent on being true to the characters and story. Instead of "show tunes," they ended up with songs that were robust, muscular, and hearty, songs that were positively luminous. A good example of this is how Hammerstein took the opening stage direction from *Green Grow the Lilacs* and turned it into his opening number, "Oh What a Beautiful Mornin'." The original stage direction reads:

> It is a radiant summer morning several years ago, the kind of morning which, enveloping the shapes of earth—men, cattle in a meadow, blades of the young corn, streams—makes them seem to exist now for the first time, their images giving off a visible golden emanation that is partly true and partly a trick of the imagination, focusing to keep alive a loveliness that may pass away . . . And, like the voice of the morning, a rich male voice outside somewhere beings to sing . . .

It's a lesson in lyric writing to see how Hammerstein took the magic of that language and the specific details from Riggs' stage direction and turned them into an enduring and now world-famous opening number. Rodgers contributed by adding the sounds of nature in his music, using a flute, a clarinet, and an oboe to imitate the sounds of birds, along with horns and open fifths, which had been established by Aaron Copland as the sound of America in *Billy the Kid* in 1938 and *Rodeo* in 1942, to create an unmistakable setting for the story: the open plains and people at one with nature. In fact, melodic fifths run through most of the melodies in the score, most notably in "People Will Say We're in Love" and "Surrey with the Fringe on Top," not only reinforcing that Americana sound but also giving the score a real sense of unity. Rodgers made his most important choice in making the first verse of "Oh What a Beautiful Mornin'" a cappella; for the audience to hear an unaccompanied voice coming closer and closer singing this faux folk song lends a feeling of realism that is rare in musical theatre. Aunt Eller sitting at her churn wouldn't hear an orchestra accompanying Curly, so neither does the audience, at least for the first verse. This plain folk sound eases us into this world and it also establishes Curly as a kind of folk hero.

Filling Out the Long Form

One of Rodgers and Hammerstein's greatest gifts to the musical theatre is the refining of long-form musical scenes, something both of them had toyed with earlier. They used it beautifully in *Oklahoma!* and achieved its complete mastery in *Carousel* in the bench scene and in "Soliloquy." Stephen Sondheim would be the one to achieve perfection in this device in *Sweeney Todd, Into the Woods, Passion*, and *Sunday in the Park with George*.

"The Surrey with the Fringe on Top" is a great example of their artistry. It starts out as a playful charm song, merely a vehicle for Curly's bragging and teasing. Rodgers draws an amazing musical picture: the sound of the horses' trot in the steady accompaniment, and in the vocal melody, the sound of various fowl jumping and scattering as the surrey comes through, jumping higher with each phrase. Hammerstein paints a highly detailed picture of the yellow wheels, the leather dashboard, fringe blowing in the breeze, isinglass curtains, lights on the side, the shiny paint job, the cats and dogs in the field, the sounds of birds and frogs, the whistle of the wind, the rattle of the surrey, the ripple of the river.

But this isn't just a musical monologue, like most songs; it's a conversation. After Curly finishes his description, Aunt Eller asks questions, Curly answers, Laurey asks more questions, and Curly answers those as well. He's accomplishing his agenda; Laurey is interested and she wants to know more. Hammerstein weaves spoken dialogue in between the singing, and now it becomes a seduction. Curly gets close to Laurey and whispers in her ear, asking her if she doesn't wish this dream would go on forever. Curly knows Laurey; she's all about wishing. Laurey is utterly caught up in the fantasy now. And the conversation becomes spoken again as music continues underneath, and the seduction turns into an argument as Laurey plays hard-to-get. But Curly manages to get back to the seduction as he sings again, now describing the ride home, as the trotting music slows down, echoing the slowing down of the horses. Eventually, the music slows down to a stop as Curly and Laurey get home from the pretend date they never went on. But the mood of seduction doesn't last once the magic of the music has stopped, and Laurey storms off, angry again.

This use of a long-form musical scene with "Surrey" not only propels the action forward and gives us important insight into characters and relationships but also establishes the language for the evening, making the wholly unnatural practice of breaking into song feel less bizarre to the audience. By weaving together song with spoken word, by making the song less formally structured, less set off from the dialogue, less artificial, the creators also made the language of musical comedy less alienating to the audience. They don't have that wall of artificiality between them and the characters (or at least they have less of it) that had always prevented real emotional involvement. It's hard to get emotionally involved in *No No Nanette* or *Girl Crazy* because they're so silly, so artificial, but *Oklahoma!* and the shows that followed its lead worked more like nonmusical plays and did a better job of involving the audience.

Like the dialogue in well-made plays, the music and lyrics in *Oklahoma!* did a lot of work, not only exploring character and plot but also establishing textual themes and creating subtle foreshadowing. For instance, Ado Annie's song "I Cain't Say No" sets up an innocent kind of sexuality that foreshadows the more serious, more dangerous sexuality of Jud and his song "Lonely Room." However, just because Annie's sexuality is innocent doesn't mean it isn't real—don't forget that Will questions the paternity of Annie's future child in "All Er Nothin'." The Act II opening number "The Farmer and the Cowman" foreshadows the increasingly dangerous rivalry between Jud, a farmer, and Curly, a cowman. When Aunt Eller interrupts "The Farmer and the Cowman" with a gunshot, it foreshadows the real violence of Jud's attacks on Laurey and Curly later in Act II. The comic mock funeral dirge "Pore Jud Is Daid" foreshadows Jud's real death at the end of the show.

Pore Jud

Jud's songs are more complex than the songs of most musical comedies of that time. With the song "Pore Jud Is Daid," Rodgers and Hammerstein created a very funny song about a very serious villain and talked about a very serious subject in comic terms, introducing one of the most serious elements in the plot without the audience even noticing. The idea of Curly suggesting Jud should kill himself is funny enough, but Curly breaking into a funeral dirge is even funnier and an economical way to establish the tension between Curly and Jud, rivals for Laurey. The mock serious tone of the song and the fact that Jud doesn't catch most of Curly's insults gives us a good laugh, but the details of the song also give us plenty of information about territory life along the way. Curly's recitative in the middle as he takes the role of the preacher is a very unusual device for a 1940s musical, but perfectly appropriate, adding a religious overtone to the moment. The song also clues us in that Curly is probably going to come out on top by the end of the story because he is more clever. He not only gets away with insulting Jud to his face; he even gets Jud to join in on the suicide fantasy. But we also feel a little sorry for Jud; he wants affection so badly he even fantasizes about suicide if it means people would say nice things about him.

After making Jud seem more human by making him the butt of Curly's joke, Rodgers and Hammerstein then show us the inside of Jud's head, a dark, frightening place indeed, and, most surprising of all, they also make him sympathetic along the way. This isn't *Girl Crazy*; this is grown-up theatre, rich, complex drama. As Jud begins his solo "Lonely Room," he describes the lonely squalor in which he lives, important details if we're to understand this man, but then he goes somewhere we don't expect: he begins talking about his dreams. Again, like any well-made play, *Oklahoma!* draws a full, three-dimensional villain. Jud is a highly sexual being and this separates him from Curly and Laurey, but it also connects him unexpectedly to Ado Annie and Ali Hakim. Jud should be dangerously attractive. He's not conventionally handsome like Curly, but there is something about him, perhaps his overt sexuality, that Laurey finds interesting. The original Jud, Howard Da Silva, was probably not the best choice for the role physically, but the handsomer Rod Steiger, who played Jud in the movie, looks like Jud should look. Ultimately, we see in both "Pore Jud" and "Lonely Room" that all Jud wants is a woman to love him and who isn't afraid of him. We feel sorry for him and it throws off the expected balance of good versus bad in the show.

Rodgers created unusual music for "Lonely Room." It's the only song in the show that's in a minor key and it's far more dissonant than any other song in the score, separating Jud musically from the other characters and giving him an aching eroticism the others don't have. Not only do we see that he doesn't belong in this community, but we also *hear* that he isn't like the others, that he is isolated from the community (which sings only in major keys), that he doesn't dwell in their world. The chord in the opening accompaniment is both dissonant and harmonically ambiguous. It's hard to tell what chord it is at first, underlining Jud's mysterious personality. Is he a villain or just a misunderstood man craving love? We can't tell and the music reflects that. And yet, when he talks about his dream of normalcy, the music changes to a major key, finally sounding more like the other characters' music, as he dreams of living in their world. Just like other brilliant dramatists, Rodgers and Hammerstein refuse to let Jud be a one-dimensional cardboard villain. Once we understand him, we may still fear him, but it's harder to hate him. Surprisingly, a lot of people cut this song when they produce the show. It's one of the most important moments in the show from the perspective of character and psychology, but they cut it anyway. And even though Rodgers and Hammerstein produced the film version, it was inexplicably cut from the movie, too.

OK Already!

The show's title song was not always a part of the score. It was written while the show was in previews out of town, partly because there were only three new songs in Act II, one of which was cut, partly because producer Theresa Helburn asked Rodgers and Hammerstein to write "a song about the land"—at least that's how she remembers it. It was written as a solo for Curly but was soon transformed into a major ensemble number. But this song was never just an excuse to sing some more. It's a symbol of Curly's new life, becoming a farmer and joining a community, leaving his free, independent life as a cowboy. And it's also about the new life of their land and community, about Oklahoma becoming a state, joining the union, becoming a part of something bigger and greater, joining "civilization." In both cases—the personal and the communal—it's about many new advantages and opportunities, but also new responsibilities. Oklahoma was one of the last two states to join the continental United States, and it was very important for the people who lived there. The song title works so well as the title of the show because it represents being a part of something bigger, giving up selfish pleasures and freedoms for bigger rewards, in the form of both statehood and marriage. Is it any wonder this song has become Oklahoma's state theme? Hammerstein made the subtle, wise choice to make the song about statehood on its surface and about Curly and Laurey and their marriage subtextually. Their union is what we've been waiting for all through the show; just as it was historically inevitable that Oklahoma would join the union, it was also inevitable that Curly and Laurey would end up together.

When the song was written, Curly sang it and a reportedly great but pointless dance solo was inserted into the middle. But this was a song about community and it made no sense to keep it so small. So it became a unison ensemble number, and then a chorus member suggested that the great voices in the cast would be better displayed in a real choral arrangement. So they called orchestrator Robert Russell Bennett in New York and told him what they needed. He jumped on a train and had the arrangement finished before he got off the train in Boston. The actors came in on their day off and learned the arrangement from the single original copy. Once it was learned, Agnes de Mille took over and staged what is now legendary: the "flying wedge." She arranged the cast in a big W formation at the back of the stage, with Curly and Laurey in front at the center point. The dancers were arranged behind them in a V formation, and the singers and other leads formed the side legs of the W. As the song progressed, the flying wedge came forward toward the audience and, finally, the entire cast gathered together at the very front edge of the stage. It was simple and thrilling, just like so many other moments in the show. The new song went in that week and stopped the show cold every night. It was just what Act II needed, both emotionally and thematically.

Déjà Vu All Over Again

The other remarkable thing about the *Oklahoma!* score is the smart, unusual use of reprises. Before this show, reprises were just a chance to repeat the hit songs in the scores to make sure people remembered them and bought the sheet music. There was no dramatic need for them. But *Oklahoma!* changed that, just as it changed almost everything else. Laurey's short reprise of "Oh What a Beautiful Mornin'" in the beginning of the show is a setup for her to insult Curly, to introduce their bickering, and it also establishes the fact that these two kids belong together. Laurey hears Curly's "music" in her head; she's thinking about him. They sing the same music and the audience registers unconsciously that they sound like they belong together—a device used, in an even more sophisticated manner, in *The Music Man*. Will Parker's reprise of "I Cain't Say No" accomplishes the same thing, while it also shows us that Will understands Annie and he knows exactly how to win her heart. Will talks her language. Both these minireprises establish the fact that these couples belong together, so much so that they even sing the same music.

The reprise of "People Will Say We're in Love" at the end of the first scene is a deft use of a reprise. Laurey refuses to break her date for the box social with Jud. Curly gets angry and storms off. Laurey cries softly to herself and sings a bit of "People Will Say We're in Love," the song in which she assured Curly she doesn't love him, even though she loves him very much. Maybe she pushed him away one time too many. Maybe she's ruined everything. She can't even finish the song because she's crying too hard. Aunt Eller finishes the scene humming the song to herself; she knows they belong together.

The second reprise of "People Will Say We're in Love" in Act II is a textbook example of how reprises would always be used after *Oklahoma!* The song is not just sung again but subtly changed so that it takes on a whole new meaning. In Act I, the song was used for the two lovers to warn each other about getting too involved, about showing too much affection. But in Act II, the song becomes a full-out declaration of love as Curly changes the song to "Let People Say We're in Love." They're both ready to express their love openly. They've grown up, no longer embarrassed for others to know of their love, ready to jump into the scary unknown of a romantic relationship. The song — their love theme — is transformed as their relationship is transformed.

And at the end of the show, there are two last reprises, this time less dramatic than just summations: first, "Oh What a Beautiful Mornin'," the anthem to the goodness and rightness of life and to this magnificent land on which they live, which will soon become a part of the United States, and then "People Will Say We're in Love" (the first version), a celebration and a reminder that yes, people *will* say Curly and Laurey are in love from now on. Like the title song does, this last pair of reprises returns to the two main themes of the show: the land and Curly and Laurey's relationship.

Dream Weaver

New York's *World Telegram* said of Agnes de Mille's dances, "Next to Mr. Rodgers . . . must stand Agnes de Mille, whose choreography . . . is actually the biggest hit of the show. [The dances] are spinetingling, out of this world."

Originally Hammerstein had planned a circus-themed dream for Laurey to end the first act, but de Mille was appalled. What did the circus have to do with Laurey's state of mind, she wanted to know. "Where's the sex?" she kept asking. She told Rodgers and Hammerstein quite emphatically that nice girls have dirty dreams. She believed that for the show to be fully dramatically integrated—Rodgers and Hammerstein's top priority for every moment in the show—the dream had to realistically explore Laurey's fears and confusion over her choice between Jud and Curly. This choice may not seem all that earth-shattering to us, but to Laurey, a sheltered farm girl of eighteen, this seems like the most important decision of her life—and it's *her* dream, *her* point of view.

It's significant that Laurey's dream focuses on Laurey and Jud, not Laurey and Curly. It's a small detail that tells us so much about her frame of mind. Jud's overt sexuality is scary and clearly dangerous, but it's also fascinating for Laurey. She's just starting to explore her own sexuality and has probably never encountered anything truly dangerous in her life. For a good girl with limited life experience, there's something terribly attractive and exciting about danger, especially when it's connected to sexuality. We see the same idea explored by Little Red Ridinghood in *Into the Woods* and by Luisa in *The Fantasticks*.

As Laurey's dream progresses, the girls on Jud's dirty postcards come to disturbing life. Laurey probably saw the postcards only once, the time she brought soup up to Jud's smokehouse when he was sick. Amusingly and appropriately, the postcard girls come to life to the tune of "I Cain't Say No." More significant, though, is not that Jud likes these girls, but that the other cowboys do, too. Does Laurey worry that the postcard girls are the kind of girls men really want, that a good girl like her can't satisfy Curly, that he and his friends would rather have whores? In the dream, Jud takes her to a saloon with "rooms" upstairs (like the rooms of "paradise" Ali Hakim described to Annie?). Significantly, in the original production, the saloon was represented by chandeliers, a few pieces of furniture, and a staircase that stood out in the middle of nowhere, not connected to anything at the top. Laurey runs up the stairs to escape Jud, but finds nothing at the top, because Laurey doesn't know what's at the top of saloon stairs and this is her dream. Curly enters, ready to kill Jud and rescue Laurey, and the music turns to "Pore Jud Is Daid," reminding us of the foreshadowing of death that song provided. All Laurey's fears of sex climax as the music turns to "Lonely Room," representing her fears of Jud, of his smokehouse, of his postcards, of his whole scary life.

Laurey's fear of Jud is terribly important. It's not just about who she'll go to the box social with; it's about facing her sexuality, about the implications of her sexuality, about whether Jud will steal her virginity, and all this is filtered through the exaggerated drama of adolescence. She genuinely fears for Curly's life, and we know that this fear may be legitimate. Her choice may be trivial to an outsider, but it's not trivial to Laurey and that's what raises the dream sequence and the entire show to a level of genuine drama. If we care about Laurey at this point, we must care about this, too. The first act ends not with the typical lovers' spat, not with a silly cliff-hanger, but instead with death and sexuality, set to horrific, dissonant musical quotations of the two most romantic songs in Act I, "People Will Say We're in Love" and "Surrey with the Fringe on Top."

In the dream, Jud murders Curly and this moment accomplishes two things. First, it makes it clear that to Laurey, this really is a life-and-death decision. Second, it foreshadows real danger for Curly and leaves us wondering if in fact Jud *will* kill Curly in real life. The earlier action of Act I sets up the very real possibility of Curly's murder at Jud's hand, and this reinforces it. The dramatic reversal late in Act II of Jud's death at Curly's hand, after we've seen Jud's plans and attempts to kill Curly, delivers the tension that keeps us interested. Contrary to Sondheim's comments, this *is* about life and death.

The smartest move in the show is that Rodgers and Hammerstein didn't end the act inside the dream. Instead, Laurey wakes and Jud is there waiting to take her to the box social while Curly looks on from the side. All the things Laurey fears are not just in the dream world; they exist in the real world, too. Laurey leaves with Jud to a very dissonant version of "People Will Say We're in Love," the music Laurey associates with her love for Curly, but now turned nightmarish and frightening. And that's how the curtain comes down.

With the dream, Rodgers and Hammerstein—and de Mille—raised the stakes and, in the process, elevated the show from a mere slice of life to a dark, psychological drama. Just as the untamed prairie of the Oklahoma territory has it dangers, so does the territory of un-bridled human sexuality. And just as the territory must be tamed by becoming a state and joining the union, so too must Jud be conquered by Curly before the show can end. The social context of the story serves as a macrocosm of the personal drama, further proof that the show's title song is an indispensable part of the show. It's also proof that *Oklahoma!* is not just about a picnic. It's a rich, complex, sophisticated work of theatre that clearly deserves its reputation for beginning a revolution.

Other Resources

There are several recordings of *Oklahoma!*. The original cast album is available on CD, with some previously unreleased songs now included. Though it's a great record of how the show was first done, the performances have no subtlety and the acting isn't all that strong. The film soundtrack is also on CD and much better. The 1979 revival cast recording is great, but the best all-around recording is that of the 1998 London cast. Some of the arrangements are a bit different from the standard rental version, but it's so much more satisfying dramatically. The film version, which is pretty faithful to the show—though missing "Lonely Room" and "It's a Scandal"—is on video. Vocal selections and the full piano score are both available, but the script is not currently in print. There are several biographies of Rodgers and Hammerstein, and most of them have good info about *Oklahoma!*, but there are two really excellent books, Max Wilk's *Overture and Finale*, which is about *Oklahoma!* and *The Sound of Music*, and Ethan Mordden's *Rodgers & Hammerstein*, a great coffee-table book with wonderful info. Both offer outstanding information on the creation of the show and its place in musical theatre history.

▟ Anyone Can Whistle

Book by Arthur Laurents
Music and lyrics by Stephen Sondheim
Originally directed on Broadway by Arthur Laurents
Licensed by Music Theatre International

Marcus Aurelius said, "The object of life is not to be on the side of the majority, but to escape finding oneself in the ranks of the insane." *Anyone Can Whistle*, an absurdist social satire about insanity and conformity, among a dozen other things, is probably the bravest show Stephen Sondheim wrote, at least until *Assassins*. It was also a spectacular flop when it first hit Broadway in 1964, running only nine performances before closing.

After writing lyrics for *West Side Story* and *Gypsy*, Sondheim had made his Broadway debut as a composer in 1962 with *A Funny Thing Happened on the Way to the Forum*, but it was with *Anyone Can Whistle* two years later that the world saw the first glimpse of Sondheim's rebel genius. The show had a book by Arthur Laurents, who had written the books for *West Side Story* and *Gypsy*, but *Whistle's* plot was too unconventional and wickedly satiric to find an audience while elsewhere on Broadway people could see more pleasant, easier to understand shows like *Hello Dolly!*.

Sondheim's score for *Whistle* was a quirky blend of the kind of dissonant, electrifying music he used more confidently in *Company* (1970) and his other later shows, along with a deft takeoff of traditional show tunes to point up the insincerity and shallowness of some of the characters. Unfortunately, since it made fun of the people in the audience, as well as the kind of show tunes they most enjoyed, the show met with more hostility than excitement. The *New York Times* began its review with the statement "There is no law against saying something in a musical, but it's unconstitutional to omit imagination and wit." John Chapman, in the *Daily News*, called the first act "joyously daffy" but didn't much like the rest. John McClain, in the *Journal-American*, actually praised the show and reported that the opening night audience liked the show so much that it cheered in the midst of several numbers. Norman Nadel, in the *World Telegram & Sun*, called the show "spectacularly original," "breathtaking," and "ingenious." But nothing can make up for a bad review in the *Times*. It closed a week later.

Yet because of a cast album recorded after the show had already closed, *Anyone Can Whistle* became a cult favorite over the years. Sondheim has admitted it has serious flaws, despite its considerable charm and humor. The show tells the story of a town that's gone bankrupt because its only industry is manufacturing something that never wears out. In order to revive her town, Mayoress Cora Hoover Hooper and her town council fake a miracle—water flowing from a rock—to attract tourists. When patients at the local mental hospital, the Cookie Jar, escape and mix with the townspeople and tourists, chaos ensues. Somehow, Sondheim and Arthur Laurents managed to shoehorn a love story in as well, between J. Bowden Hapgood, a psychiatrist who isn't really a psychiatrist, and Fay Apple, a nurse at the Cookie Jar who disguises herself as a miracle verifier sent from Lourdes. In addition to the outrageous subject matter and sharp social commentary, the three-act show also included a groundbreaking, thirteen-minute integrated musical sequence that ended the first act. *Whistle* was not just breaking the rules of traditional musical comedy, it was thumbing its nose at them—and, unfortunately, also at its audience.

It didn't help that the show's competition on Broadway that year included more traditional, crowd-pleasing musicals such as *Hello Dolly!, Funny Girl, Fiddler on the Roof*, and others. With a delicious sense of irony, Sondheim rewrote history in one scene of his 1981 showbiz musical *Merrily We Roll Along*. The central character, a Broadway composer named Frank Shepard, gets his first hit show on Broadway in that same 1964 season. As he and his friends celebrate their success in the theatre lobby with the song "It's a Hit," his producer declares their hit show is even better than *Funny Girl, Fiddler*, and *Hello Dolly!* combined. *Anyone Can Whistle* was finally vindicated, if only fictionally. Yet in the ultimate twist of fate, *Merrily We Roll Along* ran only sixteen performances.

The Trouble with Hapgood

Anyone Can Whistle is really two musicals, two very different, not entirely compatible musicals. It's part absurdist social satire, breaking the fourth wall, acknowledging itself as theatre, rejecting naturalism and sometimes even conventional logic; and part romantic musical comedy, complete with love songs and a happily ever after for the hero and heroine and even the villains. So many people have tried to stage the show but have crashed and burned because they couldn't reconcile the two distinct styles. The show's primary problem is beautifully illustrated by its title. Originally it was to be called *The Natives Are Restless*, but then the title changed to *Side Show* (promotional materials still exist with that title), and we can guess that it was more absurdist at that point. When the title was changed to *Anyone Can Whistle*, after one of the love songs, it represented a shift in the show's focus, away from wacky anarchy and more toward romantic love story. Yet with so much satirical material left in the show, that change in focus only left audiences confused.

Unless a director can bring the show's two "personalities" together into a unified whole, the show can't work. Since the biting absurdism can't become romantic comedy, the only solution seems to be to treat the love story as absurdist. Arthur Laurents has said that the show should've ended without the romantic love duet "With So Little to Be Sure Of." But losing Fay and Hapgood's resolution would cause lots of problems as well. As with *Cabaret*, it's almost as if the show's creators wanted to be daring but were afraid of being too daring so they stuck some traditional musical comedy moments into the show to mollify the audience. It didn't work, commercially or artistically, which is not to say the show isn't good, but it is problematic.

Even the basic structure of the show is strange. First, it's in three acts, which is very rare for musicals. Second, the central conflict established in the first song—the town is starving—is resolved in the second song with the fake miracle. Then we get what is *really* the central conflict of the show: the hospital patients (the Cookies) mix in with the tourists, and the town council needs to separate them because if the Cookies drink the water from the fake miracle and don't get healed, then everyone will know it's a hoax. In a way, this becomes a metaphor for the biggest problem with the show, that the absurdist satire, personified by the Cookies, is hopelessly mixed up with the traditional Broadway musical, represented by the "normal" people. And then, there's *another* central conflict, which is Fay's inability to express her feelings to Hapgood. The show can't even figure out which is the central conflict, who is the protagonist, and what needs resolving.

There's No Tune Like a Show Tune

The score also has a split personality, though with better reason. Sondheim uses traditional show-tune styles for the insincere characters. Cora and her town council sing old-fashioned show tunes—all with a wicked Sondheimian twist, of course—and these songs connote shallowness, insincerity, artificiality, and deceit (what does this say about Sondheim's feelings toward old-fashioned show tunes?). Sondheim has used this kind of pastiche (the use of older traditional song forms as commentary) in many of his shows. It distances us from what's happening, as we become more aware of the music as *music* instead of as accompaniment to a character's thoughts and words. He has used pastiche in "You Could Drive a Person Crazy" and "What Would We Do Without You" in *Company*, in half the score of *Follies*, in *Assassins*, and in other shows. In every case, the use of pastiche removes the song from the strange reality of musical comedy, in which people break out into song and no one notices, and it turns the song into a commentary.

In contrast, songs about genuine emotion in *Anyone Can Whistle* are set to the more romantic, complex, rich music we've come to know as distinctly Sondheim. The music for Fay and Hapgood's songs sounds a lot like the ballads in *Company* and *Into the Woods*. It's an interesting way to separate the characters into two camps—good guys and bad guys—but it emphasizes the show's biggest flaw and we have to ask if Sondheim's intentions are really ever communicated to audiences. Perhaps this conceit works better today than it did in 1964, with more sophisticated theatregoers, who are more attuned to the subtlety and complexity of Sondheim's music.

Old-Fashioned Show Tunes

The first time we hear singing in the show is in "I'm Like the Bluebird," sung by the Cookies in the style of a children's song. It's only a fragment, but we'll hear it again later. The first full song in the show is Cora's "Me and My Town," a brassy, bluesy, old-fashioned show tune full of Gershwinesque harmonies and intricate, clever rhymes. To emphasize Cora's duplicity, the song keeps switching back and forth between traditional show tune and a fiery Latin beat in the middle mambo section. The central joke of the song is a lyric full of tragic, depressing news about the town and its people, set to a jazzy, upbeat, Broadway torch song that asks for pity for the rich and powerful Cora. The funniest and most startling aspect of the song is the fact that backup singers appear for no dramatic reason whatsoever to sing the song with Cora. Sondheim is reminding us not only how artificial Cora is but also how artificial musical comedy is. At the end of the song, Sondheim returns to Cora's bluesy show-tune melody, this time combined with the mambo beat underneath. It's a great, splashy opening number that manages to be somewhat disconcerting as well.

The next song, "Miracle Song," is another pastiche, this time in the style of a revival meeting gospel number. It starts like a hymn in both its tempo and its modal harmonies, then moves into an upbeat, full-throttle gospel choral number, complete with a lead singer and responses from the "congregation." The lyrics are hilarious, demonstrating that Cora and her town council are far more excited by the miracle's inevitable financial rewards than by the miracle itself. Treasurer Cooley welcomes the "pilgrims" to the miracle, tellingly rhyming "Hear ye the joyful bells!" with "Fill ye the new motels." Meanwhile, Cora's contempt for the townspeople is reinforced with her lyric:

> Come and take the waters
> And with luck you'll be
> Anything whatever, except you.

The use of pastiche in the music comments on the characters who are singing. Even the townspeople are painted as insincere, implying that though "water that you part" and "water that you walk on" aren't real miracles, this water from a rock is. The song's lyric repeats the phrase "The Lord said . . . ," making it sound even more like a religious song, and thereby commenting on the mindlessness of the religious beliefs of the masses. Again, it's easy to see why audiences were put off by the show. It ridicules deeply and widely held convictions and institutions that are the very bedrock of our society. That the satire is often on the mark just makes it worse.

Strike Up the Band

The song "There Won't Be Trumpets" was cut in the original production because it came after a long, brilliant comic speech by Fay. The song is good, and it's Fay's only song in Act I, but it's an anticlimax coming after that speech. It provides some setup for Hapgood's subsequent entrance, but the scene works just as well without it. In the rental materials for the show, the song is not listed in the musical numbers at the front of the script, but it has been reinstated in the text of the script. Whether or not it belongs there is open for debate. This is the first song in the show (if it's used) that is not pastiche. It begins with a furious, dissonant introductory verse, somewhat reminiscent of music from *West Side Story*, then segues into the rich, romantic music Sondheim writes so well. The lyric contains very little rhyme. Sondheim has said that in his work, rhyme connotes intelligence and mental agility; the lack of rhyme indicates more emotional, less intellectual content. This is a song about Fay's deepest emotional hopes and beliefs and therefore the lyric is simple and straightforward, without Sondheim's usual verbal gymnastics.

It's interesting that in the second verse of the song, Sondheim adds a strong march feel to the accompaniment, even though the lyric is saying there *won't* be trumpets (or drums). The point is that when Fay's hero comes, she won't need trumpets to generate excitement; his presence will be enough. True to his lyric, the orchestration for this song is conspicuously lacking trumpets. So as she talks about his arrival, about what he'll be like, the music builds in intensity and excitement without resorting to the use of trumpets. The fanfares in the orchestration, usually reserved for trumpets, are played here by woodwinds and the xylophone, which sounds like a glockenspiel, a staple of marching bands. Orchestrator Don Walker does use brass in the song but only the low brass, mainly horns and trombones.

Not Simple

"Simple," the thirteen-minute climax of Act I, is anything but. In this musical sequence, the town council demands that Hapgood figure out who in the crowd are Cookies and who are tourists or townspeople. Hapgood breaks everyone up into two groups, Group A and Group One, but he refuses to say which group is sane and which is insane. The basic frame of this song is classic, dissonant Sondheim music, but the various sections frequently use both pastiche and parody of other musical styles to satirize and blow holes in a myriad of social institutions.

The musical and verbal chaos of this extended musical scene builds until Hapgood looks out at the audience and declares, "You are all mad!" The circuslike music from the overture, which probably made more sense when the show was called *Side Show*, is heard once again, and lights come up pointing into the audience's eyes, blinding them as the stage lights go down. When the stage lights come up again, mere seconds later, the cast is seated in theatre seats on stage, laughing, applauding, and pointing at the audience in amusement. There is a blackout and the first act is over.

Who is being watched and who is doing the watching? Who is sane and who is insane? Who are the real fools? As interesting as this bizarre finale is, will an audience understand Sondheim and Laurents' point? Were audiences for the original production hostile because they *didn't* get it or because they did?

Act II

After the "A-1 March" at the top of Act II, the Lady from Lourdes enters—actually Fay in disguise—and is soon flirting with Hapgood. Before we know it, the two of them are singing the show's first love song, "Come Play Wiz Me." This song is a foxtrot, a style that Sondheim loves and has used in several of his shows. Even when he was writing only lyrics, he used the foxtrot, as in both "Some People" and "You'll Never Get Away from Me" in *Gypsy*. "Come Play Wiz Me" is a sophisticated, sexy song, full of witty lyrics, puns, and even a couple instances of the French lyrics being played against the English ("In time, mais oui, we may."). Sondheim's affection for blues notes is evident here. It's significant that when Fay sings the title phrase, the note on "me" is a blues note, and it's also a false relation—a B-flat in the voice against a B-natural in the accompaniment. Perhaps setting "me" on a false relation is some kind of comment on the disguised Fay's "false relation" with Hapgood. The song is also teeming with syncopation, delayed downbeats, and blues harmonies, a kind of risqué, urbane song we might have otherwise expected to be Cole Porter's, especially since Porter loved incorporating French phrases into his lyrics. Again, because the characters are playing around here and are not expressing genuine emotion, the music is a (semi)traditional show tune and not the kind of full romantic music Sondheim saved for genuine emotions.

The title song, "Anyone Can Whistle," is one of those songs of genuine emotion, no artifice, no cleverness, so it's pure romantic Sondheim. There's no pastiche here, no commentary. This song has the simplest accompaniment in the score, a musical illustration of the lyric that describes the kind of easy things that Fay longs to be able to master. As with the other emotional songs in the score, there is only minimal rhyme and none of the witty puns and internal rhymes the other songs have. For those who have criticized Sondheim and his work for being too cold, too bereft of real emotion, this song stands as proof that they're wrong. Fay is a character whose feelings are so deep, so profound that she is terrified of them, paralyzed by them. Instead of yet another trivial, cliche-ridden love song about moons and stars (yes, *West Side Story*'s "Tonight" is such a song, but in that case the writers *intended* for these love-struck children to be capable of only clichés), Sondheim has written a gut-wrenching song of real emotional muscle, a song about personal complexity, about how real people feel in the real world. Like Bobby in *Company* and George in *Sunday in the Park with George*, the depth of Fay's own emotions is the most terrifying thing of all. All three of these Sondheim characters find it safer and easier to choose to subvert and submerge their feelings. It's been said that nothing is sadder than seeing someone else trying to hide his or her sadness, and that's ultimately what makes Bobby, George, and Fay so much more moving than tragic characters in other musicals. Yet we return to the same question: does this belong in an absurdist social satire?

After a brief return to Cora and another of her pastiche numbers, this time the Sousa-esque "There's a Parade in Town," the show comes back again to the love story as Fay and Hapgood decide what to do about the Cookies' predicament, a plot element that has been mostly ignored since Act I. Again, the next song, "Everybody Says Don't," is a non-pastiche number. Aside from Fay and Hapgood's first song in which they flirt playfully, with Hapgood not yet knowing who Fay really is, none of their music together is pastiche. This is an indication to us that their relationship is something to be taken seriously, but that also makes it even harder to fit them into the larger context of the show. "Everybody Says Don't" sits on a driving accompaniment rhythm that is close to the foxtrot tempo we heard earlier, and the vocal line is almost a patter song. Because this is more a song of philosophy than of deep emotion, the lyric is clever and full of rhyme. "Anyone Can Whistle" was a song about Fay's fears; this is Hapgood's song about conquering those fears. It follows dramatically, and this song seems to fit the style and plot of Act I better than the rest of Act II does.

Everybody Should Have Said Don't

At the end of the act, Fay destroys the Cookies' records one by one, "freeing" them by erasing their identities as mental patients. The "Don't" ballet is a musical and choreographic dramatization of this concept, as we see each Cookie break free and dance around the stage when his record is destroyed. The "Don't" ballet—which was written by dance arranger Betty Walberg, not by Sondheim—is an extremely long, very strange piece. It starts with a parody of Gershwin's *American in Paris*, played by a muted trumpet, then moves into the accompaniment vamp from "Everybody Says Don't." At one point, it imitates the *West Side Story* prologue musically and percussively, and it's unclear whether this is an intentional imitation, as a joke or maybe as some kind of commentary on theatre dance music at the time (this was seven years after *West Side Story* opened), or if Walberg did this unconsciously. She uses lots of heavy jazz chords that again sound more like Bernstein's *West Side Story* music than like Sondheim's music for *Anyone Can Whistle*. It all ends with another quotation of the *American in Paris* imitation, first by the trumpets, then the piccolo. It even ends with big, full orchestral Gershwin chords.

Because the show is such a gleefully nasty satire most of the time, it's tempting to think this is a clever parody of *An American in Paris* and *West Side Story*. But what is it making fun of? The music of Bernstein and Gershwin? Or is it poking fun at Jerome Robbins' groundbreaking choreography for *West Side Story*? Neither seems appropriate here since all the other targets in the show are public institutions that deserve the satiric spears. And though Sondheim uses other musical theatre forms in his songs, he never parodies them; he always treats them with respect, developing them, using them to comment on the action, not on the song forms themselves. Yet how would parodies of Bernstein and Gershwin comment on the characters or institutions in *Anyone Can Whistle*?

Act III

Act III returns us to the antagonists of the Act I plot—Cora, Schub, Cooley, and MacGruder—who got almost no time in Act II. They need to destroy the miracle and blame it on Hapgood. This will cause the town to turn against Hapgood and keep the Cookies from ruining their fake miracle and exposing Cora and the council as crooks and fakes. "I've Got You to Lean On" starts out as musical dialogue, similar in style to sections of "Simple," which makes dramatic sense and provides some musical continuity. Then the main body of the song moves into a perky foxtrot rhythm, matched with funny, biting lyrics and plenty of internal rhyme. The third section returns to the kind of musical dialogue that opened the song, this time accompanied by the kind of modal harmonies that were used, though more slowly, in the "Miracle Song," as the conspirators decide to publicly denounce Hapgood as an enemy of God and the church. The subtext of the lyric is hilarious. The men show their political cowardice and their willingness to let Cora take the heat if the plan fails when they sing, "When everything's hollow and black, you'll always have us at your back." In response, Cora lets them know she won't be indicted without naming names. She sings, "What comfort it is to have always known that if they should catch me, I won't go alone." The song ends with a old-fashioned soft-shoe dance break.

When the council turns off the miracle and declares it Hapgood's fault, the crowd turns on Hapgood, while a variation on the "Simple" accompaniment plays as underscoring. Hapgood and Fay discover Cora and Schub's deceit, and Cora orders them both out of town, to underscoring reminiscent of the "Miracle Song." Cora is back in control. Fay wants to expose Cora to the town, but Hapgood won't help her. He thinks that will only cause more trouble for Fay and him and won't accomplish anything. Feeling betrayed, Fay erupts into the angry "See What It Gets You," a song combining the pseudofoxtrot rhythm of "Everybody Says Don't" with a driving, erratic bass line. Hapgood has convinced Fay to risk her quiet life, her security, but once she's done it, he's not there to back her up. Fay even quotes—sarcastically—"Anyone Can Whistle" to finish this song, but this time it's in a fast, agitated, unnatural tempo, with the woodwinds quoting "Everybody Says Don't" in between vocal lines. Sondheim has brought together Fay and Hapgood's relationship musically: the foxtrot accompaniment of "Come Play Wiz Me"; Fay's first emotional song, "Anyone Can Whistle"; Hapgood's response, "Everybody Says Don't"; and, finally, Fay's counterresponse, "See What It Gets You." Though the Fay and Hapgood subplot may not sit too comfortably on the rest of the plot, it certainly makes a complete musical story in and of itself.

The act continues with "Cora's Chase," a lengthy musical sequence consisting of a gleefully nasty waltz sung primarily by Cora ("Lock 'em up, put 'em away . . ."), as suspected Cookies are rounded up and arrested, alternating with extended instrumental dance breaks. In the midst of it all is a comic a cappella quartet version of Cora's main melody, treated with solemn religious reverence; then it speeds up as it returns to the manic pitch of the rest of the piece. Toward the end, the chorus appears, singing frantically "Run for your lives, run for your lives," a kind of precursor to *Sweeney Todd*'s "City on Fire"; the lyric even mentions fire. Cora and Schub tell Fay that they'll lock up whatever forty-nine people they want, innocent or not, sane or insane, unless Fay reveals the names of the real Cookies. She has no choice, so she does. As the Cookies are assembled, they reprise their theme song, "I'm Like the Bluebird."

The last song in the show, "With So Little to Be Sure Of," returns to Fay and Hapgood's romantic subplot and the romantic Sondheim style of music that has accompanied it. The song starts with a quick quote of "Come Play Wiz Me," a reminder of how all this started— in case you'd forgotten—and then the main body of the song is one of Sondheim's most lush, beautiful melodies. But again, we have to ask if it belongs in this show. After a few more pieces of incidental music while the plot ties up loose ends and one more rendition of "I'm Like the Bluebird" from the Cookies, the show is over and Hapgood and Fay walk off into the sunset together to an instrumental quote of "With So Little to Be Sure Of."

Mad as Hell

The old cliche that only the insane can see clearly is embodied by Hapgood. He is our hero, the only one who can cut through all the crap, who can see how absurd it all is. And late in the show, we find out he's a patient in the Cookie Jar and not really a doctor—because, of course, all doctors are fools. In the opening scene, the townspeople are described in the stage directions as wearing stylized rags and clown wigs, yet when the Cookies, the insane, enter, they are described as pleasantly dressed and smiling. Even the official name of the Cookie Jar, Dr. Detmold's Asylum for the Socially Pressured, shows the authors' bias against the socially conventional view of sanity and insanity. In the interrogation, Cora thinks George is crazy because he doesn't have headaches and backaches, like "normal" people do, we presume. The show goes to great lengths to condemn conformity and makes the questionable and subversive assumption that anyone in an asylum is really just a nonconformist or freethinker. Fay describes the Cookies as the people "who made other people nervous by leading individual lives." Schub says that safe (i.e., conformity) is sane, and Hapgood replies, "Not always." Hapgood tells us at the end of the first act that we are all mad. He tells Fay that the world made the Cookies crazy. He says, "I was probably the craziest man in the world. Because I was not only an idealist, I was a practicing idealist!" Being crazy is portrayed as somehow braver, more noble, and infinitely preferable to being sane.

At the same time, psychiatry is immediately suspect, since its purpose is to cure insanity and being crazy is a good thing. In a big slam against the methods of psychiatrists, Dr. Detmold, the symbol of conventional psychiatry, says, "Psychiatrists do not fraternize with patients . . ." Hapgood lampoons these methods and doublespeak when he rationalizes calling George "Hapgood":

> Calling the patient by my name, he identifies with me immediately, we have an instant transference and thereby save five years of psychoanalysis.

Of course, the mere fact that Hapgood, a patient himself, can pass so easily for a doctor suggests that psychiatrists know nothing anyway. The Cookies love him because "Hapgood has no answers or suggestions, only a lot of questions." The harshest condemnation of doctors is their comparison to the 1950s greatest evil, Communists, when Hapgood says, "I am not now nor have I ever been a member of the medical profession," echoing the watchcry of Senator Joseph McCarthy's House Un-American Activities Committee.

Sondheim even takes direct aim at McCarthy and his anti-Communist witch-hunts. In the interrogation, Schub declares that Hapgood is "boring from within," the common accusation of communists, and then Schub actually calls Hapgood a communist, which

Hapgood ridicules. MacGruder says his occupation is fighting the enemy. Hapgood asks "What enemy?" and MacGruder replies, "What year?" Unfortunately, McCarthy had been toppled years before *Anyone Can Whistle* opened, so the satire was a bit dated, but it was on target nevertheless.

Absolute Power Corrupts Absolutely

The show's creators apparently think as little of politicians as they do of doctors. Every politician portrayed is corrupt, greedy, and generally amoral. Of course they're also ultimately incompetent. The politicians all have money, especially Cora, while the townspeople starve to death. Schub's proof that his plan will work is that it's unethical. Yet we, the audience, are indicted for putting people like them in office. Cooley reminisces about the good old days, when the populace was "normal and frightened." In the interrogation, George says he votes, but "only for the man who wins," a shot at modern political polls and ignorant voters. The "A-1 March" is a parody of the lack of substance in two-party politics. The greatest indictment of politics is that Hapgood, a mental patient, was once an advisor to the president. The plot development in which the town council sets up Hapgood as the reason the miracle water stops is an illustration of how badly the public needs a scapegoat when things aren't going well.

For God's Sake

Anyone Can Whistle's other great target is religion—not God, really, just religion. The "Miracle Song" is the centerpiece of this attack. The satire begins with the crass materialistic manufacture of a "miracle" to attract "pilgrims." Cora and her council and their commercialization of religion are the fictional counterparts of the bevy of televangelists practicing today, some of whom even own their own cable networks. They make millions—some billions—by literally selling religion and religious merchandise. In *Anyone Can Whistle*, they're selling the privilege to partake of the miracle water and be cured. They tell the pilgrims they can partake of the miracle for a modest fee. When business booms, Cora decides they're so prosperous they could issue stock. We laugh at this line, but how different is it from Pat Robertson's multibillion-dollar Christian Broadcast Network? As with most religious peddlers, this crew contends that its miracle is the greatest of them all:

> There's water that you part,
> Water that you walk on,
> Water that you turn to wine!
> But water from a rock—Lord! What a miracle!
> This is a miracle that's divine,
> Truly divine!

In other words, parting water, walking on water, and turning water to wine aren't really miracles, at least not miracles that are *truly* divine. Cora and her cronies are dismissing the miracles of Jesus as minor accomplishments beside their own. As outrageous as this seems, it's not all that different from what actually happens in the God business. Many a preacher claims that his religion is the only real one, that other religions are false, that believers in other religions will necessarily burn in eternal damnation.

Cooley, the treasurer, used to be a preacher himself, thereby tying money and religion together again. Cooley and Schub actually discuss licensing and merchandising rights for the miracle and for Baby Joan, who "discovered" the fake miracle rock. During the interrogation, the show returns to the subject of religion during Cooley's interview. We find out that Cooley was thrown out of the pulpit "because I believed . . . in God and they only believed in religion."

Later in the show, the council actually declares that God turned off the miracle waters because there are sick people running loose in the town, infecting the town, just as one prominent real-life televangelist once declared that Florida was hit by a hurricane because God was angry at America's acceptance of gays and lesbians. The council decides to label Hapgood as an enemy of heaven and an enemy of God himself, just as today's religious conservatives do with anyone who disagrees with them. Hapgood and the Cookies become the convenient scapegoats for the townspeople to hate and blame for their perceived misfortune. As ridiculous and contrived as this all seems, it's exactly what happens in the real world. It's just hard for us to believe people can be that manipulative and hateful. This is perhaps *Whistle's* most accurate and therefore most dangerous satire.

The *Is* Have It

Along with exploring conformity and nonconformity, *Anyone Can Whistle* also explores identity. So many of the characters in the show indulge in role playing: Hapgood as a doctor, Fay as the Lady from Lourdes, the Cookies as pilgrims, Cora as a caring civil servant, Cora and her council as heroes, and most startling, the actors as the audience at the end of Act I. Fay's inability to have fun except in costume is a comment not only on restrictive social mores and roles but also on theatre itself. Hapgood calls the Cookies by his own name, swapping their identities with his own identity, which is already not real; or perhaps it's *more* real after the swap, since he's actually a Cookie. The transposition of actors and audience at the end of the first act is one of the most provocative moments in all of musical theatre. Who is the spectacle and who is the observer? The audience is traditionally considered the observer, but theatre—and especially satire—is the true observer, watching and commenting on real life, as represented by the real people in the audience. The characters onstage are crazy, but art is just imitating life; the *real* crazies are in the real world, and maybe they are there in the audience.

During the interrogation, June and John mix up the stereotypical gender roles, with John as June's secretary even though he still pays for her dinners. They both refer to each other and to themselves in the third person and apply the wrong gender pronouns to each other. Soon after that, Schub says he saw a man cross over from one group to the other, but Hapgood tells him it was a woman. Gender roles have been skewed, along with everything else. And June and John also serve as a commentary on marriage; as a couple, June and John have lost their individual identities. The old-fashioned cliche "A woman's place is in the house" is set to rhyme against "And that is where you hang your spouse." This smashing of gender roles and loss of identity is briefly touched on again later in the show, when Hapgood says, "I chased four women in my life—and every one of 'em caught me and tried to change me."

All There in Black and White

Anyone Can Whistle takes only one shot at racism in our culture, but it's a big shot and it's well aimed. In the interrogation, Hapgood interviews a black man named Martin. Martin's watchcry is "You can't judge a book by its cover," a clear enough condemnation of racism. But it is immediately twisted, first by bad grammar, then by a ridiculous stereotypical "Negro" dialect. *Cover* becomes *cubber*, a once widely used attempt at southern black dialect that Sondheim is parodying. It sounds silly to our ears but this was once considered standard practice in lyrics by Ira Gershwin and other top lyricists. In *Porgy and Bess*, in the song, "I Got Plenty o' Nuthin'," the word *heaven* becomes *hebben*; and in "It Ain't Necessarily So," the word *devil* becomes *debble*, which is strange, since the characters sing *V* sounds in other moments in the show.

Hapgood then asks Martin what he does for a living, and Martin replies, "Going to schools, riding in busses, eating in restaurants." It becomes clear from this line that Martin's watchcry is a reference to the civil rights movement that was still going on in 1964 when *Anyone Can Whistle* opened and to the attempts at desegregation and the ending of discrimination based on race. A big part of the movement involved various sit-ins, in which black activists deliberately broke the segregation laws by going to "whites only" schools, riding in the front of buses instead of the back, where they legally belonged, and eating in "whites only" restaurants. Of course, great strides had been made by 1964, so that's why Hapgood comments that Martin's line of work was getting rather easy. Martin replies, "Not for me. I'm Jewish," invoking yet *another* group suffering from virulent racism in the 1950s and '60s. On top of everything else, Sondheim and Laurents named the character Martin, after Martin Luther King Jr. The interview with Martin is capped off with the most brazen satire in Hapgood's syllogisms:

> *The opposite of dark is bright,*
> *The opposite of bright is dumb.*
> *So anything that's dark is dumb—*

And Martin finishes it, with one more stereotype:

> *But they sure can hum.*

When the lines are repeated the second time, Martin ends with a new line, "Depends where you're from," commenting on the fact that racism was still worse in certain parts of the country, even though the Supreme Court had outlawed segregation ten years earlier, in 1954.

To Produce or Not to Produce

Now ask if you should produce *Anyone Can Whistle*. Yes, you should, providing your audience is open-minded enough to enjoy an interesting, funny musical with some relatively serious flaws. Even if your audience is confused by much of the show's story, by the scattershot, hit-and-miss satire, and by the Marx Brothers–style anarchy of "Simple," there are still plenty of surefire laughs, some beautiful songs, and the opportunity to say they've seen this rarely produced Sondheim gem. It will take some serious effort to make sense of the script and score and decisions will have to be made about how to fuse the show's two disparate styles, but despite its problems, it is a remarkable piece of musical theatre, remarkable for its ambitions, its brazen bucking of convention, its considerable charm, and the fact that it was the first Sondheim show that really gave us a glimpse at the genius of his later work. Just as it's fun to see Shakespeare's early plays as much for their promise of later greatness as for their own strengths, *Anyone Can Whistle* provides a similar joy. And it's still a better musical than two-thirds of what Broadway has turned out in the last fifty years.

But one of the fatal flaws of *Anyone Can Whistle* is that it takes aim at too many targets. It satirizes religion, politics and government, psychiatry and doctors in general, tourism, marriage, gender roles, racism, and more. The satire is generally very funny, very wicked, and usually on target, but the audience can get lost trying to register all the satire while it's keeping track of who's the hero and who's the villain, keeping up with the French dialogue, paying attention to various disguises and alter egos, and trying to figure out whether the show is absurdist social satire or romantic comedy.

Other Resources

The script for *Anyone Can Whistle* is not in print and is available from Music Theatre International only when you produce the show, although perusal scripts are available if requested. The piano-vocal score and vocal selections were published but may be difficult to find these days. The original cast album is available (it was recorded after the show had already closed in 1964), and the CD reissue includes tracks not originally released on LP, including the full "Cookie Chase" and "There Won't Be Trumpets," which was cut in previews. The

1995 Carnegie Hall concert performance, starring Bernadette Peters, Madeline Kahn, and Scott Bakula, is available on CD as well. Though the 1995 recording is a more complete recording of the score, it is missing the joy and lunacy of the original cast album, so that many people having heard only the later version find the comedy a bit heavy. The original cast—Angela Lansbury, Lee Remick, and Harry Guardino—really captures the spirit of the show better and that version is a lot more fun. The song "There's Always a Woman," which was written for Fay and Cora but cut from the Broadway production, is on the 1995 recording, as well as on the *Unsung Sondheim* CD from Varese Sarabande.

 # Hair

Book and music by James Rado and Gerome Ragni
Music by Galt MacDermot
Originally directed on Broadway by Tom O'Horgan
Licensed by Tams-Witmark Music Library

On February 2, 1962, the moon, Mercury, Venus, Mars, Jupiter, and Saturn all aligned in the constellation Aquarius. All seven of these heavenly bodies had not come together for twenty-five hundred years. Many people believed it was the dawning of a new age, the age of Aquarius, symbolizing a pooling of everyone's creativity, an age of communalism.

When the rock musical *Hair* opened, John J. O'Connor wrote in the *Wall Street Journal*, "No matter the reaction to the content . . . I suspect the form will be important to the history of the American musical." And it was, paving the way for the nonlinear concept musicals that dominated musical theatre innovation in the 1970s: *Company, Follies, A Chorus Line, Working,* and others. And yet, some Broadway establishment figures refused then and now to accept this radical departure. Even today, some people can't see past the appearance of chaos and randomness to the brilliant construction and sophisticated imagery underneath. In 1996, while reviewing *Hair*'s godchild, the rock musical *Rent*, Howard Kissel wrote in the *New York Daily News* that *Hair* had been nothing more than "formless amateurism." Even as recently as the summer of 2000, one hapless reviewer in St. Louis wrote of the show, "*Hair* remains a musical theatre anomaly, a freaked-out mish-mash of psychedelic-babble . . . You'd have to be stoned to have written it and it would help if you're watching it."

Back in the late 1960s, the artists of off Broadway and off off Broadway had been complaining that professional theatre was dead, and even worse, that it was boring. *Hair* was the revolution they had been waiting for. With very little plot, a unit set, plenty of four-letter words, explicit sexual content, rituals, drugs, lyrics that didn't rhyme, music that didn't follow the rules, and the sound of genuine rock and roll on the Broadway stage for the first time, this musical knocked Broadway on its collective ass. Not only did many of the lyrics not rhyme, but many of the songs didn't really have endings, just a slowing down and stopping, so the audience didn't know when to applaud. Other songs segued directly into the next number, so the audience didn't have time to applaud. The show rejected every convention of Broadway, of traditional theatre in general, and specifically of the American musical. And it was brilliant.

Most surprising of all, it was an enormous hit. Director Tom O'Horgan said at the time that he saw *Hair* as a once-in-a-lifetime opportunity to create "a theatre form whose demeanor, language, clothing, dance, and even its name accurately reflect a social epoch in full explosion."

The show opened first at Joseph Papp's Public Theatre in October 1967 for a limited, eight-week run. When its run ended, Papp and independent producer Michael Butler moved the show to the Cheetah, a New York disco. Papp then pulled out, and after massive revisions including thirteen new songs, new cast members, a new director (O'Horgan), a new choreographer (they wanted the movement to look more spontaneous, less choreographed), and the addition of designers Jules Fisher and Robin Wagner, Michael Butler moved the show to Broadway, opening it in April 1968 at the Biltmore Theatre. Butler's astrologer picked the opening date to ensure a successful run. *Hair* acted as a launching pad for the careers of Diane Keaton, Melba Moore, Donna Summer, Tim Curry, Nell Carter, Peter Gallagher, Joe Montegna, Ben Vereen, Cliff DeYoung, Meat Loaf, and many other performers who went on to great success.

Hair criticizes and satirizes racism, discrimination, war, violence, pollution, sexual repression, and other societal evils. It is a psychedelic musical, in the true sense of the word, perhaps the only one ever on Broadway. The show is made up of a barrage of images, often very surrealistic, often overwhelming, coming at the audience fast and furious, not always following logically; but when taken together, those images form a wonderful, unified, and ultimately comprehensible whole. At its best, the show really can cause the kind of euphoria in its audience that one usually associates with psychedelic drugs. As with most satire, *Hair* makes fun of racism, war, sex, and other things by carrying them to ridiculous extremes, as in the songs "Sodomy" and "Colored Spade." *Hair* shocks audience members, though that is not really its goal, by challenging what they believe, by showing how absurd, how offensive, how nonsensical, and in some cases, how dangerous are the behavior and language that society calls normal. And the show asks some good questions: Why did we send American soldiers halfway around the world to Vietnam to kill strangers when there was no direct threat to our country? Why can't we talk openly about sex? Why are certain words "dirty" and other words that mean the same thing acceptable? Why are there so many offensive words for black people but hardly any for white people? Why are so many straight people interested in what gay people do in private? If the Constitution guarantees free speech, why can't we burn the flag? Is it right to protest and refuse to follow laws that are unjust?

The Hippies

The hippies of the 1960s were the second generation of the "beat" movement of the 1950s. Interestingly, most hippies didn't call themselves "hippies"; they called themselves "freaks." They were in a counterculture movement that actually included many separate submovements: the drug culture, nudists and naturalists, vegetarians, "Jesus freaks," communes, environmentalists, Krishna followers, mystics, and many others. The thing that united them was their rejection of the mainstream culture, the culture of their parents. And they weren't all kids; the hippie movement started in the early '60s and, by 1969, many hippies were in their thirties or older. In fact, the older hippies were often revered as tribal wise men. The hippies were about nonviolence, individualism, a rejection of materialism, about spirituality but also a rejection of institutionalized religion, and above all, about the desire to reach a higher, purer level of consciousness. Their drug use was not just an escape; it was also a means to help them find the spirituality they believed their parents had lost in the meaningless hypocrisy of organized religion. Most hippies differentiated between good and bad drugs. The good drugs were mind-expanding, psychedelic drugs, like marijuana, peyote, and LSD, that helped them find spirituality. The bad drugs were those used only for escape, like alcohol, nicotine, tranquilizers (like valium), cocaine, and heroin. The abuse of prescription drugs by adults is satirized in Act I as two mothers—played by men—bemoan their rebellious daughters and

Berger responds by offering tranquilizers to several famous authority figures who were having trouble with rebellious kids—Rabbi Schultz (a high-profile Jewish political figure), the Rockefeller Foundation, President Nixon, Vice President Humphrey, and the Pope. The hippies condemned this kind of drug use. Notice that the drug trip song "Walking in Space" in Act II of *Hair* says explicitly that the two reasons for taking the drugs are total self-awareness and meeting God. Paul McCartney said in one '60s interview, "God is the space between us. God is the table in front of you. It just happened I realized all this through weed."

It's not surprising that the hippie movement sprung up. After World War II, America went through a very strange time. There was prosperity like the country hadn't seen in quite some time and material wealth was at an all-time high, but there was also the threat of nuclear bombs. In addition, the women who had learned during the war that they could work, that they could participate actively in society, that they could have lives outside the home, were all now thrust back into the roles of wife and mother. After having discovered genuine independence and freedom, they were now put back into their old repressive roles. After relative social chaos during the war, the already repressive American society became even more repressive to try to restore the prewar social order, which was, of course, impossible. The genie could not be put back in the lamp. As there had been during other times of social upheaval—such as the turn of the century and the Depression—there was a real friction between the demands for conformity and conservatism and the instinctive human need to express oneself, made even worse by the taste of freedom women had gotten while their husbands and boyfriends were off fighting the war. There was also a new sexual freedom knocking at America's door, courtesy of the invention of the birth control pill.

The baby boomer children growing up in the fifties had all the consumer goods they could want but found little to feed their souls. They had had extremely permissive childhoods and were then expected to fit into a repressively conformist adult world. Their parents taught conservative values while the parents' own social drinking reached heights not seen since the 1920s. Also, many more kids than ever before were being sent to college, where they were learning to question everything, to form their own opinions about the world. They found that the liberal arts education that their parents so wanted for them turned out highly educated men and women with no real-world skills, lots of unanswered existential questions, and no preparation for getting a job and starting a family. Even worse, these kids left college with endless possibilities before them—too many possibilities, it turned out. Whereas earlier generations had been locked into taking over family businesses, the baby boomers had more freedom in choosing their futures and no guideposts, and in many cases, the wide array of choices proved overwhelming.

Along with all this, the black civil rights movement was gaining steam and all these disillusioned kids found a strong, viable model for social protest. Following the example of Martin Luther King Jr. and other great black leaders, the youth of America, especially those on college campuses, started protesting all the things that they saw wrong with America: racism, environmental destruction, poverty, sexism and sexual repression, violence at home and the war in Vietnam, depersonalization from new technologies, and corruption in politics. The hippies' predecessors, the beat generation, had created a far less political counterculture. But the escalation of the war in Vietnam, the expansion of the draft, more aggressively enforced drug laws, and increased antiloitering sweeps in parks and public spaces forced the hippies to become political, and a new underground press sprung up. Contrary to popular opinion, the hippies had great respect for America and believed that *they* were the true patriots, the only ones who genuinely wanted to save their country and make it the best it could be once again.

Another difference between the beats and the hippies was the audience for their respective art. The beats' chosen art forms were poetry and jazz, and they readily admitted that their art was elitist. The hippies, on the other hand, were determined to create art of the people and their chosen art form, rock/folk music, was by its definition populist. Due in large part to Bob Dylan, country music also became a big part of the hippie music movement, as represented in *Hair* by "Don't Put It Down." But possibly the biggest difference between the music of the hippies and the music of the beats was that the hippies' music was often very angry, its anger directed at those who would prostitute the Constitution, who would sell America out, who would betray what America stood for—in other words, directed at their parents and the government.

In 1967, twenty thousand people gathered in Golden Gate Park in San Francisco for the world's first Be-In. (The term *be-in* became very popular and was later parodied in the title of the TV show *Laugh-*

In.) Despite the hippies' anticapitalist leanings and alongside their populist intentions, major record labels got the message and immediately signed several San Francisco bands to gigantic advances. In early 1967, Brian Jones of The Rolling Stones told one interviewer that things were changing, that the world "was about to enter the age of Aquarius. There is a young revolution in thought and manner about to take place." By 1968, high school teachers were teaching Bob Dylan's lyrics as poetry in English classes and psychedelic artists like Peter Max were designing mainstream advertisements.

The reason the creators of *Hair* gave their musical its title was that long hair was the hippies' flag—their "freak flag," they called it—their symbol not only of rebellion but also of new possibilities, a symbol of the rejection of discrimination and restrictive gender roles, a philosophy celebrated in the song "My Conviction." It symbolized equality between men and women. In addition to the long hair, the hippies' chosen clothing also made statements. Drab work clothes—jeans, work shirts, pea coats—were a rejection of materialism. Clothing from other cultures, particularly those of the Third World and Native Americans, represented their awareness of the global community and their rejection of U.S. imperialism and selfishness. Simple cotton dresses and other natural fabrics were a rejection of synthetics, a return to natural things and simpler times. Some hippies wore old World War II or Civil War jackets as way of co-opting the symbols of war into their newfound philosophy of nonviolence. On top of all this, nudity was a big part of the hippie culture, both as a rejection of the sexual repression of their parents and also as a statement about naturalism, spirituality, honesty, openness, and freedom. The naked body was beautiful, something to be celebrated and appreciated, not scorned and hidden. They saw their bodies and their sexuality as gifts, not as "dirty" things.

Experimental Theatre and the Bantu

In addition to the social influences of the '60s, *Hair* also came from New York's experimental theatre movement. In the late '60s, when *Hair* was created, this movement had been going on for quite some time, led by directors such as Joseph Chaikin, Peter Brook, Jerzy Grotowski, and Antonin Artaud; writers such as Samuel Beckett, Jean Genet, and Eugene Ionesco; companies such as the Living Theatre, the Group Theatre, and the Open Theatre; and theatre spaces such as

Joe Cino's Caffe Cino and Ellen Stewart's LaMaMa Experimental Theatre Club. The theatre works created during this time were based heavily on improvisation, on group creation, on ritual, on exploring new ways to communicate with an audience, and on new ways to involve an audience directly in the act of performance. The creation process, often done in extended workshops, was as important—or, in some cases, more important—than the actual presentation of the work. They rejected the conventional notions of director, playwright, script, rehearsal, and character.

Ritual was important to *Hair* because of its roots in experimental theatre but also because of its spiritual roots. The show's opening number, "Aquarius," is a ritual summoning of the tribe, a formal calling together of the members of this group of hippies. In the original Broadway production, when the song began, the hippies were out in the audience mingling with audience members. They froze and then began moving to the stage in slow motion, coming together on stage and forming a large circle, a potent symbol of life that would be used throughout the show. Ritual is used in many moments in the show, in the mock Catholic mass of "Sodomy," in the Be-In, in the passing of the joints before the trip, in the marching and chanting that happen throughout the show.

Another area the experimental theatre movement was exploring was the idea of words as sounds, as percussion, or as background noise, divorced from literal meaning, something Gertrude Stein had played with earlier in the century. In songs like "Ain't Got No Grass," "Three-Five-Zero-Zero," and "The Bed," words come at the audience like a freight train, so fast, so quirky that no audience could ever catch it all or comprehend it all. But the purpose of these lyrics isn't just to be comprehended; they are to be enjoyed as abstract sounds. Toward the end of "Ain't Got No Grass," the lyric deconstructs itself into a list of words and phrases based on the sound *pop*. The words don't make complete sense; they have become percussion. They are no longer meaningful words; they are now just sounds. *Hair* was the first impressionist Broadway musical, in which lyrics, dialogue, plot, and character were often not drawn conventionally; they were implied, suggested, abstract. Just as the impressionist painters created only the impression of form and structure, left to be interpreted and synthesized by the eye and mind, *Hair* did the same thing with the art of theatre.

Hair director Tom O'Horgan was very directly involved in the experimental theatre movement—and after *Hair*, would go on to bring that philosophy to the Broadway production of *Jesus Christ Superstar* as well. Both Gerome Ragni and James Rado, *Hair*'s authors, came out of this world, too, although both had also had mainstream success as actors on Broadway and elsewhere. In fact, Rado's initial dream was to become a mainstream Broadway songwriter in the Rodgers and Hammerstein tradition. Interestingly, neither Ragni nor Rado were hippies themselves (and only two of the original Broadway cast were), but the authors found the hippie counterculture fascinating and once they decided to write *Hair*, they spent all their time in Greenwich Village with the hippies, doing research. Off-Broadway producer Eric Blau, who would go on to create the cult hit musical *Jacques Brel Is Alive and Well and Living in Paris*, introduced Ragni and Rado to composer Galt MacDermot, who agreed to set their bizarre lyrics to music. Blau was the show's first producer, but when Papp guaranteed an eight-week run at the Public Theatre, Blau encouraged Rado and Ragni to take it; Blau could guarantee only an opening, no more.

MacDermot had been born in Montreal but went to college at Capetown University in South Africa. He brought this African influence to the music of *Hair*, using the rhythms of the rituals of the Bantu tribe, the driving pulse of African music, and the habit of musically setting stresses on unexpected syllables, as in "What a Piece of Work Is Man," "Ain't Got No Grass," and other songs.

A Really, Really Brief Look at the War

In its first, 1967 version, *Hair* was almost exclusively about the war in Vietnam. It was only when the rewrites were done as they moved the show to Broadway in 1968 that other issues were added and made more prominent. Vietnam was a major issue in the hippie movement, and though its prominence was reduced in the second version of the show on Broadway, it still formed the backdrop of the only real story line in the show, that of Claude going off to war; and an understanding of the background of the war is important to an understanding of *Hair*.

Of course, it's important to remember that people still disagree not only on interpretations of the war and motivations for the war but also on actual facts about the war. It's impossible to find two reference sources today that tell the exact same story.

Vietnam had been a possession of France since the late nineteenth century. During World War II, the French gave Vietnam to the Japanese. Toward the end of the war, a Vietnamese leader named Ho Chi Minh established a government headquartered in Hanoi, in the northern part of the country, with a constitution based loosely on the U.S. Constitution (he was an ardent admirer of Thomas Jefferson). But after the war was over, Churchill insisted that Vietnam should return to French "ownership," against the wishes of the Vietnamese people, and the French invaded to take the country back.

In 1954, a Vietnamese communist faction under the leadership of Ho Chi Minh rose up against the French and finally drove them back out of Vietnam. An international conference in Geneva, Switzerland, that year negotiated a cease-fire and decided to split the country in two, leaving the northern half of the country to Ho Chi Minh. The conference also demanded that free elections be held in 1956 to reunify the country. But the leaders in the south refused to hold the elections because they knew how widespread support was for the increasingly communist Ho Chi Minh. The United States supported this refusal because there were politicians in the United States who were so terrified by communism, so obsessed with its perceived threat that they believed the United States had to prevent the communists from taking over Vietnam. These politicians believed that there was a secret international alliance of communist countries, and that if Vietnam fell to the communists, they would then systematically take over the world, country by country, until the United States itself fell to communism. Of course, these politicians were wrong; there was no such international threat or alliance.

Based on this unfounded fear, the United States went in and set up a pseudodemocratic puppet government in the southern part of the Vietnam in 1956, claiming rule over the entire country, but Vietnamese in the north refused to recognize this government; it actually had very little power outside the city of Saigon. In addition, some of the South Vietnamese saw the Americans as no different than the French, just another foreign power who wanted to control them. In the early 1960s, a coalition of South Vietnamese communist groups, called the Vietcong, which were basically independent of the communists in North Vietnam, though connected in some ways, rose up in the south against the U.S. puppet government.

In 1964, the North Vietnamese fired on U.S. personnel, and President Johnson convinced Congress to give him free rein to take "all necessary measures" to retaliate, an act that was unprecedented and arguably unconstitutional. Some historians believe Johnson needed the war in order to energize the political right wing, to jump-start dormant patriotism, and to galvanize the American people behind his social programs and his dream of the Great Society. Unfortunately, it would not end up working the way he had planned. Johnson began by ordering the bombing of North Vietnam.

Then in 1965, the United States sent the first combat ground troops—thirty-five hundred men—into South Vietnam to fight the two enemies, the Vietcong and the North Vietnamese. Anti-war protests, marches, and demonstrations began in America around 1967, due in large part to the fact that this was the first war ever broadcast on television. The coverage wasn't what we're used to today, with correspondents reporting from the rooftops of hotels. During the Vietnam War, the reporters and cameramen were in combat with the ground troops, beaming home pictures of blood and carnage, bringing the full force of the horror of war into American living rooms. Most Americans had never seen war like this. It was real like it had never been before. The protests escalated and continued throughout the rest of the war. The Pentagon learned its lesson and never allowed such open access to the press again, and not surprisingly, there have been virtually no major antimilitary protests since then.

By 1969, with no victory in sight, President Nixon talked about plans for U.S. troop withdrawal, promising to end the war within three years. In 1973, a cease-fire was agreed to and most of the U.S. ground troops left Vietnam, but the bombing of North Vietnam continued. Eventually, in 1975, the North Vietnamese took Saigon, the biggest city in the south, renamed it Ho Chi Minh City, and effectively "won" the war, forcing the United States to pull out completely. Interestingly, once the communists took over, the U.S. politicians were proved wrong. Instead of communism spreading across Asia and Europe, the communist countries started fighting with one another and Vietnam got into a bloody war with communist China.

During the Vietnam War, more than 47,000 Americans were killed in action and more than 303,000 were wounded in action. The South Vietnamese suffered about 200,000 killed and 500,000 wounded. The North Vietnamese and the Vietcong suffered about 900,000 killed and an unknown number wounded. More than a million Vietnamese civilians were killed. The financial cost of the war ended up being about two hundred billion dollars.

The legacy of the war is that America lost its innocence. It was no longer the unquestioned Good Guy in world affairs. The reception for troops returning from the war was not always friendly. Many Americans felt the war was immoral, and America's long-held image of itself as global champion of the oppressed was replaced by an image of America as bully, interfering where it had no business, killing innocent men, women, and children, and lying about it all to the public.

Three-Five-Zero-Zero

Once Congress had given President Johnson the power to do pretty much anything he wanted in Vietnam, he decided to send in ground troops to secure air bases and begin a full-scale ground war, marking the official escalation of the war. On the morning of March 8, 1965, three thousand five hundred Marines—the first U.S. ground troops of the war—came ashore near the Da Nang air base, welcomed by Vietnamese girls and four American advisors holding a bedsheet proclaiming "Welcome to the Gallant Marines."

But, interestingly enough, that may not be what the song "Three-Five-Zero-Zero" in *Hair* refers to. Jim Rado has said that the song was inspired by an Alan Ginsberg poem. Ginsberg's "Wichita Vortex Sutra," written in February 1966, contains almost all the freaky, violent, surrealistic images in the song "Three-Five-Zero-Zero," often quoted word for word. In the poem, General Maxwell Taylor proudly reports to the press that three thousand five hundred of the enemy were killed in one month. He repeats the number, digit by digit, for effect: "Three-Five-Zero-Zero." In addition to the many other images from the poem that found their way into the song, Ginsberg also refers to 256 Vietcong killed and 31 captured, which became 256 *captured* in the song lyric. Though the song starts out somber and intense, spilling out Ginsberg's images of death and dying, it turns midway into a manic dance number, an absurdist celebration of killing that echoes Maxwell's glee at reporting the enemy casualties, commenting on the Happy Face that the U.S. government tried to put on the ever-diminishing returns of the war in Vietnam. While our soldiers—and theirs—kept dying, Washington tried to whip up World War II–style support for the war among Americans. But we had seen the war on our TV screens this time, and we weren't celebrating.

Let the Sun Shine In

References to the war are peppered throughout the *Hair* script. The only dramatic through-line in the show focuses on Claude's dilemma over whether to go to war or burn his draft card. In addition to being the focus of the conversations about Claude going to the induction center to be drafted, the war is an ever-present image in the show. During Claude's Act II drug trip, the images of war pile up in both comic images and disturbingly dramatic images. In most productions of *Hair*, it's made clear that Berger gives Claude a special joint before the trip in Act II, one presumably laced with more powerful hallucinogens than the others. Since the hippies believed that some drugs (LSD, peyote, pot, and others) opened and expanded the mind, increasing the power of the mind, helping the user reach higher consciousness and greater understanding, we can assume that Berger gives Claude a more powerful drug specifically to help him make up his mind, to clear away his indecision about Vietnam.

The trip begins with the song "Walking in Space," most of which describes the sensations of being high, but there are a few references to the war here. Once the song ends, everything else in the trip is triggered by Claude's fear of going to war. The first images are of young men, Claude among them, jumping out of a helicopter into the jungles of Vietnam. When Claude lands, he sees two American soldiers chasing a Vietnamese peasant. He turns around and sees George Washington and his troops, retreating from an attack by Native Americans. The next image is of Ulysses S. Grant assembling his troops, which include Abraham Lincoln, John Wilkes Booth, Calvin Coolidge, Rhett Butler and Scarlett O'Hara, and General Custer, all symbols of war in Claude's mixed-up, drugged-out mind. Also among Grant's troops is Aretha Franklin, a wonderful nonsequitur that might represent Claude's knowledge that the draft is racist—or it might just be the kind of random image a drugged-out mind conjures. Grant's troops dance a minuet for a bit and then are attacked by African witch doctors—probably a reference to Hud, who is referred to as the boogeyman in Act I—and the witch doctors kill everyone but Lincoln. Hud becomes LeRoi Jones, the black social activist, writer, and publisher, and he confronts Lincoln (played by a black woman, by the way), threatening to harpoon him/her, making fun of the black separatists of the '60s who refused to allow whites to participate in the civil rights movement. Lincoln calms Hud/Jones down and proceeds to deliver a crazy, soulful Gettysburg Address.

The trip continues as the killing of war comes to the forefront of Claude's mind. A succession of comic stereotypes murder one another—first monks, who are killed by Catholic nuns, who are killed by astronauts, who are killed by Chinese, who are killed by guerillas, who are killed by a Native American. This sequence is played three times, forward and backward, as the trip spins out of control. The action continues as Claude's parents appear with a drill sergeant and have a conversation with a suit Claude has left behind, the only thing that remains after Claude is killed in war. The tribe members begin playing children's games that escalate until they all end up murdering one another. The song "Three-Five-Zero-Zero" begins and the tribe becomes the walking dead, advancing on the audience, accusing it of complicity in the horror of war. By the end of the song, everyone has died again, in agonizing, slow deaths. Two tribe members have been watching all this from a platform above the fray and they sing "What a Piece of Work Is Man," an ironic tribute to the majesty and nobility of mankind, sung as the two tribe members walk through the battlefield of murdered bodies. A short section of "Three-Five-Zero-Zero" returns, and the trip ends.

The finale, "The Flesh Failures," summarizes the themes of the show, particularly the insanity of war and our consumerist culture, that we are obsessed with comfort as people are being murdered in southeast Asia. We pass each other on the street, the song tells us, bundled up in our designer clothes, purchased specifically to display our level of wealth and success, too busy to stop and connect to each other, too busy to help the homeless lying on the street, too preoccupied with our superficial lives, our appointments, our scramble to accumulate possessions—a theme *Hair*'s descendant *Rent* would return to. Yet somewhere inside, buried beneath all this, hidden deep down, there is greatness in the human race, such potential—but we have failed. We have failed by succumbing to comfort, to the demands of the flesh, instead of aiming for something higher.

Claude comes forward, now dead, killed in Vietnam, invisible to the tribe—just as returning Vietnam vets were "invisible" in American culture—and as he reprises his theme song, "Manchester, England," the tribe sings in counterpoint "Eyes Look Your Last," a musical setting of a speech from *Romeo and Juliet*. The words are Romeo's, spoken after he finds Juliet's (apparently) dead body and just before he takes his own life. The last line of this section, "The rest is silence," is Hamlet's last line before dying at the end of *Hamlet*. We are killing ourselves, the tribe is telling us. After another verse of "The Flesh Failures," the show finishes with "Let the Sun Shine In."

But "Let the Sun Shine In" is not the happy song most people think it is. It's a call to action. The members of the tribe are begging us, the audience, to change things, to stop the killing, the hatred, the discrimination, the destruction of our world. They are saying that we are in a time of darkness—as described in detail by "The Flesh Failures," "Easy to Be Hard," and other songs—that it is now time to let the sun shine in and change things. It's significant that the lyric doesn't say the sun is already shining and everything is going to be fine. It says we have to take action, we have to *let* the sun shine on the darkness around us, and the implication is unmistakable: if we don't let the sun shine, it will be the end of us.

The Tribe

The cast of *Hair* is called the Tribe, and in each production of *Hair* around the world, the cast chooses a tribe name, generally naming itself after a Native American tribe. The practice is not just cosmetic. This show, perhaps more than almost any other, really is an ensemble piece, one in which the entire cast must work together, must like one another, and often within the show, must work as a single organism. All the sense of family, of belonging, of responsibility and loyalty inherent in the word *tribe* has to be felt by the cast. And the mere choosing of a tribe name begins that process in a very real way.

Like those in Stephen Sondheim and George Furth's musical *Company*, the characters in *Hair* are greatly—and intentionally—underwritten. Much of what is important about the characters is in the subtext, hidden below what feels like very casual, even trivial conversation. It's the job of the actors and the director to read between the lines, to discover the relationships, the loyalties, the tensions, the love, and the deep connections among the characters.

George Berger and Claude Bukowski (presumably named for beat generation poet Charles Bukowski) form the center of the tribe and the show. Berger is a manic master of ceremonies and the leader of the tribe. He leads the tribe and the audience through the craziness of Act I, but in Act II he fades into the background to some extent as Claude's story takes center stage. While Act I is Berger's act as he introduces the tribe, its philosophy, and its way of life, Act II belongs to Claude, his drug trip, and his decision to go to war, where he will die. Berger and Claude are two halves of one whole. Claude is the intellectual half, the introspective one, the voice of reason, morality, spirituality, guilt. He's the one who tries to *understand* everything around him, including that which is not understandable, and that's his downfall. He says several times in the show that he is "Aquarius, destined for greatness or madness," but in actuality, he is destined for both. His greatness is in forcing the tribe through his death to confront the evils of the world; his madness is his decision to become part of the machinery of war. If Claude is Aquarius (Jim Rado, one of the show's authors, who played Claude on Broadway, was also an Aquarius), then this is Claude's show, and the opening number is summoning him. Notice that the tribe's final good-byes to Claude are done while singing "Aquarius."

Berger, on the other hand, is the animal half, focused on instinct, courage, pleasure, primal urges. But those primal urges are not just for food, water, and sex; they are also to protect the tribe, to be its leader. Only together, do Berger (the id) and Claude (the superego) make one healthy person. This is a common device in literature, most recently used in the novel and film *The Fight Club* and also used in the late 1960s in "The Enemy Within," an episode of the original *Star Trek* series.

With this in mind, it's interesting that both Berger and Claude want Sheila, since they are two halves of a whole. Berger wants Sheila only for the physical pleasures of sex, nothing more, while Claude wants her for the spiritual pleasures of pure love. Only together do they make the perfect lover. Sheila loves Berger but Berger's only interest in her is physical. When she brings him the shirt in Act I, his violent reaction speaks volumes. He feels smothered by her. He doesn't want gifts. He doesn't want commitment and he doesn't want the depth of feeling that he sees in Sheila. Like men have done for centuries, his reaction to the smothering love she gives him is to become a jerk, to treat her badly in order to get her to leave him alone. He explodes at her over nothing—and in an early version of the script, brutally rapes her—hoping that she'll hate him, hoping that she'll crawl away, licking her wounds, giving him at least temporary freedom. She tries to hang on, tries to laugh off his insults, but eventually she lashes back with the song "Easy to Be Hard." She doesn't understand him. Each time they have sex, each kind word he says to her gives her hope that he really does love her, but he doesn't understand that he's sending these signals. To him, it's just sex. To her, it's love. In the earlier, off-Broadway script, Berger cares so little for Sheila—or at least, so much more for Claude—he even asks Sheila in Act II to sleep with Claude before he goes off to war.

What a Piece of Work Is Claude

Some people see Claude as Hamlet, the melancholy hippie, prisoner of indecision. In fact, there are several Shakespearean references in the show. In the original off-Broadway script, Claude recites a speech from *Hamlet* to Berger after the trip, a speech in which Claude/Hamlet marvels at the nobility and great potential of mankind but confesses that he sees the world as nothing but a barren wasteland. Galt MacDermot later set this speech to music for Broadway and called it "What a Piece of Work Is Man." It was inserted into Claude's trip, still serving basically the same purpose, but now sung by two other members of the tribe as part of Claude's hallucination—so, arguably, still coming from Claude.

After the trip, as Berger and Claude are waking up, Berger says, "Face reality, Shakespeare." Is that just a coincidence or does Berger know Claude's trip included a speech from *Hamlet*? Does Berger possess some kind of Shakespearean magical powers that allow him to see inside Claude's mind? And if he can, was Berger manipulating Claude's trip like a latter-day Prospero to persuade him not to go to Vietnam? "What a Piece of Work Is Man" also serves as proof of how literate Claude is; if *Hamlet* shows up in his trip, Claude must be familiar with the play and its themes. And of course, by this logic, Claude has read Allen Ginsberg's poem "Wichita Vortex Sutra," on which the other song in the trip, "Three-Five-Zero-Zero," is based—further proof that many of the hippies were well educated and well read.

Finally, as Claude is killed and comes back to the tribe, now invisible as he always wished, he sings a reprise of "Manchester, England" as the tribe sings in counterpoint "Eyes Look Your Last." This section ends with Hamlet's last words before he dies, "The rest is silence." There's another quote from *Hamlet* that precedes the song "Mess O' Dirt," which was cut from the show.

And just as Hamlet was fascinated with plays and players, Claude is fascinated with film. In his Act I introduction song, "Manchester, England," he lists his heroes, the legendary film directors Frederico

Fellini, Michelangelo Antonioni, and Roman Polanski. In both the Broadway and the off-Broadway script, a scene is included in which Claude even makes Sheila act out a scene from a screenplay Claude has been writing about the tribe, just as Hamlet writes a play about the murder of his father by his uncle. "The Flesh Failures" makes a reference to film as well.

Claude Hooper Bukowski Superstar

But while some people see Claude as Hamlet, others see him as a Christ figure, and there are even more references to Jesus Christ in *Hair* than there are to Hamlet. Several times throughout the show, Claude talks about wanting to be invisible, wanting to know what people are thinking, and wanting to perform miracles. Midway through Act I, Claude enters, saying, "I am the Son of God. I shall vanish and be forgotten." Is this a comment on organized religion losing touch with God and forgetting the true meaning of Jesus' teachings? Following this comment, Claude comes through the audience and the tribe, "blessing" people as he goes. Later, he compares his hair to Jesus in the song "Hair." At one point, Jeanie says that "Claude is hung up on a cross over Sheila and Berger." After the trip he says he wants to hang on a cross and eat cornflakes. At the end of the show, when Claude returns to the tribe for the finale, he says, "Berger, I feel like I died." Like Christ, Claude has died and has returned, and like Christ, Claude is the Chosen One, the one member of the tribe chosen (literally, by the draft board) to give his life for the others. In the last moment of the show, Berger forms a cross over Claude as the final lights fade.

In addition to these very obvious moments, there are other, less direct references. Like Christ, Claude is sent to his death by the government. Like Christ, Claude suffers through enormous confusion and conflict over what to do—Claude throughout Act I and specifically in "Where Do I Go"; Christ in the Garden of Gethsemane. Just as Claude's parents disapprove of him and his lifestyle, there is evidence in the Bible that Jesus' mother and brothers thought he was out of his mind and an embarrassment to the family. And just as the second half of the Bible (the New Testament) focuses on Jesus Christ, the second half of *Hair* shifts its focus almost exclusively to Claude and the story of his death and (metaphorical) resurrection.

It's important to remember that Jesus was not just the Son of God; he was a radical political activist in the same spirit as the political activists of the 1960s. He was the center of a great revisionist social movement that rejected the social and spiritual status quo, dozens of small messianic groups each thinking its leader was the messiah the Jews had been waiting for. As he preached, Jesus roamed the country, living a life of relative poverty, taking handouts of food and shelter from strangers, picking up supporters and adherents as he went, speaking on social and spiritual issues, challenging the authority of the government and the ruling classes, declaring that things must change. When the crowds grew too big to fit inside churches, Jesus began speaking outside in large open areas, and thousands would gather to listen to him and to commune with one another and nature, not unlike the be-ins of the '60s. The hippies' trip the night before Claude goes off to his death in war could even be compared to the Last Supper.

Furthermore, if Claude is Jesus, then Berger is John the Baptist, and Jeanie is Mary Magdalene. Even Claude's and Berger's names, by accident or not, are similar to their Biblical counterparts: Claude and Christ, George Berger and John the Baptist. Berger's first speech to the audience deals a lot with water, creating an arguable connection to John the Baptist. At one point, one of the tribe members actually cites John the Baptist as his hero. In fact, the historical John the Baptist was a lot like Berger, wild, out of the mainstream, roaming the countryside, a strong and harsh critic of the government and of the church. Like the hippies of the 1960s, John the Baptist believed the church had lost touch with God, that he and his followers had to totally discard accepted mainstream religion in order to find God. John the Baptist wore camel skins and ate bugs and wild honey. He had wild, long hair and a long, unkempt beard. He was a first-century hippie, vigorously rejecting the establishment and the moral and political status quo. Just as Claude is drawn to Berger, so was Jesus drawn to the radical revolutionary John the Baptist, a charismatic young man declaring philosophical war on the church, the government, and other adult institutions. And like the hippies, most of the followers of John the Baptist were very young.

And like Mary Magdalene loved Jesus, Jeanie loves Claude, but he can't return her love. Because Claude is the emotional and moral center of *Hair*, Jeanie is by extension the most important female character in the show, even though it might not appear that way at first glance. She acts as a Greek chorus several times throughout the show, explaining things to the audience, identifying characters and relationships, but she also gets a solo introduction song in Act I, "Air," along with the other leads. It's through her that we feel the tragedy and the anguish of those Claude will leave behind. There are cryptic references throughout the show that Jeanie may be psychic in some way, or at least some kind of hippie mystic, that she knows Claude will end up going to war, and that she might know that Claude will die in Vietnam.

It may even be that Jeanie is denying the fact that Claude is the father of her unborn child only to free him from any responsibility, since she knows he doesn't really love her. It's probable that they have slept together. Though there's nothing in the text that says this explicitly, Jeanie and Claude allude to this in their conversation before the be-in, and it's certainly an interesting idea for the actors to explore. Though Claude is in love with Sheila, Jeanie is in love with Claude and, along with Berger, she will suffer the greatest loss when Claude dies. It's hard not to see parallels to Mary Magdalene, and the content of lost gospels rediscovered in 1945 implies there might even be romantic parallels. These new papyrus texts have holes and gaps in them, but some scholars maintain that these texts describe a romantic relationship between Jesus and Mary Magdalene. Unsurprisingly, this is hotly contested among biblical scholars.

Like Mary Magdalene, who was called both prostitute and saint, Jeanie provides a symbolic bridge between sexuality and spirituality, between the pleasures of the flesh and the cultivation of the soul. (Perhaps she should be the one to sing "Sodomy.") Jeanie is promiscuous, already pregnant by "some speed freak" when the show begins, but she is also the one who invites the audience to the be-in, an event of spiritual exploration and awakening. She brings Claude a book on astral projection, and as mentioned earlier, she seems to have mystical powers. But even beyond all that, Mary Magdalene would have been right at home with Berger and the tribe. She grew up in Magdala, a small fishing village that was a hotbed of rebel activity against the Roman Empire. She came from a well-to-do family just as many of the hippies came from upper-middle-class families. And, in fact, Mary Magdalene was not a prostitute, even though she was characterized as such for centuries, just as the hippies were often characterized as sexual deviants and hedonists. Some texts suggest that she did have a considerable sexual appetite and, because she was well-off enough that she didn't have to work, she might have practiced what the hippies of the 1960s called free love. And for that she was considered a sinner by her contemporaries. Like the hippies, Mary Magdalene was an independent thinker who met Jesus, a radical political activist, and joined his movement, a movement dedicated to finding enlightenment, rejecting old social norms and rules, and discovering the answers to the great existential questions; the parallels to the tribe in *Hair* are obvious. After Christ's crucifixion, and after Mary's subsequent preaching and evangelism, she retired to a secluded wilderness where she lived out her remaining years. Some accounts say that each day she was carried up to the heavens by angels to listen to the music of the heavens, an experience probably akin to astral projection, a practice Jeanie is very interested in.

In the Name of the Father

LeRoi Jones, black social activist and writer, wrote in the 1960s, "God has been replaced, as he has all over the West, with respectability and air conditioning." *Hair* reflects that view of American society in the 1960s. It exposes the dark underbelly of organized religion as it satirizes its hypocrisies. In the song "Donna," it's unclear whether Berger is singing about looking for a girl named Donna or, in fact, looking for the Virgin Mary, the Madonna. The song starts with a slight variation of "once upon a time" and the last line of the song actually replaces the words *my Donna* with *Madonna*. Could Berger be talking about *the* Madonna, the "sixteen-year-old" Virgin Mary? Could this song be about his search for true spirituality as symbolized by Mary, his inability to find that spirituality in the hypocrisy and institutionalization of organized religion? And could that "disfigured" spirituality be represented by the "tattooed" Donna? After all, the song catalogs all his attempts to find spirituality in India, in South America, and through psychedelic drugs in San Francisco. In the second part of the song, when he calls Donna psychedelic, perhaps he's telling us he found the Virgin Mary—and God—through psychedelic, mind-expanding drugs (which was the goal of the drug users, after all), and it was only through the drugs that he could "evolve" into a more spiritual being.

Just a few minutes after "Donna," the tribe performs the song "Sodomy," a mock religious hymn cataloging sex acts that organized religion condemns: fellatio, cunnilingus, pederasty, and masturbation. It satirizes religion's preoccupation with sex, "unspeakable" acts that nonetheless fill the Bible (making it as R-rated as *Hair* itself), acts that continue to embarrass the modern-day Catholic church. The audience flinches when pederasty is mentioned, but do we too easily forget that the sexual repression of the Catholic church drives too many priests to molest altar boys over and over still today? Before the song, Woof poses as a priest and says, "This is the body and blood of Jesus Christ. And I am going to eat you. I swear to tell the truth, the whole truth, and nothing but the truth, so help me God. In the name of the Father, the Son, and the Holy Ghost. Amen." In one short speech, he pokes fun at the solemnity of priests and religious rituals, the cannibalistic implications of communion, and the all too blatant exceptions to the constitutional separation of church and state in America. He sings "Sodomy," skewering the sexual hypocrisy of organized religion, concluding with a reference to the Kama Sutra, an ancient text that celebrates sex rather than denigrating and trying to control it.

The song "Ain't Got No" also makes two religious references. The song is a list of things the hippies "ain't got," with responses shouted out by the tribe. When the soloist sings that he has no faith, the tribe shouts out, "Catholic," suggesting that the Catholics have lost their faith, have lost touch with God in the morass of manmade ritual that defines the church (already satirized in "Sodomy"). At the end of the song, when the soloist sings that he has no God, the tribe shouts "Good." But we learn throughout the show the tribe is in fact very spiritual, so this reference means only that it's a good thing to lose God *as defined by modern religions*, a false God, a God loaded up with man's baggage and distanced from real spirituality and faith. But *Hair* doesn't limit itself to Christian spirituality. The mantra chanted before the song "Don't Put It Down"—"om mane padme hum"—is a scared Buddhist mantra to Avalokiteswara, the Buddhist savior and protector.

As evidence of the spiritual side of the hippie culture and of *Hair*—and despite, or perhaps because of, the show's criticism of organized religion—the original Broadway cast celebrated its third anniversary in May 1971 by holding a very special mass at the Cathedral of St. John the Divine in New York City, presided over by Gerome Ragni's brother and other clergy. For the occasion, Galt MacDermot wrote a new Mass in F, and instead of hymns, he used songs from *Hair*, sung by the Broadway cast and several New York choirs. The mass was released on an album called *Divine Hair/Mass in F.*

Hippie Get Your Gun

So why does Claude choose to go to war? After so much pressure from the tribe to burn his draft card, after his terrifying hallucinations about agonizing death during the trip, why does he go to Vietnam? In a literary sense, he is destined to go. He's the Chosen One, the one who will sacrifice himself for the others. But on a personal level, Ragni and Rado have painted a portrait of a very real, very complex person. From the very beginning of the show, we find out that Claude is searching for fulfillment, trying to find himself and his place in the world. In fact, that is why he has joined the hippies. In his first song, "Manchester, England," Claude says that he "dropped out," as hippie and drug guru Timothy Leary advocated, but that his life is still unfulfilling. He asks Timothy Leary directly in the song why this is, why his life should still feel so meaningless when he has followed Leary's instructions. Like the title character in *Pippin*, Claude is on a quest to find the meaning of life, and like young men throughout the history of the world, Claude realizes that war might just be the thing that makes a man of him, that shows him who he really is. Although for Pippin, war is just a comic sketch performed by a troupe of players, for Claude, war is very real. He might find out who he is, but he might also get killed. After the trip, Claude realizes that although war scares him, nothing else in life has proved satisfying.

But here *Hair* breaks the rules again. Instead of finding his true self deep in the jungles of Vietnam, instead of experiencing revelations about himself, instead of gaining elusive wisdom about the nature of life, Claude is dropped into Vietnam and instantly killed by a North Vietnamese sniper. There is no romance here, no literary devices, no triumph for our hero. He just gets shot and dies in the jungle, running away, screaming like a frightened child. It reminds us that war is not like a John Wayne movie or a romance novel. War is death.

All There in Black and White

Hair challenges nearly everything we complacently accept as ordinary in life, all the things we just don't think about. It shoves them in our face and demands that we look at them. Racism, obscenity, sexual repression, and other issues are all laid bare before us, rejecting the restrictions of "polite society."

Racism is the most American of all issues. It was an issue when the Declaration of Independence was written. It split the nation during the Civil War and again in the 1960s. In the song "Colored Spade," Hud lists every racist label and stereotype ever thrown at him, to show how horrible, how ridiculous, how offensive they all are. He confronts the audience members with words and phrases and stereotypes they might have actually used—or allowed others to use—and he claims them for his own. When we hear them all together, when we realize how many more labels there are for blacks than for whites, they become ridiculous. They lose their power.

In "Dead End," the black tribe members list signs we encounter every day—Dead End, Keep Out, Don't Walk, No Standing, Keep Off the Grass, and others. And the fact that these warnings are being sung by black men and women raises them to the level of metaphor. This is the world black Americans face every day, in employment, in housing, in pay, in opportunity, and not just in 1968 but still today.

At the beginning of Act II, two songs, "Black Boys" and "White Boys," make a powerful statement without the audience even noticing. It was surprising enough, especially in 1968, for women to objectify men the way men had been objectifying women for centuries, but it was even more surprising that they were doing it across race lines. Three white women sing about how much they love black men, and then three black women sing about how much they love white men. The songs are funny, seemingly harmless entertainment. But there were states in the 1960s where interracial marriage was still illegal. It wasn't until *Star Trek* in the late '60s that television saw its first interracial kiss. These two charming songs are more subversive than the audience realizes. And though racism is far less prevalent today than it was in 1968, there are still comparatively few interracial couples in America and, except in the biggest cities, those that exist still turn heads when they walk down the street. We haven't come as far as we'd like to think.

The trip makes some interesting commentary on race. When General Grant lines up his troops, not only are the genders reversed (women as Lincoln, Booth, Coolidge, Gable, etc.), but so is race in at least one case. A black woman plays Abraham Lincoln and a blond girl plays Lincoln's shoeshine boy. Like the song "Colored Spade," "Abie Baby" is another politically incorrect comedy number, in which three black tribe members sing joyously about being freed by Lincoln, in a stereotypical Hollywood black dialect. While the singers continue in the background, the black female Abe Lincoln recites a contorted Gettysburg Address, peppered with modern black references.

Though it's common today to practice color-blind casting—ignoring an actor's race when considering him for a role—*Hair* forced this upon audiences, demanding that they think about the social roles separating the races, demanding that they see these separations as arbitrary and ridiculous. It was jarring to see a white girl shining shoes, but had it been a black man, we might not have even thought about it. It's odd to hear a black woman recite the Gettysburg Address but there's no reason that she shouldn't. As she quite correctly points out, they are "*all* our forefathers." But most disturbing is that as startling as this must have been in 1968, it's still more surprising today than it should be.

And Love Will Steer the Stars

It's impossible to describe the experience of performing *Hair* to someone who hasn't done it. I was highly skeptical of the many people who told me their lives were changed by working on this show. Until I worked on it. From the choosing of the tribe name to the overwhelming rush of emotion in the show's finale, it is an experience unlike any other. Not only does it bond each member of the tribe to every other member (and this includes actors, director, designers, musicians), but it bonds each tribe to all the other tribes around the world, past and present. It centers people, changes them, guides them toward balance in their lives, guides them back to paths in their lives they've forgotten or abandoned, guides them toward a deeper spirituality. Even the most cynical among us is transformed by *Hair*. It holds a mystical, primal power that is impossible to explain. Just as it is utterly unique in so many concrete ways, it is just as unique in all the unexplainable ways.

Other Resources

The script of the original off-Broadway version of *Hair* was published but is currently out of print. You may be able to find it in used-book stores or on the web. Also out of print, but worth finding, are two books about the show, Barbara Lee Horn's *The Age of Hair: Evolution and Impact of Broadway's First Rock Musical,* and Lorrie Davis and Rachel Gallagher's *Letting Down My Hair*. Davis was an original

Broadway cast member and her book describes the entire process of the creation of the show. Vocal selections are commercially available, but the full score and the Broadway script are available only through Tams-Witmark, which licenses performances.

There are many recordings of the score available on CD. The best is the original Broadway cast album, but the 1993 London revival cast album contains new music that has now been incorporated into the standard rental version. The original off-Broadway cast album, which is very different, and a recording of songs cut from the show called *DisinHAIRited* are both only on out-of-print LPs, but both are worth finding. There is also an active and invaluable e-mail discussion list about *Hair* on the Internet that can be accessed at <www.jabberwocky .com>. This discussion list counts among its members dozens of actors, directors, and designers who have worked on *Hair*, as well as members of the original Broadway cast. Past posts are archived on the website. Members of the list helped me immeasurably in researching *Hair* both for the production I directed and for this chapter.

Jacques Brel Is Alive and Well and Living in Paris

Music and original French lyrics by Jacques Brel
Concept, English lyrics, and additional material by Eric Blau
  and Mort Shuman
Based on the writings and commentary of Jacques Brel
Originally directed in New York by Moni Yakim
Licensed by Music Theatre International

More than any other piece written for the musical stage, *Jacques Brel Is Alive and Well and Living in Paris* utterly defies description. It is an evening of independent songs, yet it is more than a revue. It doesn't have a plot or an immediately recognizable cast of characters, so it's not really a book musical. It has been called the world's first librettoless musical. In reality, it is a one-man musical with a cast of four. Two women and two men portray one character: the real-life folk singer–poet Jacques Brel. The words are Brel's; the opinions, insights, and razor wit are Brel's. The underlying, sometimes nearly hidden optimism is Brel's. In a sense, the show is more a character study than anything else, but is it a character study of Jacques Brel the man or of western civilization at the end of the twentieth century? Eric Blau, one of the creators of the show, said that Brel writes about the way we live in a world we did not create.

Jacques B. Nimble

Every rule in the theatre, no matter how hardcore, must eventually be broken. At one time, we thought every musical had to have a story, then along came *Company* and *A Chorus Line*, which had situation and characters, but no story. We once thought that when there was a story, it had to be told in chronological order, then along came *Merrily We Roll Along*, with a narrative that ran backward. It had always been accepted—and still is today—that poetry makes rotten lyrics, and lyrics make rotten poetry. Poetry is words that make their own music, that require contemplation and reflection; one quick hearing of those words, complicated by music, makes it impossible to hear them and digest them completely. On the other hand, lyrics are written to be coupled with music, and when you read them on the printed page, the rhythm is often hard to discern, rhymes don't always make sense, and the simplicity that makes some songs so powerful (like "Oh What a Beautiful Mornin'" and "Morning Glow") seems silly and unsophisticated. Even the best lyrics, like those of Stephen Sondheim, usually don't work half as well as spoken or written text. They were created to work with music and they are incomplete without it.

Yet the lyrics in *Jacques Brel* shatter the conventional wisdom. The words have all the complexity and beauty of poetry, and yet they work as lyrics. They are instantly comprehensible on one level, while later reflection reveals even more depth under the surface. This anomaly may be due partly to the fact that these songs were not written as poetry or as theatre lyrics; they were written to be sung in clubs and coffeehouses in France and Belgium. They are a strange hybrid of eighteenth- and nineteenth-century art songs coupled with 1960s protest songs. And like some art songs and protest songs, many of these songs are written so that syllables that would naturally be stressed fall on unstressed beats in the music, throwing the natural sound of the words off a bit, making the audience listen more closely, making it impossible to hear them passively. The song "Madeleine" is hilarious and also bittersweet on first hearing, and then terribly tragic on further reflection. The nature of each song changes the more you think about it. In a way, the performance is only the beginning of the life of the songs, because they stay with you and their words echo in your mind over time, your understanding and their impact transforming and evolving over time.

Coming to America

Jacques Brel was born in Belgium in 1929 but moved to Paris as a young man to be a singer and songwriter. By the early 1960s, Brel had established a reputation as one of France's greatest writers and interpreters of modern songs. (In France, the writing of popular songs is much more respected than it is here in America, and serious poets and playwrights write pop lyrics.) Though Brel himself insisted his lyrics are not poetry, they have an intensity of images, uncommon rhythmic patterns, and a sophisticated structure that confirm his stature as a major artist.

In 1957, the first American recording of Brel's songs was released with only moderate success. In 1961, singer Elly Stone began singing two of Brel's songs, "Ne me quitte pas" ("Don't Leave Me") and "La valse á mille temps ("The Waltz in Thousand Time")," in an off-Broadway show called *O, Oysters!*. Though the show did not run long, Stone continued to perform the Brel songs. In 1968, Eric Blau and Mort Schuman built an off-Broadway musical using twenty-six of Brel's songs, and they called it *Jacques Brel Is Alive and Well and Living in Paris*. It ended up running for five years. After its off-Broadway run, the show enjoyed a limited engagement of four weeks on Broadway, and several Broadway producers asked for an extended run, but the show's producers refused. Broadway was not the place for this show. It's been revived twice in New York and has been produced around the world. A film version was released in 1975, which included an appearance by Brel himself singing his best-known song in France, "Ne me quitte pas," a song not in the stage show. Since the show first opened, Brel's songs have been recorded by artists as diverse as David Bowie, Judy Collins, and Barry Manilow, and the show continues to be produced throughout the world. Brel died in 1978 at age forty-nine, but the show's title didn't change.

It's still accurate.

E Pluribus Unum

So if this is a show composed of twenty-six separate, independent songs—twenty-six one-act musicals—what makes it hang together as an evening? Does it, in fact, hang together as an evening? First of all, as discussed earlier, this is one man's philosophy, Brel's thoughts about the world and about being alive, specifically about the struggle to survive in our modern world. It is a kind of character study, though not in the sense we're used to. It doesn't describe his life explicitly like *Give 'Em Hell Harry*, *Tru*, or other one-character plays do, although it does describe his life subtextually in "Brussels," "Jackie," and other songs. It's closer to Jane Wagner's one-woman show *The Search for*

Signs of Intelligent Life in the Universe, one person's two-hour riff on Life, the Universe, and Everything. We get to know Brel's personality, his politics, his fears, and what he cherishes. We get a glimpse of how much he misses the simplicity of his childhood in "Jackie" (it's not a coincidence he chose his own name for this song). We get a glimpse into his feelings about war and his fears of growing old. We see his (mostly negative) feelings about family in "Timid Frieda" and "Funeral Tango." These are not just Brel's random thoughts, though; every song is about our struggle to survive, either literally or spiritually. The show's creators chose these songs from the Brel canon because they do have that common thread among them; and that ever-present survival subtext helps make the show a lot less dismal than it might appear on the surface.

But practically speaking, how does that make the show a compelling, unified evening of theatre? There are several small devices, including the way some of the songs are grouped thematically around topics like death ("Statue," "The Desperate Ones," and "Sons Of"), false or bad love ("Alone," "Madeleine," "I Loved," "Mathilde," and "Bachelor's Dance"), and the way time turns the tables ("Brussels," "Fanette," "Funeral Tango," and "Middle Class"). There are also themes that connect nonconsecutive songs over the course of the show, like growing old ("Alone," "Bachelor's Dance," "My Death," "Amsterdam," "Old Folks," and "Middle Class"), sex ("I Loved," "Timid Frieda," "My Death," "Girls and Dogs," "Jackie," "Amsterdam," "Fanette," "No Love, You're Not Alone," and "Next"), and war ("Marathon," "Alone," "Statue," "Sons Of," "The Bulls," "Brussels," "Next," and "If We Only Have Love").

Most importantly, there is an overall dramatic arc to this show. The central theme of the show is that no matter how overwhelming life can get—and it can get *really* overwhelming, Brel tells us—we have a strength and a survival instinct that gets us through even the worst of it. The opening song, "Marathon," acts as an introduction to this idea and as a table of contents for the show's topics. The other songs catalog for us the things that make life overwhelming: war and death, drugs, family, money, love and marriage, and the relentlessness of time. At the end of the show, all these things explode in the insanity and chaos of the penultimate number, "Carousel." Then the conflict, the tension, is resolved in the last song, "If We Only Have Love." We not only come to understand what Brel thinks is wrong with the world but also where he thinks the solution lies. Like any good satirist or commentator, he takes aim at himself along with the rest of us, and we get to know his philosophies, his sense of humor, and his unwavering faith in human nature to do good and come out on top.

Still, the show's structure doesn't make it easy to engage and hold an audience. The coherence of the evening isn't always apparent until "Carousel," the second-to-last song. Up until that moment, the show has to move like lightning to create the sense of overwhelmingness that the songs describe. Like *Songs for a New World*, this is a show that is not necessarily understood on a conscious level. Like *Passion*, it's a show about relentlessness that must be relentless itself in order to make the audience feel what the characters feel. At intermission, an audience seeing *Jacques Brel* should be a bit dizzy, not quite sure what it has seen and where it's heading. By the end of Act II, it all becomes clear.

Triple Play

More than most pop songwriters, Brel used triple time—a waltz or variations of a waltz—in a lot of his songs. "I Loved" is a triple-time lullaby, as is "Timid Frieda," in both cases as ironic commentary on the lyrics. "The Desperate Ones" is in the style of the gentle waltzlike piano pieces called *gymnopédies* that the turn-of-the-century French composer Erik Satie wrote. "Sons Of" starts out as a triple-time lullaby but transforms itself into a frightening grand waltz as it repeats over and over the list of young men who go to their deaths during wartime. "Amsterdam" is a sailor's sea shanty in 6/4 time, a variation of triple time. "Old Folks" is a slow, endlessly repetitive triple-time lullaby, with an accompaniment that ironically echoes Braham's lullaby as it describes old people going to their final sleep. "Marieke" is in 12/8, a variation of triple time. "Fantine" is a slow, sad waltz. "No Love, You're Not Alone" is a waltz that builds and grows like "Sons Of." And "Carousel" is a mad waltz gone out of control, spinning and speeding wildly as it gets faster and faster and finally explodes, bringing together all the waltzes that have gone before it. More than a third of the *Jacques Brel* score is in triple time, which is extraordinarily rare for pop songs or theatre songs, and "Girls and Dogs" acts as a bridge between those songs and the rest of the score. "Girls and Dogs" is in 7/8, each measure counted as 1-2-3, 1-2, 1-2, combining triple time and duple time in one song.

Marathon

The show opens with "Marathon," a comic, absurdist tour of history that also acts as a kind of table of contents of the entire show, chronicling war, pop culture, social attitudes, political movements, and the remarkable ability of human beings to survive any obstacle throughout this century, all the topics that will be explored in greater depth in the rest of the show. It makes fun of the ridiculous, shortsighted, bullheaded way humankind stumbles through history, usually only choosing the right path by accident. Above all, this is a song about survival. No matter what horror presents itself—the mass murders of Hitler and Stalin, the catastrophes of stock markets crashes, wars—human beings survive. We go on, even with the knowledge that as we overcome one horror, another is surely looming in the distance.

"Marathon" is one of the songs in the show with a text that has very little relation to the original French text. The song's original title was "Les flamandes," and it was a scathing satire of the restrictive morality of Brel's native Belgium. It was a song so antiestablishment that the Belgian government denied Brel permission to perform the song at his concerts in Belgium. Of course he performed it anyway. Though the show's creators and translators, Eric Blau and Mort Shuman, wrote an entirely new, unrelated lyric for this music, there are still two interesting connections between the French lyric and the English lyric. First, they share a structural device. "Les flamandes" traces the girls' restrictive lives at ages twenty, thirty, forty, fifty, and so on until they're one hundred. Similarly, "Marathon" traces the progress of America in the twentieth century through the 1920s, 1930s, 1940s, and so on up to the millennium. Also, the chorus of "Les flamandes" keeps returning to the idea that the girls dance every Sunday to attract a husband; and "Marathon" returns in each chorus to the phrase, "But we keep on dancing . . . ," in this case referring to both our determination to survive and our tendency to ignore or dilute reality whenever we can.

In its English form, "Marathon" is a catalog of America in the twentieth century, an appropriate opening for the show that follows. The song's humor and its horror come from the way the lyrics couple the mundane with the horrific: "Dempsey-Tunney, Sacco and Vanzetti," or "Breadlines, shanty towns, Frankenstein's Bride." The historical, cultural, and pop culture references pour out of this song in an unending stream, some obscure, some obvious, but all of them so fast that the listener barely has time to register the ones he knows before two more have already passed him by.

"The twenties roar" is a reference to the common label the Roaring Twenties. "Bath tub gin" was illegal homemade gin often made or kept in the bathtub during Prohibition in the 1920s. "The road to sin" is probably a reference to the slogans of the Women's Christian Temperance Union, which was trying to stop the consumption of alcohol, as well as a joke on the popular 1927 Broadway play *The Road to Rome*, by well-known playwright Robert Sherwood. "Charles A. Lindbergh" was the first man to fly solo across the Atlantic, in 1927. "Dempsey-Tunney" refers to the famous 1927 boxing match between former heavyweight champion Jack Dempsey and the current heavyweight champion Gene Tunney. "Sacco and Vanzetti" were the two anarchists falsely accused and arrested in 1920 of bank robbery and murder because of propagandist leaflets in their car, and they were prosecuted as "Reds." They were convicted and given the death sentence. Despite worldwide protests over lack of evidence, public demonstrations, the requests of sixty-one law professors, and the confession of another man clearing their names, they were still executed in 1927. In 1977, the governor of Massachusetts granted them posthumous pardons.

"Black, black Monday, and the market drops" refers to the great stock market crash of 1929. On Thursday and Friday, October 24 and 25, stock prices had dropped drastically, so the millionaires started buying everything up, partly in order to save some of the companies from going under. On Monday, everyone saw how much buying was happening and they, too, started buying at the low prices. At the end of the day on Monday, October 28, the millionaires dumped everything they had bought; this was Black Monday. They turned a tidy profit, but when the market opened Tuesday morning, there was widespread panic and the market crashed. This lyric line, more than any other, encapsulates the whole idea of the song, of the endless, often repetitive parade of the mundane and horrific over time, because "Black Monday" also refers to October 19, 1987, the second time the stock market crashed, twenty years after this show was written.

"The thirties scream" is a reference to the rise of fascism and political extremism around the world, and the subsequent murder of millions of innocent people. "The horsemen ride," in addition to being a biblical reference, is also a reference to the four horsemen of the apocalypse, four players on Knute Rockne's champion college football team at Notre Dame University, the "four horsemen" label coming from the world-famous 1918 antiwar novel of the same name and the 1921 film based on it.

"Orphan Annie" is of course the title character in the newspaper comic strip "Little Orphan Annie." A radio show based on the comic strip, which began in 1924, debuted in 1931 on the NBC Blue Network, sponsored by Ovaltine. "Daddy Warbucks dies" refers to the demise in the '30s of the Robber Barons, the ruthless millionaire businessmen. In 1933, President Roosevelt signed into law the Glass-Steagall Act, which forbade banks to deal in stocks and bonds (which millionaire J. P. Morgan had been doing), and the National Industrial Recovery Act, which established "codes for fair competition," collective bargaining, shorter work hours, and fixed pricing.

"Breadlines, shanty towns" were the results—and symbols—of the Great Depression. "Frankenstein's Bride" appeared in the famous 1935 film *The Bride of Frankenstein*, a sequel to the extremely successful 1931 film *Frankenstein*, both from Universal Studios, which went on to make many more monster movies.

"Adolph Hitler and the Siegfried Follies" is a satiric reference to the German dictator, comparing his goose-stepping Nazi soldiers to the strutting showgirls of the Ziegfeld Follies on Broadway. The "Siegfried Line" was a western German battlefront in World War II. "Josef Stalin and a bag full of jollies" refers to the Communist dictator of the Soviet Union, who manufactured an artificial famine in the Ukraine in 1932 to starve out those who would not join him, exterminating 6.8 million people, from 1936 to 1938, in an effort to liquidate his enemies.

"Call your broker and buy marzipan" is a comic reference to the fact that money and stocks and bonds were no longer worth anything in the 1930s, so an investor would have been just as well off buying candy as stock. Marzipan is a candy made from sugar and almond paste.

"The forties burn because the trumpets blare" is a reference to the destruction of European cities during World War II. "The Yanks are coming, coming over there" is a reference to the United States joining World War II in 1941. The line is a lyric from the song "Over There," written in 1917 by George M. Cohan about World War I, and it's probably used here to again point out the repetitive nature of human history. "Auschwitz" was a Nazi concentration camp in World War II. "Edelweiss" is the national flower of Austria, the country that joined Hitler a bit too eagerly in World War II, and it's a flower that grows only in the highest mountains of the Austrian Alps. This lyric was written after *The Sound of Music* had played on Broadway, so the writers knew the audience's association with this flower through the song "Edelweiss."

"Drang und sturm" is a reference to Sturm und Drang, a nineteenth-century German literary movement, literally, "storm and stress," characterized by extreme nationalism, impetuousness, and an opposition to societal norms. The "Manhattan Project" was the U.S. government's project to develop the atomic bomb. "Robert Oppenheim" (actually Robert Oppenheimer) was the leader of the Manhattan Project, which developed the atomic bomb in 1945. "God makes mushrooms" is a reference to the mushroom-shaped clouds of the atomic bombs, and maybe also to the use of mushrooms as a mood-altering drug. " . . . Like a lollipop" is a reference to drugs like LSD that were ingested by licking them off a piece of paper or a lollipop. In other words, the lyric is saying that peace is not real; it's imaginary and it doesn't last. No matter how secure we may feel for the moment, the feeling—like being high on drugs—is an illusion and only temporary.

"The eighties bang and the nineties whimper" is a reference to T. S. Eliot's 1925 poem *The Hollow Men*, part of which reads, "This is the way the world ends / Not with a bang but a whimper." "The century hangs" is a reference to the Bible-based belief that the world will be destroyed at the end of the millennium.

Alone

Like "Marathon," the song "Alone" also acts as a kind of table of contents for the show, dealing with more specific issues than "Marathon," which is drawn in much broader strokes. In the first stanza, the singer's view of love as a game that is ended with lies connects to the next song, "I Loved," which describes a once immature understanding of love. We don't treat love with the care and respect we should, these songs say. The second stanza of "Alone" refers to the thrills and speed of modern life that we all crave, a theme that will reappear in "Carousel" in Act II. Like the singers of "Fanette" and "Jackie," the third stanza of "Alone" describes our penchant for living—and hiding— in the past instead of dealing with the realities of the world around us. We enjoy too much wallowing in lost love at the expense of feeling real emotion, it says. Interestingly, the male singer of "Alone" shares all these things with the female singer of "I Loved," but though she has grown up and faced her immaturities, he has not.

The next two stanzas of "Alone" talk about our tendency to solve problems with guns, to make snap decisions about complex issues of right and wrong, and then to storm into difficult situations, declaring ourselves on the moral high ground—all issues that are taken up again in "Statue" and "The Bulls." But this tendency of ours applies not only to war but to other situations as well. How often do our preachers mark one group or another as immoral, as dangerous to the American way of life? Once it was freed slaves, then Jews, then blacks again, then feminists, then gays; and each time, Bible verses are offered up to prove that this stand is a moral one. They acquire fame, money, and power, yet they know these gains are ill-gotten. Echoing the themes in "Jackie," "Alone" says money and power do not bring peace of mind, do not bring real security, only more doubt and fear.

The result of this is articulated in the sixth stanza: we all end up confused about what is right and wrong. We find ourselves or our loved ones demonized by those who say they represent God and morality. And though the preachers fill their lives with various kinds of insurances—going to church and reading the Bible to insure they'll go to heaven, putting their millions in the bank to insure they can live comfortably—still, deep down, they're afraid that someone will steal their money or their cars, that their daily, secret indiscretions may be made public or may keep them out of heaven. So how do we react? We all stay locked in our houses, suspicious, rarely letting anyone in, physically or emotionally, keeping ourselves alone and isolated out of our fear and our conviction that it's every man for himself.

Ultimately, we grow old and find that no amount of money, power, or fame can fight back death. As Brel says in "My Death," in "Old Folks," and in "Sons Of," no one is safe from growing old and dying. And the only thing we can take with us is the good or evil we did while we walked this earth. If we've spent our life in the pursuit of only our own interests, when it comes time to cash in the chips, we will truly be alone.

The singer observes that though we know there are horrible things happening in the world, we most often stay at home in our cocoons, preferring not to get involved, not to risk our own safety or comfort in the interest of doing what's right. And when some of us get to be rich and famous, powerful and influential, it doesn't really matter because it's all been done for selfish reasons. At the end of the song, the singer asks what he has done to deserve this spiritual and emotional isolation and loneliness. His tragic flaw is precisely the fact that he doesn't know.

Ultimately, though, the message we get from this song is the exact opposite of its literal theme. Because the feelings the singer articulates in this song are universal, we really *aren't* alone; because we all feel this way at some point in our lives, that shared experience keeps us from really being alone. There are millions of other people in the world who feel exactly as we do, and this song reassures us that our fears and anxieties are shared ones. In fact, we are not alone, and neither is the guy singing this song. The act of singing it, the act of articulating what he feels, has connected him to the rest of us.

Madeleine

With "Madeleine," Brel sets up a cheery song about young love, then methodically subverts every one of our expectations about what a love song should be. Like so many Brel songs, "Madeleine" is about the dark side of love, the pain and blind optimism of unrequited passion.

To introduce the idea of four actors playing one character—or one composite perhaps—all four sing this first-person narrative. The lyric uses first-person singular pronouns despite the four voices harmonizing. There is a rule that an audience will accept any device or artifice in a musical as long as it is introduced within the first ten minutes. This is one of the few rules the creators of *Jacques Brel* did follow. Four voices portray one person here, early in the show. Once this dramatic device is established, we accept it for the rest of the show. Four actors singing this man's sad tale reminds us that Brel represents us all. We have all pursued, hoped for love that would not or could not be returned. In fact, as we watch two men and two women sing this song, we must consider the possibility that the narrator could be a woman, and the unrequited love could be a question of sexual orientation.

The narrator is in love with a woman named Madeleine, a woman he waits for every night, a woman who never comes. As the song begins, he tells us that he waits for her every night and of his romantic plans for the evening. At first we assume that he and Madeleine go out every night together, first to Joe's for french fries, then to the movies. In the second verse, we discover that it's getting late and Madeleine isn't there yet. It's also raining and our narrator hasn't the sense to come in out of the rain, for fear that he might miss Madeleine when she arrives. Eventually, he decides she's not coming tonight. So he decides to go home, but he'll be back tomorrow night. And we realize that he's there every night and every night he gets stood up.

Madeleine doesn't love him. She's not his girlfriend. She may not even know him. As the songs ends, we find we know this man better than we thought. His love is not real; it is obsessive, irrational, self-delusional. As if the narrator weren't already screwed up enough, Brel adds even more neurosis to his character. At no time during the song does the narrator ever blame Madeleine for anything. It's always his own fault or the fault of Madeleine's family, never her fault. Despite the awful way Madeleine treats him, he still sees her as perfect; he says he knows that she's too good for him. In the third verse we see this illustrated most potently. He says he only has himself to blame, perhaps for Madeleine's not showing up, perhaps for him catching a cold, or who knows what else. He even mocks his own obsession, saying he must have called her name a thousand times since he's been standing there, perhaps blaming that obsession for driving her away. Since it's not her fault, since she's not to blame for him standing in the cold and rain, he doesn't have to forgive her for standing him up. And he'll be back there the next night, going through the exact same thing, illustrated by the device of repeating almost exactly the first-verse lyric in the last verse. It's sad because it's so hopeless, but it's funny because we've all been there.

I Loved

The relationship described in "I Loved" has failed for two reasons. First, the singer had an immature idea of what love is. The lyric starts by listing the magical, fairy tale symbols that she associated with love. She believed that there was just one special man for her, that she only had to wait for him and that they would find each other because they were fated to be together.

Then she meets a man who fits the ideal in her head. He fits all the wild romantic notions she's read in stories and seen in movies, but they have passion, not love. Everything is extreme. Nothing is real. And on top of everything else, he's a lying, cheating jerk. One of the most telling lines in the song is the idea that this man loved the singer like a poet would love her. It's significant that he does *not* love as a normal person loves. She saw him as the mysterious, impossible-to-understand artist, as a god who could throw lightning bolts. She never saw him as a man. A woman can't love a god.

Having extreme passion can be wonderful, but when the good side is extreme, the bad side probably is, too. There is a price to be paid for that kind of too-good-to-be-real romance. There was no trust; she was constantly afraid that he would leave her. That's not love, but it did fit the romance novel ideal of love, the tragic heroine who is left by the man she loves to suffer evermore, to live alone with her memories of the passion, to be the subject of torch songs sung by Billie Holliday.

But now she's grown up. Like Clara in the musical *Passion,* she knows the difference between passion and love. Looking back, she realizes that the romance was not as life-transforming as she had expected, and that losing him did not destroy her utterly as she perhaps had hoped it might. She ended up being not a tragic heroine, but instead just a woman, an adult who will endure other loves and other losses and still wake up the next day. She is an adult and her fantasies are gone, for better or worse. No matter how devastating it seemed at the time, it was just another day in her life, inconsequential enough that she can't even remember his name anymore.

It's interesting that at no time during the song does she ever say that she loved *him*. She loved the symbols, the trappings of romance, but never him. She even loves some of the memories of places where they made love, but not him and not his love. Though her lover was in control when they were together and when they broke up, he's not anymore. She's in control now. He has no power over her. The title "I Loved" holds the meaning of the song—there is no object, no *whom* she loved. Unlike most love songs, this is about what and how she loved, not whom she loved. Brel tells us all we need to know in his title, but it's not until the end of the song that we realize it.

Mathilde

"Mathilde" is another twisted look at love. The spoken line that precedes this song is from Aristophanes' comic play *Lysistrata*: "Women bring many things. Who can deny that? But surely it's not peace that we bring." And to illustrate that statement, the singer of "Mathilde" tells us about the woman who dumped him, who broke his heart, who destroyed his life—and who is coming back to him. And even though he knows she's going to break his heart again, he still wants everything to be perfect for her. Despite the pain she caused him, he still loves her and some part of him still thinks he might have her again. Is this love? Or is it some sick kind of dependence? Has he decided, consciously or subconsciously, that he deserves this pain or perhaps that he'll never find what he wants so he'd better settle for what he can get? Once again, Brel paints an all too real and familiar scenario and shows it for the insanity it is, cutting through all the self-delusion.

The spoken line before "Mathilde" makes the first conceptual bridge between the songs about love and the songs about war. *Lysistrata* is a play about a city full of women protesting war by denying their husbands sex until they stop fighting. The creators of *Jacques Brel* have adroitly linked the battle of the sexes with their antiwar message, two of the three most prominent themes in the show.

Bachelor's Dance

"Bachelor's Dance" is about a man who can't find a girl because, like the singer of "I Loved," he's created an idealized partner in his mind that he'll never find in real life. This is a song about the objectification of women, about idealized women, women who don't really exist. The woman he's looking for is wise, soft-skinned, loving, good at keeping house, good at mothering, and she'll keep looking better and better as she ages. Not only is the woman of his dreams unreal, so is the picture he has of domestic life. Sadly, the man who will settle only for perfection will always be alone. It's fitting that this song is sung by the same actor who sings "Alone."

This song traces the phases of his life, from young love, to blissful, middle-aged domesticity, to comfortable old age. But as he grows old, he does not mature. (Isn't it interesting that the women in the show mature, but the men don't?) At each stage, the women who would love him are rejected because they don't measure up to the ideal in the singer's head. At the end of his life, he finds himself still alone, still looking, having let his entire life pass him by without knowing the joys of sharing a life with someone he loves. And all he can ask is why his dream girl never came.

Timid Frieda

"Timid Frieda" is a song about freedom and the costs and dangers of that freedom. It's about growing up and making a life, living independently, learning life lessons the hard way, away from the repression of family and old-fashioned moral codes.

The first verse of the song describes Frieda's arrival in the big city, the magic and glitz of it all in her eyes, her fear of this strange new world. She wonders if the denizens of this world will accept her and if she will find the freedom and independence she seeks. For the first time, we hear the line that will transform throughout the song, "There she goes with her valises held so tightly in her hands." Here her tight grip illustrates her fear; later it will illustrate excitement, and later still, determination and her newfound independence.

The second verse describes her excitement upon joining this new world. She finds self-respect, perhaps for the first time, and she discovers that the petty concerns of childhood really are inconsequential. She realizes she belongs here and that this is where she will make her life. The third verse gives us a glimpse into the world she has left. She says she won't go back there where they don't need her (or want her?), where all they do is berate her with scoldings and meaningless, ready-made, one-size-fits-all platitudes. Her home life was constricting. The "little lessons and platitudes from cans" are the empty cliches passed down from generation to generation, the prefab rules and restrictions that are mindlessly repeated without ever being reexamined to see if they still apply. Finally on her own, Frieda is free of the irrational repression that drove her from her home and family. Here on the street, there's an excitement and freedom she never had at home. As the third verse ends, Frieda's stranglehold on her valises shows us her determination to make a new life for herself.

The fourth verse gives us more insight into the new life Frieda has chosen. She is now living "on the street where the cops all perish," a place of danger, risk, and, yes, excitement. The contention that those cops "can't break her" might also imply that she is involved in illegal activity, perhaps prostitution. The lyric goes on to say that "she can take her brave new Fuck-You stand" against the cops. There's a strong case to be made that Frieda has become a hooker, a life that scares her but also exhilarates her; she's scared, but her senses are heightened. Has the repression of her home life driven her to the extreme rebellion of selling sex? Could the line about the cops perishing be a reference to *la petit morte* ("the little death"), a French literary phrase meaning orgasm? In other words, is she giving the cops freebies?

The reading of Frieda as a prostitute is certainly not the only possible interpretation of this song, but it does make sense. If we accept this premise, her home life and family make more sense, the danger of the streets makes sense, and the references to cops make more sense. After all, why would the cops *want* to "break her" if she weren't involved in illegal activity?

Finally in the last verse, the singers ask that if we see Frieda, to leave her alone, to allow her to make of her life whatever she wants. Is Frieda really just one woman, or is she an archetype, a symbol of many women? The original French title is *plural*: "Les timides," meaning "the timid ones." The lyric makes no judgment of Frieda's career choice and it seems to disapprove heartily of the way her family has treated her. Interestingly, the music is a simple waltz, sounding almost like a lullaby. Perhaps it's telling us that this is the message we're sending to our children, that if we are suffocating them in our moral repression, their natural inclination will be to go too far the other way, into a life of dangerous rebellion. Whatever the song's moral stance, it clearly believes that people should be left to their own choices. Like the several songs preceding it, this song is about passion and lust without love, a theme Brel returns to often.

It's worth noting that Brel's original French lyric aims in a different direction. It begins by comparing "The Timid Ones" to falling leaves being blown about, folding into themselves, at the mercy of the fates. It describes their sheltered lives, their need to hide, to be hidden and protected from the world. They're afraid to take or even ask for what they want, and when they find someone they are just used and discarded. The last line of each verse, "A valise in each hand," says that they have no home, no place that is their own, no safe haven to return to when the world gets too cold. The French lyric connects deeply with the lyric of "The Desperate Ones." The English lyric is a logical extension of the French lyric, instead of a direct translation; Timid Frieda was once one of the timid ones, but she took control of her life, rejected that which was destructive in her life and set out on her own. Though her life may be decadent and unsafe, it is still her life, and it's the one she chose.

My Death

"My Death" is not as dark and foreboding as it sounds. This song is not about the dark shadow of death as much as about growing old and the inevitability of death. The point of the song is that death is unavoidable, that it looms over us all like a shadow, but—and this is important—it usually waits until we've each lived a full life and done most of the things we wanted to do. The song isn't about death *stalking* us (the usual portrayal); it's about death *waiting* until we're ready. In a way it's a perfect companion piece to "Old Folks" in Act II. The most important lines of the song are repeated several times:

> But whatever is behind the door,
> There is nothing much to do.
> Angel or devil, I don't care,
> For in front of that door, there is you.

In other words, it doesn't matter that death will eventually come to each of us. There's nothing we can do about it; we can't escape or cheat death. What matters is that before we go through that metaphoric door into death, we enjoy the things that lie on this side of the door, in life. Death is even connected to sex in the second-verse references to arms and thighs and fingers, perhaps another reference to le petit mort, or orgasm.

Death in this song is not evil. It is not the frightening shadowy figure with a scythe. It is a kind but uncompromising force, one that is patient, that waits to allow the singer and her friends to live their lives and have fun before they die, yet it is still something we can't escape. It's not something we can understand (as illustrated by the images of magicians), but that's okay. We don't need to understand it. We just have to accept that death informs everything; it is a part of life that can't be separated out. The constant references to the passing time echo the same phrase in "Old Folks." It connects to the old silver clock in "Old Folks," to the chronological structure of "Marathon," to the descriptions of the phases of life in "Bachelor's Dance," and to the ever-present use of past tense in almost all the songs about love. Time and death are the two most prevalent themes in this show, and they converge here. Death is almost friendly; there is a kind of security knowing what's to come and knowing that it won't take you before your time. It's interesting that this song should come after "Timid Frieda" (in a direct segue, without stopping), a song about a girl in the dangerous, maybe fatal, twilight world of the Big City.

Jackie

"Jackie" is a song about a man who wants desperately to return to the simple, protected world of being a child, away from the responsibilities and complexities of being an adult. Each verse sets up a fantasy scenario in which the singer dreams up a life for himself, each time more fantastic than the one before. Yet none satisfy him. He dreams of being a singer and a drunken gigolo in the first verse; then a rich and famous recording artist, a high-class brothel owner, a drug dealer, and even ruler of the world in the second verse; and finally an omnipotent god in the third verse. But in every verse, no matter how extreme the fantasy, no matter how rich and powerful he is in each scenario, he still prefers the thought of going back to his childhood. He wants to return so badly he would settle for being a child just for an hour a day, just a short escape to recharge his psychic batteries. Despite the brisk tempo and high energy level, this is an extremely sad song. This is a man who can't be happy, whose happiness is all in the past tense. And the last line of each verse even denigrates the life he longs to return to:

> If I could be for just one little hour
> Cute, cute, cute in a stupid ass way.

It's interesting that before he slips into his imagination in each verse to return to his childhood, he needs some sort of mood-altering drug—alcohol in the first verse, opium in the second, and actual death in the last verse.

The Statue

"The Statue" raises some interesting and difficult questions about honoring war heroes. This is a song about glorifying war and about the necessity and danger of illusion. The singer of this song is a man who was killed in the war (he doesn't say which war, and though we can assume from certain references it's one of the World Wars, the song applies to other wars just as well), and he's angry at the person who wrote the inscription on the statue erected in his honor. The statue says the singer was a paragon of honor and virtue, but in reality, he admits, he was a liar, a cheat, and an all-around jerk. The inscription says that he was most beloved by God, but in reality, he admits, he only prayed to God when it suited him, and he even prayed to Satan when he thought it might help. The inscription says the singer died like a hero, but in reality, he admits, he only went to war because he had nothing better to do with his life, because he thought it might help him get girls, and he died from incompetence, not out of bravery or sacrifice.

The singer knows that the statue is not just a memorial but is also a recruiting poster, an invitation to kids to join the army, to become heroes themselves, and have statues erected in their honor. Yet the singer knows firsthand that war is not like the movies, and that if they erect a statue to honor you, you won't be around to enjoy it. He also knows that most of the kids who go to die on the battlefield, kids who die more bravely than he did, won't be honored. The singer wants to protect them from the lie, from the glorification of war. He doesn't want his name to be used to recruit kids to go to war and be killed. He doesn't want to be an accomplice in their deaths. But there's nothing he can do. He can tell the kids to get away from this statue, tell them not to read the fictionalized inscriptions, but they can't hear him. He's dead.

It's interesting to notice that Brel quotes a bit of the melody from "The Battle Hymn of the Republic" in the vocal line in each verse to underline the false glorification of war (and perhaps to give America a little extra blame for that glorification?). The central idea of this song is a sentiment expressed in several Brel songs: soldiers are ordinary people having to survive in extraordinary circumstances. Despite the statues and memorials, despite the John Wayne movies and *Hogan's Heroes*, the men and women laying down their lives in the name of war are neither heroes nor clowns (as the lyric says in "If We Only Have Love"). And in a way, the fact that they are ordinary people makes their victories and even their survival all the more impressive. Brel finds a difficult moral question in the act of war, and he objects to dressing it up and making it seem like something it is not.

Like many Brel songs, this one is built on a tragic irony. In this case, this man led a dishonorable life but he is now trying to do the honorable thing, by telling the kids the truth, by telling them not to believe the lies on his statue. The irony lies in the fact that they can't hear him because he's dead. By getting himself killed, through incompetence and apathy, he not only provided the propagandists with recruitment material, he also forfeited the opportunity to set the record straight.

Some directors have experienced a problem with one word in the lyric. The singer refers to the man who "wrote" things on his statue, and many listeners today think he's talking about graffiti. The singer is really talking about the man who carved the inscription on the base of the statue. This problem has been solved by simply substituting the word *carved* for *wrote* in the couple of instances in which it occurs.

The Desperate Ones

"The Desperate Ones" is a song about a different kind of victim, not those killed in war but those who are killed—or who take their own lives—because of the indifference of those around them. They may be the homeless, who have no voice, no power or influence; they go through their lives without making a sound, without calling attention to themselves. They may be the men in "Alone" without friends or family. They may be the ones success forever eludes, who suffer wordlessly behind their desks and computers, never given the chance they need to succeed, to realize the American Dream, finally just too depressed to keep going.

They are the ones who kill themselves and no one notices. They made no difference when they were alive and their deaths mean nothing either. Their fates were sealed long ago; they could never be the winners. "Their footsteps sing a song that's ended before it's begun." They find in suicide a peace and a calm, an end to the suffering, which exists nowhere else for them:

> And underneath the bridge
> The water's sweet and deep;
> There is the journey's end,
> The land of endless sleep.
>
> . . . .
>
> On the bridge of nevermore
> They disappear one by one,
> Disappear without a sound.

The lyric says, "They cry to us for help. We think it's all in fun." Like the people in "Brussels," we choose not to see that which we don't want to see. We talk of love, of compassion, of all Americans sharing in the American Dream, but it's only talk. As Brel says, we know the verb *to love* but we don't really know *how* to love. And what's most tragic is that when these people, the desperate ones, are gone, we never miss them. Death on the battlefield can be horrific, but perhaps this is even worse.

Sons Of

Several songs in the show are about war, exposing the false romanticism and reminding us of the harsh realities, but "Sons Of" takes the issue out of the larger social context and puts it into a personal context. The singer is not a mother or a sister. She is not someone who has lost a loved one to war. She *is* war, first the sweet seducer, set to the pretty, lullaby music of the first verses, later the mad killer, set to the crazed, grand waltz of the last verse. As the music changes from innocent to manic, war itself transforms from the opportunity for heroism to the indiscriminate killer of young men and women. The first verse doesn't mention death, only children, the hope of the future. It's not until the second verse that the lyric speaks of them vanishing. The images grow darker. In the third verse, the reality hits us: some of our children went to war, and some of them never returned; of course, this song was even more potent in the Vietnam years. The last verse returns to the words of the first verse, now set to the macabre, throbbing death waltz. The song even refers to itself—to lullabies— in the third verse. The first verses are the lullabies, the false lulling to sleep of our fears, the fraudulent promises of greatness. We're sucked in by the lullaby—by this song itself—and we lose our children.

The song touches on an idea that was explored in "The Statue" and will be returned to in "If We Only Have Love": that war does not discriminate, that it kills rich and poor alike, educated and uneducated. When the shrapnel flies, the rich kid will die as quickly as the poor kid. The song reminds us that when war breaks out, the greatest cost is in human lives. And the people who die aren't just abstract, faceless numbers and they aren't "troops"; they are our neighbors, our children, and our friends.

The song talks of generations, of the circle of life ("sons of your sons"). Ultimately, the song says that no matter who dies, whether it's someone famous ("sons of tycoons") or anonymous ("sons of the farms"), a child or relative or someone you don't know ("sons passing by"), a worker, an artist, or a soldier, it's always a loss for us all when a young man or woman goes to fight and does not come home. They are all our sons. The nightmare fears of the children become the nightmare fears of us all. As the music gets bigger and louder with each verse, it illustrates the mounting cumulative death toll of human lives lost to war. Harmonically, the music doesn't end. The last chord of the song sounds like it should go on, illustrating the idea that war never ends, that our human propensity to war is eternal.

Amsterdam

Act I closes with "Amsterdam," a song about disillusionment and regret. The singer is a sailor who looks back on his life and finds nothing of value. He began as an idealistic young man with romantic dreams of the life of a sailor (perhaps he was one of the kids who saw the inscription on "The Statue" and believed its lies), but he will end his life in a dirty bar in a drunken fight, not bravely on the battlefield, not in sacrifice for a fellow soldier. He will never become the man he wanted to be. The last lines of the first verse, "There's a sailor who's born on a muggy hot night by the dawn's early light," mark this young man's new life as a sailor. He has begun over, been born again, into the service of his country (hence the phrase from the "Star-Spangled Banner").

But the idealistic young man finds exactly the opposite of what he expected: drunken old men with rotted teeth, seedy bars, and whores. The other sailors can think of only one thing—sex—and they'll do anything to get some. So they go off with the whores, having long forgotten their idealism (or more poetically, "they've forgotten the tune"), the reason they joined the service, each one of them led only by his penis. And soon, the idealistic young man becomes just like the others.

In the third verse, we return to the present as the narrator sits and tries to drink away his memories of who he once was and what he once wanted to become. He tries to drink away the world in which he now lives. At the end of the song, we find that he was also once in love, probably in love with one of the whores he met; but like most whores, she only loved him as long as he was paying, until it was time for the next customer. So now he drinks to that unfaithful love. And there he sits in the port of Amsterdam, his own personal hell on earth, the place where he lost his ideals, where he lost his soul.

The Bulls

Act II opens with "The Bulls," a song about our insatiable appetite for violence and bloodshed. The first line of the song says so much: "On Sundays, the bulls get so bored when they are asked to show off for us." Later, "show off" becomes "suffer," and finally "drop dead." The absurdist image of the bulls getting bored with dying is a way for Brel to point out the foolish consistency of our culture and our species. It's always the same and has been since humans first walked the earth. We never tire of blood. This song is particularly potent for an American audience, brought up on horror movies, action/adventure movies, ultraviolent cartoons and video games, violent comic books, TV cop shows and "reality" shows, professional football and boxing, and kids roaming our city streets with automatic weapons. When we're not becoming so inured to violence that none of it seems real anymore, we're romanticizing it in movies starring Arnold Schwarzenegger. "The Bulls" describes the transformation of grocery clerks into Don Juan, Garcia Lorca (the famous Spanish poet-playwright), even Nero, the minute they step into the ring to torture and kill the bull. It's interesting that none of these three figures are real heroes, the implication being that the toreadors may be romanticized but they are not heroic, just murderous. The lyric even wonders what the bulls are thinking. Are they dreaming of a hell made for the sadistic men who would torture them?

The song's final lines completely change the meaning of the song—something that happens in many Brel songs. Suddenly we find that the bullfighting is only a metaphor for war, that the sadistic toreadors are standing in for the politicians who declare war but do not fight themselves, that the defenseless bulls sent to certain death represent the young men and women sent to their deaths fighting wars they didn't start—the boys in "Sons Of." More than any other song, "The Bulls" illustrates Eric Blau's remark that Brel's songs are about how we survive (or don't) in a world we didn't make. The hell for toreadors that the bulls dream about is really a hell for war-declaring politicians and generals. The silly girls screaming in the stands represent the American public cheering military battles and triumphs, making a hero of the president when he flexes America's muscle by sending troops to battle, yet ignoring the veterans of Vietnam because there was no romanticized triumph.

Old Folks

"Old Folks" is a song about time—the loss of it and the tyranny of it. Like its companion piece, "My Death," it realizes that death is inevitable, that it cannot be cheated, and though it will wait, it won't wait forever. Every day we slip closer and closer to its grip, without ever really knowing just how close we are at any given moment.

The old silver clock mentioned repeatedly in the lyric is a concrete symbol of the ever-forward movement of time. Yet though we can see on a clock both how far we've come and how far we have yet to go, in life we can only see how far we've come. The repetitiveness of the music and the backup singing conjure the steady ticking of the clock and illustrate the old folks' mundane life, every day the same, actions repeating endlessly without variation, like the swinging of a clock pendulum.

The first verse identifies the Old Folks; they are all of us, rich and poor. As many of the songs in the show tell us, no one escapes death, and most of us do not escape growing old. These are the people whose best years are behind them. Like the main characters in Sondheim's *Follies*, and the characters in other songs in this show, they can't deal with the present so they choose to exist in some foggy, half-remembered, happily romanticized past. Yet they find the clock ticks too slowly for them; their lives are no longer what they want them to be, and living is now just waiting for death. Just like in "My Death," the lyric of "Old Folks" has the old silver clock saying, "I'll wait for you."

All the joys of their lives are done: their books are no longer exciting, the piano stands unused, their pets have died, their happiest moments are only in old photos and songs. Their only reason for going out is to pay their last respects to someone even older than they are, who has died as they surely will. Their main activities for the day are looking out a window, sitting in a chair, or staying in bed. Perhaps the most disturbing line in the song is "They hold each other's hand, like children in the dark, but one will get lost anyway." Is the lost child the one who dies or the one who survives alone? Or is it referring to one of them losing his mind to Alzheimer's? The lyric says, "The other will remain, just sitting in that room which makes no sound." Is this the survivor, or is death the room which makes no sound?

Marieke

"Marieke" is a song about loss, a song that takes a very different view of death, this time of premature death from the point of view of the survivors. Marieke is a woman's name, but she represents anyone we've lost: a spouse, a child, a lover or friend. This song is about how life goes on and how the world is not quite the same once that loved one is gone. This lyric is in three languages. The verses are in English. The choruses are in a variation of Dutch, called Flemish (exactly as Brel wrote them), a language spoken in Brussels. But the choruses also contain some phrases in Brel's original French.

A rough translation of the first chorus, which is all in Flemish:

Without love, warm love,
Blows the wind, the silent wind.
Without love, warm love,
Cries the sea, the grey sea.
Without love, warm love,
Suffers the light, the dark light;
And grates the sand over my country,
My flat land, my Flanders.

The second chorus, a mix of Flemish and French, is a variation of the first chorus:

Without love, warm love,
Blows the wind; it is finished.
Without love, warm love,
Cries the sea; it's already finished.
Without love, warm love,
Suffers the light; all is finished;
And grates the sand over my country,
My flat land, my Flanders.

The third chorus, all in Flemish, conjures much darker, more fatalistic images:

Without love, warm love,
Grins the devil, the black devil.
Without love, warm love,

Burns my heart, my old heart.
Without love, warm love,
Dies the summer, the sad summer;
And grates the sand over my country,
My flat land, my Flanders.

The repetition of the phrase "Come back again" echoes the phrase "Come on, love," which is repeated so much in "No Love, You're Not Alone." Both songs are about lost love, about people who aren't willing to accept the loss they've suffered, who can't face reality.

Some productions cut this song because of its Flemish lyrics. With every other song in the show translated into English, it seems odd to sing one song with lyrics the audience can't understand. The show's creators chose to keep this lyric largely in two foreign languages because they felt the sounds of these languages were so beautiful, and the experimental theatre movement at that time was very interested in language as abstract sound. But is that sufficient justification, and does it alienate the audience? Some of Brel's audiences in France, and all of them in Belgium, understood the passages in Flemish, so this song about Belgium took on greater meaning in its native tongue; but American audiences have no idea what the Flemish passages say. There are a few lines of spoken text in the show before the song that give a rough idea of the Flemish lines, but despite the beauty of Flemish, it still seems odd to translate an evening of French songs into English except for one. There is a textual progression through the three choruses that is interesting and poetic, and to deny American audiences the opportunity to understand these poetic words is problematic.

Brussels

Just before the song "Brussels," there is a spoken line that sums up the theme of the song: "And sometimes the songs were sung, between the acrobats and the jugglers, in music halls built long ago. Everybody heard the songs—but nobody listened." Like "Marieke" and other Brel songs, this is about denying reality.

This is another Brel song dripping with irony. On the surface, the carefree life of pre–World War I Brussels seems an idyllic one, full of happy people, music, and a trouble-free existence. But we come to understand over the course of the song that the happiness was a false one, an artificially created happiness used to shut out the harsh realities of the world. World War I was exploding around the people of Brussels and they pretended nothing was happening, that they were somehow protected from the violence. Instead of preparing for the inevitable, preparing to defend themselves, they sang, danced, and had sex. When the Germans rolled into Brussels and occupied the city in 1914, no one was ready and their carefree world collapsed.

The singer compares prewar Brussels to the silent movies—innocent, unsophisticated, artificial, somehow unnatural. Like Berlin before World War II, the people of Brussels focused on pleasure, which led to a kind of irresponsibility and decadence (as portrayed in the musical *Cabaret*). This is another song about the romanticism of war and the way people can ignore the horrors around them. The references to World War I as fun, as a game, are the whole point of the song. War is not romantic, Brel is saying (again). It is not heroic. War does not "save the world"; on the contrary, it kills millions of people. To treat it as romantic is foolish and dangerous, hence the reference to the grandfather and grandmother having no brains. To underline this foolishness, the show's creators even made up a new word, *brustled*, when they translated the lyric.

The end of the song builds to a manic climax, modulating up a key to build excitement, then suddenly it breaks apart and the singers run out of steam like windup toys. This is a musical representation of the peak of the party atmosphere in Brussels in 1914 as the German tanks rolled in and stopped the party, a kind of social coitus interruptus, somewhat as it happened in Berlin and other places around the world in other times. Too often, we don't see war or other social upheaval coming until it's here, and even when it arrives, we try desperately to pretend it's not here. This song is a cautionary statement telling us to keep our eyes open, to learn from the past (a theme from "Marathon"), to be forever vigilant.

No Love, You're Not Alone

According to Eric Blau, the singer of "No Love, You're Not Alone" has lost the man she loves to alcohol and/or drugs. In an attempt to work her way back into his life and heart, she offers herself as a friend. She thinks that if she is allowed to be his friend, her broken heart will be healed, yet we know it won't. Even if he allows her friendship, she still won't be for him what she once was, and this substitute relationship won't make up for the one that has been lost. Though he will get everything he wants out of this new relationship—love, companion-ship, a friendly shoulder to cry on, and yet no real intimacy or re-sponsibility—she will not. She is willingly putting herself into a re-lationship in which she will give love but will not get it in return.

She makes references to their former life together, to their love-making. Ironically, all the sorrow and loss she sees in him are really her own. She says that maybe he feels too much, yet she's the one whose emotions demand more than she can have. She says perhaps he prays too much, yet she is the one who is praying for something that won't come to pass. Ultimately, in reassuring him that he's not alone, she's really trying to convince herself. At the end, desperate to go back to what she once had, she says:

> The newsreel of our life,
> I'll play it in reverse.
> Your pain will fall away,
> We'll relive yesterday,
> And start where we began, love.

But this is what *she* wants, not what he wants. If they went back to yesterday, the pain would fall away for her because she would have what she's lost: his love.

Next

"Next" is the most disturbing of the songs about sex, turning up the heat one more notch above the song before it. "Next" describes a man's first experience with sex, but this is no ordinary first time. The singer says he was just a kid when his "innocence was lost" (or was it taken?), and though many of us use that phrase to describe having sex for the first time, we don't mean it like he does. His first time was with a pros-titute in a mobile whorehouse sponsored by the army, no tenderness, no pretense of affection, just an impersonal assembly-line fuck. He describes himself standing in line with all the other soldiers, naked except for an army towel around his waist. The experience forever changed sex for him. For the rest of his life, he has associated sex with that awful moment, his lieutenant pushing the line along, shouting "*Next!*", the men shuffling along waiting to be called, him being thrown into the arms of a uncaring woman.

But perhaps this song is about more than the specific situation described. Perhaps it's also about the way modern society has made sex into a business, in our TV shows, on our billboards, in our magazines, in almost every aspect of our culture. Our children are exposed to sexuality everywhere they turn. It's impossible to avoid it, impossible to preserve their innocence. Perhaps the army-sponsored whorehouse represents the way the media, advertisers, and even the government force kids to become aware of sexuality long before they would otherwise, through child beauty pageants, designer clothes for kids, sensuous Calvin Klein ads featuring nubile young people, and a parade across our television screens of sexually active teens on the daytime talk shows. How many millions of kids accessed the transcripts of the Monica Lewinsky sex scandal through the Internet?

How ironic that the government, the supposed bastion of discipline and enforced morality, would sponsor a mobile whorehouse; and yet how appropriate that when it did, it would also destroy sex by making it mechanical and perversely uniform, forcing this most unmanageable, instinctive act into a cold, orderly structure. At the end of the song, the singer says he'd happily maim or kill himself to escape the lifelong torture of remembering that day in the army every time he's with a woman. Not only was that day a nightmare for him, but he must live it over and over, for the rest of his life.

Carousel

The show ends with two powerful songs. The first, "Carousel," is the culmination of everything that precedes it, a kind of summation of the insanity of the evening and of our modern world, the swirling together of all our neuroses, addictions, hostilities, and posturing. We've spent the evening listening to Brel observe that which is most absurd and dangerous in human nature, and in this penultimate song, we see it all come together and literally spin out of control. "If We Only Have Love," which immediately follows, will be the answer to how we can keep the carousel of our collective life from spinning off its base and crashing down around us. If "Marathon" was a table of contents, "Carousel" is the climax of our madness, and "If We Only Have Love" is the resolution.

Brel's original French title for "Carousel" was "La valse á mille temps," a pun title. Normally, a waltz would be "á trois temps" (i.e., "in three time," or as we would put it, in triple time). "La valse á mille temps" literally means "The Waltz in Thousand Time," which would mean a thousand beats to each measure, an appropriately absurdist comment on the craziness of our modern world. And yet Brel's original French lyric is less about the insanity of modern life and more about love and lovers and how they can live their lives in the music of a love song. In Brel's lyric, "Waltz in Thousand Time" says that in each beat of the waltz, young lovers can live a lifetime.

But the creators of *Jacques Brel Is Alive and Well and Living in Paris* had to create a dramatically satisfying conclusion for their show, so they took liberties with this number, as they did with "Marathon." The imagery in the English lyric is all about our often unreal, deceptively packaged, substance-free world. The carnivals are our infomercial political conventions, our high-profile religious organizations spending more effort on fund-raising and TV shows than on healing society, our ridiculously combative government, our citizens' cutthroat battles to seize control of local governments and school boards—all things richer in glitz than in content. The cotton candy described in the song is the empty calories of television and movies, of bland pop music and celebrity magazines. The fortune tellers are the endless parade of self-proclaimed experts telling us our society is being destroyed by gay marriage, telling us salt will kill us, telling us exercising our abs will lead to happiness and success, telling us the world would face its fiery end in the year 2000. The lines that sum up this song and the show as a whole come at the end of the first stanza: "And the whole world madly turning, turning, turning 'til you can't see."

It's not hard to see our presidential and congressional candidates as crazy clowns chasing brass rings. It's not hard to see our siliconed, nipped-and-tucked movie stars as Kewpie dolls with painted faces. It's not hard to see infomericals, pyramid schemes, and other get-rich-quick opportunities as tricky shell games and missing peas. The missing peas are the promises of riches—or beauty or a washboard stomach—that never existed to begin with.

The point of this song is our disorientation. How can we keep our balance in a world so full of lies and intentional misrepresentation? There may never be a better metaphor for the bedlam of our world than a carousel that never stops, spinning faster than we want it to, making us a little queasy, wishing there was some way to get off of it. But there's only one way to stop the carousel, the song is telling us, only one way to get off this horrific ride. Our only hope is to stop everything and reevaluate the mess we've made of our lives. We can stop the carousel, if we only have love . . .

If We Only Have Love

After an evening of cynicism, wicked satire, and biting social commentary, this final song takes us by surprise, this simple anthem of love. But this isn't a song about holding hands and teaching the world to sing in perfect harmony. This is a song about surviving. Through almost every song in the show, there is a shred of hope underneath the darkness, behind the bitterness. This last song says that there is always hope, that we will always survive, no matter what seemingly insurmountable obstacles may be placed in our way. The song is not as simplistic or sappy as it might at first seem; and it shows us that the rest of the show is not quite as dark and hopeless as it first seemed. Just as "Marathon" serves as a table of contents, this song becomes a kind of epilogue, a summary of the show, again touching on all the same subjects that were mentioned in the opening number and then explored in more depth over the course of the evening.

This song is not about romantic love or even the love of family and friends. It is about tolerance, respect, the love of the human race. The first line says it all: "If we only have love, then tomorrow will dawn." No matter what the odds, even when millions of souls are murdered in concentration camps, even when bombs are dropped and Armageddon seems at hand, still the sun comes up in the morning and the human race marches on. We will survive.

The song tells us that if we can only be tolerant of each other and embrace our differences rather than letting them separate us—"to embrace without fears"—then we'll be all right. So much death and destruction throughout the centuries have been done in the name of God. But if we just use our faith ("the hymn that we shout") to heal and help rather than to condemn and divide, we'll be all right; "we can reach those in pain, we can heal all our wounds." If we could do this, then religion could have real meaning again ("Then Jerusalem stands"). We have to learn to solve problems and disputes without resorting to sending young men off to war to kill one another in foreign lands, without monthly shootings in our schools ("We can melt all the guns"), a subject that is dealt with in great depth throughout the show.

Ultimately, we are done the most damage by the people who want power and control over their fellow humans, the politicians who use their countries and their citizens for personal gain, the preachers who use their pulpits to become rich and politically powerful, the people who feign morality in order to impose their values on others. If we all realize our basic humanity, our limits, our ultimate insignificance in the sands of time, only then will we be "tall as the pines, neither heroes nor clowns." We must recognize what is good about being human, what we all share, how we all need and depend on one another, and how anyone trying to exalt himself above others will only cause pain and suffering.

We can't forget, however, that every sentence of this lyric beings with "if," warning that this better tomorrow is not a sure thing. It's interesting to note that Brel's original French title is "*When* We Only Have Love," not *If*. Unlike Brel's version, the English lyric never says that any of this *will* happen, that humanity *will* ever get past its innate aggression and thirst for violence. So some of the cynicism that runs so rampant throughout the rest of the show remains present here, and it may be more the perspective of the translators than that of Brel himself.

Brel sees a future that is better than our present, and he maintains less skepticism than his translators that we can attain it. He believes it will come. Frank Galati, director of the epic American musical *Ragtime*, described his show in terms that apply to *Jacques Brel* as well, and to this last song. He said *Ragtime* is about "our ability, as a people, to face ourselves in times of crisis and dig deep for what is best within us. It is the only thing that will save us." What makes *Jacques Brel* so passionately loved by so many people is its universality. It is about struggle, deep, personal struggle and collective social struggle, and we all need to know when we turn out the lights at night that we are not alone in our struggle, that others share that struggle with us, and that just as they have survived, we will survive, too. The love in "If We Only Have Love" is not the love of silly '70s pop; it's the shared humanity that reassures us in our darkest times that we are not alone.

A Friendly Warning

There is a great danger in staging *Jacques Brel Is Alive and Well and Living in Paris* without careful consideration; this is not like any other show, and it can't be approached or staged like any other revue. For the same reasons that complex music distracts an audience from lyrics, complex staging—or random wandering around the stage—does the same. This is a show about ideas. Like most of Stephen Sondheim's musicals, *Jacques Brel* should be physically minimalist. The audience will not get bored if the actors stand or sit still. Most of the audience members have not heard these lyrics before and they're going to need fierce concentration to digest Brel's ideas. Some of these songs demand movement, but some work best in stillness.

When I directed the show, several of the songs seemed impossible to stage. We couldn't figure out how to physicalize them. "Carousel" especially was turning out to be a major headache. Finally, we realized that our mistake was in looking for clever staging ideas. What we should have been doing was trying our best to understand the central message of each song, then create staging that helped communicate that. In the case of "Carousel," instead of trying to create some choreographic carousel onstage, we went back to the lyrics. This is a song about being overwhelmed, about social and historical perpetual motion, about the way history repeats itself. It's also the climax of the tension that has been created through the other songs. So we devised a set of gestures taken from the other songs we had already staged, and we put them together into a six-measure movement pattern that repeated endlessly throughout the song. Since this pattern would be performed against eight-measure sections in the music, the gestures and music would almost never line up right, creating tension between what we heard and what we saw. The cast stood in a diamond floor pattern and the only visual variety was that with each repetition of the pattern, the cast rotated positions onstage. As the song sped up, so did the gestures and the revolutions of the cast, until they became almost a blur of movement. We had created physically the ideas that propelled the song—repetition, motion, tension, and a kind of visual summary of the rest of the show. It turned out to be dazzling.

Other Resources

The original off-Broadway cast album of the show is available on CD but does not contain three songs from the show—"The Statue," "Girls and Dogs," and "Middle Class." And the arrangements on the cast album add a flute and trumpet to the band, which are not in the performance rental materials. The added sound is nice, but the original arrangements, with only piano, guitar/mandolin, bass, and percussion, are very strong arrangements, in many cases more subtle and more beautiful than those on the cast album, and there's no need to change them. The movie soundtrack was released on LP with full orchestrations, but it has not been transferred to CD; you might find it in used-record stores. The movie soundtrack contains both "The Statue" and "Middle Class," as well as several other songs added for the movie that are not in the show. Fortunately, the cast recording of the 1994 London revival is available in a two-CD set, and it's the only recording of the entire stage score. It's a little odd hearing these French songs, which were interpreted and translated by Americans, sung by British singers. But it's still a great recording and the only place to hear all the songs in the arrangements audiences actually heard onstage.

There are also recordings available on CD of Brel himself singing his songs in French; these are often very different arrangements, but it's fun and illuminating to hear Brel's interpretations of his work. The film version has not yet been released commercially on videotape, but it is shown on PBS from time to time, so some musical theatre fans have it on tape. There are plans to release the film on videotape sometime soon, but I don't know when. Eric Blau wrote about the experience of creating the show in a book called *Jacques Brel Is Alive and Well and Living in Paris,* which also contains all the English lyrics and the original French lyrics. Vocal selections have been published but these are very different, simplified arrangements, with none of the key changes and musical climaxes. Some theatre companies have used the vocal selections instead of the real score because it's easier, but they do a great disservice to the show's wonderful arrangements—and it's a violation of the licensing agreement.

Both the script and score are available only from Music Theatre International, which licenses the show. Unfortunately, there is no piano/vocal score; there is only a conductor's score with piano, percussion, bass, and guitar all scored on the same page, but *no* vocal lines at all. It's tough to use this for accompanying the show, but there's no alternative. It's also worth noting that the script and handwritten chorus books differ on numerous lyrics so that it's sometimes difficult to know which version is the definitive version. From a practical standpoint, the rental materials make it tough to learn the score, but with the help of the cast album, it all eventually makes sense and the pieces fall into place, and the joy of performing these songs is well worth the effort.

7 The Ballad of Little Mikey

Book, music, and lyrics by Mark Savage
Originally directed in Los Angeles by Robert Schrock,
with additional direction by Mark Bringelson
Licensed by Belvedere Productions, Los Angeles

Gay literature underwent a profound change sometime in the early 1990s. Before that time, most gay stories were about how hard it is to be gay, about how hard it is to come out of the closet, about facing rejection and discrimination, about trying to find love in a world that hates homosexuality. But at some point in the last decade of the millennium, things really changed for gay Americans. Suddenly being gay wasn't so outrageous. Suddenly there were gay characters all over mainstream TV—about two dozen of them in some seasons. Suddenly kids were coming out of the closet in high school, and some kids were never even *in* the closet. There were suddenly gay high school proms, gay high school students forming gay student clubs, gay celebrities and politicians—even Republicans—coming out of the closet publicly in record numbers.

Gay literature and theatre turned a corner. Instead of stories about being gay and dealing with the pain of being an outcast (as in *The Boys in the Band* and *La Cage aux Folles*), stories were now being written about finding love, building relationships, family, work, friendships. Though the main characters were gay, the stories weren't about being gay. Now they were about gay people facing the same problems, obstacles, and dramas straight people face. Gay humor changed, too. At the same time, there was an explosion of gay comedians on the comedy club circuit. Comic novels, sitcom jokes, and other forms of gay-oriented humor turned the same corner that literature and theatre had. Instead of making fun of themselves (the old "I'll make fun of myself before you have a chance to"), gay comedians and writers were now laughing more at the antigay religious extremists who were losing ground every day and at the ordinary, day-to-day craziness of being human, whether gay or straight. Instead of having one topic to explore—being gay—there were now dozens of topics: dating, love, marriage, family, work, politics, and of course, sex. Some of what the gay community found funniest was just how ordinary gay lives could be. Especially after years of hearing how deviant they were, gays found stories about gay couples arguing over who should take out the trash funny precisely because they were so ordinary.

The Ballad of Little Mikey

The Ballad of Little Mikey is particularly interesting in regard to this change in gay literature and theatre. As the show opens, Mikey, a gay man in his thirties, has been offered a high-paying, mainstream job, but to take it he will have to give up the gay-oriented nonprofit law project he runs and the other political projects he's involved in. As he prepares to do this, he looks back over his life and the path he's taken to get to where he is. The show divides its time between the present and flashbacks set in 1979 and 1980. The scenes in the past seem on the surface to conform to the older kind of gay literature, in which the topic is being gay and the difficulties gay people face, while the scenes in the present are about relationships and other issues—*not* about being gay. In fact, a straight couple could play the scenes in the present without rewriting a word. *Mikey* straddles two very different time periods in a way that embodies this change within its own structure.

In the scenes in the past, Mikey has to deal with figuring out he's gay in high school; being in love with another guy who's not ready to admit his own homosexuality; going to college and finding a gay community that seems very foreign and intimidating to him; looking for sex in a hostile world that demands that gay sex be hidden and cloaked in anonymity; learning about gay culture, a culture not inherited from the family as other cultures are, but instead consciously passed down through social structures outside the family, constantly reinvented; and foremost in this story, confronting the divisive and aggressively hateful world of politics. Mikey wonders if he wants to be like the other gay men he meets, whom he perceives as effeminate, catty, bitchy, something less than manly. He has been brought up to believe that a man must behave a certain way, and he's not ready to give up that preconception. As in the old school of gay storytelling, Mikey questions whether he really wants to be gay.

In contrast, the scenes set in the present deal with entirely different issues: the process of trying to salvage a long-term relationship during which Mikey and his partner, Steve, find they want different things; the desire to "settle down" and have a "normal" life after years of chaos and adventure; the realization that Mikey and Steve really want the same life their parents had; and the understanding that though marriage can be difficult and frustrating, there are compensations that make it worth the struggle. These are the kinds of issues the new gay literature deals with, the same issues straight couples face.

The Ballad of Little Mikey straddles two very different historical and cultural periods while it also straddles two literary periods, and the contrast between those periods serves not only as a history lesson for those in the gay community too young to remember the historic riots at the Stonewall Inn (the New York gay bar) but also as a great literary tour of where we've been and how far we've come. It also charts the change in many gay individuals in America, like Mikey, once focused so intently on their own gayness (which manifested itself either in the tremendous and constant effort to stay closeted or in political and social activism), now more focused on starting families, having children, building lives more in synch with the traditional American Dream. Mikey's job with the law ·project represents the gay world, while the new job he's been offered (as an entertainment lawyer) represents a new world in which orientation is mostly irrelevant. *Mikey* the musical ultimately finds itself to be a bridge between the past and future for gay-themed musicals, in part because (unfortunately) musical theatre is always the last storytelling form to adapt to new trends and forms. Perhaps *Mikey* takes the older shows, like *La Cage aux Folles,* and links them to the new shows, like *Rent* and *A New Brain,* in which main characters can be gay and yet their orientation is never an issue.

We'll Have a Gay Ol' Time

Because *Mikey* was written in the 1990s, even the scenes in the past are not really just about being gay. Whereas the central journey in older gay shows and literature was always about coming to terms with being gay or overcoming obstacles facing gays, *The Ballad of Little Mikey* is about a different kind of journey. Mikey's journey is not just about learning to be gay or about joining the gay community; it's bigger and more universal than that. It's a journey we all take. It's about growing up, finding one's place in the world, and learning that there are things in the world bigger and more important than our own personal wants and needs—a journey that gay men and lesbians take, certainly, but one that is taken by many people, gay or straight. As part of that, Mikey is also on a journey of discovering what it means to be gay, but that journey ends midway through Act II. If that were the central journey of this story, the show would end after the Mikey protests the movie *Cruising*, and it doesn't. Mikey still has to declare his place in the world. He has to come out to his parents ("Oh Mom, Oh Dad") and make the decision to attend law school and dedicate his life to helping others by becoming a full-time activist.

Finally, at the end of the show, Mikey has dedicated his life both to helping others and to sharing a life with Steve; and *that* is the culmination of his journey. That is the Holy Grail he seeks. Only then can the show end. Being gay is not his destination; it is merely the world in which he makes his journey. In *The Wizard of Oz*, getting through Oz is not Dorothy's goal; finding herself and her place in the world is. Oz is just the environment in which she makes that journey, just as the gay community is the environment in which Mikey finds his way in the world. In a very real sense, this story is not a gay story. It is a story about becoming an adult. It just happens that the hero is a gay man.

What gives this show a sense of unity is that though there are two narrative threads going on—Mikey's dilemma over the new job in the present and his quest to find himself in the past—they are in some ways the same journey. In the past, Mikey must find his place in the world, where he belongs and what he is meant to do. In the present, he has already found his place in the world, but he has lost his way in some respects and needs to find his way back. He's getting burned out by the law project and getting more pressure from Steve to get a "real" job. The law project has invaded his life with Steve and is keeping Steve from his dream of owning a house. Despite Mikey's usual self-reliance, he has only kept the law project going by draining Steve's checkbook. Mikey has to find his way (or his way back) to a place where he can do the good he wants to do, rejuvenate himself, and stop draining Steve's bank account. By the end of the show, both of Mikey's journeys are ended. In the past, Mikey has found his place in the world, and in the present he and Steve have made a compromise that will allow the law project to continue without the destructive consequences.

Sex

One of the greatest concrete differences between older gay shows and *Mikey* is the willingness of *Mikey*'s author, Mark Savage, to deal head-long and unapologetically with gay men as sexual beings. Though William Finn's musical *Falsettos* addressed this to a limited extent, most musicals that do deal with gay issues treat gay men as sexless (like *La Cage aux Folles*), presumably because the authors think that gay men as sexual beings are just too frightening for mainstream audiences. Yet in *Mikey*, Savage dives into sexuality with honesty and abundant good humor. The show's second song, "Tap," lampoons and celebrates serial sex in public restrooms, not because it's admirable or preferable to monogamy, but merely because it was a part of some gay lives, especially in the pre-AIDS 1970s, and because Mikey has to discover that he can't find fulfillment in that world. He has to be dissatisfied there so that he will continue his quest to find fulfillment elsewhere.

In a sense, "Tap" is an absurdist minimusical all its own, able to stand independently, and yet very much a part of the fabric of Mikey's story. It uses one of the most reliable devices for introducing an audience to a foreign world: a newcomer. Mikey comes to the world of bathroom sex as an outsider, and as he learns the ropes, so does the audience. This device is also used to introduce characters and themes in *1776*, *The Best Little Whorehouse in Texas*, *Camelot*, *Brigadoon*, *The Music Man*, and other shows. Mikey is the audience's surrogate and the audience must find this situation as overwhelming and freaky as Mikey does. To sugarcoat the staging of "Tap" destroys its purpose in the story; if the audience is a bit uncomfortable watching it, it's serving its purpose. Hopefully the generous humor of the piece and its whimsical absurdism will keep people from being *too* offended. Reactions will depend on how close individual audience members are to the place in their lives where Mikey finds himself; the audience as a whole will probably be just as split as Mikey is himself ("This is really gross. But it's kinda neat," he sings). But because Mikey is trying to find a place in the world where he can fit in as a gay man, he is willing to ignore his reservations. For some straight members of the audience, the kisses between men throughout the show may actually be even more distressing than the bathroom sex because the kisses are real—two men are actually kissing there onstage—but the bathroom sex is only pretend.

One of the charges leveled most often by religious extremists against the gay community is that gays are promiscuous, indulging in wild, anonymous, unprotected sex; usually they say this about gay men more than lesbians. This charge sounds sillier and sillier as the gay community fights for legal marriage rights and the right to adopt children. But the reason the antigay forces believe this is because at one time, a small but very visible part of the gay community *was* very promiscuous. In the mid- and late 1970s (the *Mikey* flashbacks are set in 1979), the dance club scene was at its height. Anonymous sex was the norm among some gay *and* straight people in this milieu. But part of the reason for this behavior in the gay community was that gay sex was forced by mainstream society to remain "in the closet." A gay man couldn't openly date another man, couldn't participate in the dating and courting rituals that straight people could. Gay men wanted love, companionship, and sex as much as straight men, but they weren't allowed to look for it or, even supposing they could find it, to enjoy it in public. They had no choice but to look for it in the back rooms of bars and dance clubs and in public restrooms, where the security of anonymity could be preserved.

Today, gay issues are being discussed in the pages of newspapers across the country, as well as on TV and in magazines, and it's now easier for gay men and women to look for dates in the open. They no longer have to sneak around, taking only what they can get, while praying they don't get seen by anyone who might know them. Part of this "respectability" is the result of the AIDS epidemic, which demanded that anonymous sex could no longer be an option for intelligent adults. Part of it is that AIDS made many gay men very sick and it was impossible for them to keep their secret. Part of it is the result of mainstream society getting past its fear of the unknown. As more people come out of the closet, their friends and loved ones see firsthand that gay people are just like straight people, and the fear of the unknown, the belief that gays are "undermining the American family," disappear. People see the truth. And the need for anonymous sex in back rooms and restrooms decreases dramatically.

So while the anonymous bathroom sex portrayed in the song "Tap" may seem distasteful or disturbing to some of us today, we have to understand the cultural and historical context of the song, how difficult it was for gay men and women to meet, how desperate gay Americans were for the same sexual freedom that their straight friends were enjoying, that was being portrayed on the big screen in straight films like *Bob and Carol and Ted and Alice* and *Carnal Knowledge*.

Form as Content

It's interesting that "Tap" is the most musically dissonant song in the show, full of chords and melodic notes that are outside the key. This is music that doesn't sound "right." It doesn't follow the standard rules of western music our ears are used to, and Savage uses this music because Mikey is in a place that isn't entirely "right" for him. He's outside his key, metaphorically. Certainly he enjoys the sex he has—even bad sex is still pretty good, as the saying goes—but it's not really satisfying to him. He complains that even after months of bathroom sex, he still hasn't really met anyone. Mikey wants love, companionship, understanding, and he finds none of those things in public restrooms. On the other end of the musical spectrum, the two songs that are the purest, most sincere expressions of love—"Just Like Our Parents" and "Oh Mom, Oh Dad"—are also the simplest musically and the most harmonically traditional.

This is a device used in other modern musicals, in which the simplest music accompanies the purest, least intellectual expressions of emotions and the most complex music accompanies lyrics with more presence of mind, with more intellect, with emotional or intellectual deception or artifice. For example, in *Oklahoma!*, Jud's complex, psychotic "Lonely Room" is the show's most dissonant music. Yet in Stephen Sondheim's musical *Passion*, "Loving You" and "No One Has Ever Loved Me" are the most sincere expressions of love in the show and also the simplest songs musically. As in Sondheim's work, the songs in which Mikey is analyzing his life are loaded with interior rhymes and double entendres:

> *When lonely and frightened,*
> *He kept his smile tightened*
> *And tried to erase any doubt of it.*
> *But when there are two*
> *And it's good and it's true*
> *Then just possibly you should be proud of it.*

He's tired of the shame
And the lies and the pain
And the sneers and remarks cutting through him.
When people start prying
And rumors start flying
What good would denying it do him?

Aside from the one cheat rhyme (*shame* and *pain*), this is a virtuoso lyric, even down to the extra interior rhyme in the last line (*good would*). When sung, this section of "The Ballad of Little Mikey" flies by at lightning speed, set to triplets so nonstop that the singer barely has a chance to breathe. Not all the rhymes may be consciously registered by the audience at that speed, but it still works to keep the momentum of the song going, to imply the chaos and overwhelming turmoil of Mikey's life and thoughts, and to imply Mikey's intelligence and quick mind. Savage uses this musical bridge twice in the song, but the first time it's only half as long as in the example above. By doubling the length of this breathless passage the second time it shows up, Savage makes us feel the escalating pressure and stress in Mikey's voice. As the first full-length song in the show, this lyric communicates not only important content in its extensive detail of Mikey's high school life but also so much more, merely through its structure and form.

In another area of lyric writing, the sexual double entendres in *Mikey* are very revealing. Generally, double entendres are the common refuge of those who really want to talk about sex but are embarrassed by it, and the lyric to "Tap" is full of them. They allow Mikey to talk about his sexual feelings, his physical sensations, without actually saying any of it out loud, without actually talking in explicit terms about his sexuality, with which he's still not very comfortable. The double entendres don't start until after Mikey has figured out what's going on in the stalls around him, but then they fly; for example, "And I feel a warmth, a glow inside me, I can feel it grow inside me"; "I know how to fill my cup"; "Anytime I need a hand"; "I've always got one ear cocked"; and all the references to the boys as toys. There are times when he talks about sex explicitly in the lyric, but it's almost always when he's talking about other people, not about himself. When he's talking about his own feelings, he has to hide behind the double entendres.

One Out of Many

Mikey represents the average urban gay man, who in the 1970s focused a great deal of his attention on finding sex partners. After decades of being denied sexual expression of any kind, some gay men went crazy during the sexual revolution, behaving like starving men at a banquet. For the first time in history, they could talk about sex, and for the first time, they saw themselves in movies, even though they were usually portrayed as psychos. They had their own pornography, just like straight people, although the straight porno market will always eclipse by far the gay porno market, all religious extremists' statements to the contrary. But when AIDS hit in the early 1980s, gay men had to reexamine their priorities. The party was over. Like adolescents, gay men had sowed their wild oats and it was time to settle down. Serious gay relationships slowly became the norm. The gay movement had come of age, and in *The Ballad of Little Mikey*, our hero follows that same path. He embodies the gay movement's wild times, eventual disenchantment, and finally the desire to couple. Mikey himself comes of age in 1980, just a year or two before AIDS was first reported in the *New York Times*. In many ways, Mikey *is* the gay movement.

One of the most interesting lines in the song "Tap" is "Make love all you want, just don't make any noise." This refers to more than just the need for discretion in public restrooms; it also refers to the entire experience of being gay in the 1970s. The self-appointed moral arbiters of our country said it a different way, but they meant the same thing: "Keep it in the bedroom where it belongs." In fact, they *still* say it. Mikey and his friends have unconsciously expressed mainstream's society's view—because they've been raised on it—that people can be gay only so long as the rest of the population doesn't have to know about it, hear about it, or see it. This view is predicated on the fallacy that to be open and honest about being gay is to flaunt it. These people conveniently forget, of course, that straight people "flaunt" their orientation all the time, by wearing wedding rings (implying to all the world that they're having straight sex), keeping spouses' pictures on their desks at work, showing pictures of their children, getting married, getting divorced.

By the time this show is over, Mikey has become exactly the kind of gay man the national religious leaders most hate, and the kind that seems to be everywhere these days, the kind that won't keep quiet, that won't hide his identity in order to keep others comfortable. Mikey has become a political activist, a protester, a challenger of antigay laws and policies. Perhaps it was during his early experience in the world of anonymous sex that Mikey learned to hate the enforced silence he would later rebel against so fiercely. Again he becomes a symbol of the gay movement itself.

Mikey and Steve

Perhaps the most controversial, most "subversive" aspect of *The Ballad of Little Mikey* is the absolute normality of Mikey and Steve's marriage. As mentioned before, a straight couple could easily play the scenes set in the present without changing a word of dialogue. Some gay activists would charge that Mikey and Steve are just imitating straight marriage, but a more convincing argument is that the basic dynamics of being in a long-term monogamous relationship just don't vary that much from couple to couple, whether the couples are straight or gay. There is a human need among many people (though not all) to couple, to share one's life, the good times and bad times, with a partner.

We don't know much about Steve and Mikey's courtship. We know that Steve met Mikey while interviewing him about the *Cruising* protest, and Steve gave Mikey his card. Mikey had to be told why Steve was giving him his card, but that also would've been the case with a straight man or woman who didn't date much. Mikey's naivete was due to inexperience, not the singular nature of being gay. Also, because they were gay, Steve was taking a risk in 1980 by giving Mikey his card. Presumably, Steve was not openly gay at his television station at that time (some journalists were coming out at that time, but not many). Later when Steve is working at the network and Mikey chains himself to the network building in protest over gay issues, Steve is fired. Mikey's actions probably outed Steve as a gay man.

Steve and Mikey have been together for a number of years. Mikey tells us he's been absolutely faithful to Steve and we can safely assume Steve has been faithful to Mikey as well. In most respects they are married, despite their lack of a legal document. Mikey and Steve suffer the same frustrations straight couples do. And Steve has a right to be frustrated. While Mikey has pursued his dream of running a nonprofit legal project, Steve has been supporting not only their relationship but also Mikey's law project, the very thing that is keeping Steve and Mikey apart, the thing that causes the most friction between them; and because Steve has to finance so much of the law project, it has become the one thing keeping Steve from realizing *his* dream of a house for him and Mikey. Steve wants Mikey to get a "real" job so that Steve can stop pouring money into the law project and they can finally get a house and settle down. Mikey has been allowed to pursue his dream at the expense of Steve's dream, and that's not fair. Still, it's important to remember that Mikey's dream is a noble one; he gets nothing out of it but satisfaction, and he helps so many people who might not find help anywhere else. That's no doubt part of what makes it hard for Steve to stop giving Mikey money; Steve knows that the money is going to help people.

In a way, Mikey's decision, which underlines every moment of the show, is not so much between a job he likes and a job he's not so crazy about; it's really a choice between saving the world, represented by the scenes in the past in which Mikey becomes an activist, and saving his marriage to Steve, represented by the scenes in the present. There's an interesting moment late in Act II when the two worlds, past and present, collide, just as Mikey and Steve's conflict comes to a head. After the flashback scene in which Mikey leads the protest against the movie *Cruising*, Steve appears in the present. He points out that Mikey is remembering the past through rose-colored glasses, that events didn't happen quite as Mikey has portrayed them, that Mikey didn't really speak with quite so much eloquence. Steve sees that in the battle between past glories and future domesticity, the past is winning; so Steve has to deglamorize the past to even the playing field. As Mikey and Steve talk, Murray Cade, the older gay activist, appears in the past and begins talking to Mikey. Mikey is in the middle of these two worlds now, being asked to make a choice between them. Just as the moment approaches when Mikey must make a decision, these two worlds collide, both conceptually and dramatically onstage. This is the first moment in the show when characters from the past and present occupy the stage together; and it will happen again in the finale when these two worlds will finally coexist peacefully. Murray wants to encourage the young Mikey as an activist, while Steve wants to encourage Mikey's more domestic inclinations. Mikey can no longer compartmentalize his life; it's time for him to figure out how to integrate his life as an activist with his domestic life with Steve.

Mikey and History

The politics of *The Ballad of Little Mikey* are often naive, but we have to remember that they are not the politics of the twenty-first century; they are the politics of 1980. Gay issues were not yet a permanent fixture on the national scene and gay activists were not nearly as sophisticated and experienced as they are now. Audiences will accept this naivete, even find it charming, as long as they aren't allowed to forget the time frame. If they forget the action is set in 1979 and 1980, Mikey's intensity and simplification of issues could seem silly.

Savage has done a good job of looking at this time and these politics objectively (especially considering he was actually there in the fray), realizing that though Mikey's passion is real, his understanding of the issues is sometimes only superficial—not only is he new at this, but he's not yet been to law school. In the scene in which Mikey and his friends protest the Al Pacino film *Cruising*, Mikey makes the standard arguments about portraying gays negatively in film; but the crowd makes intelligent and legitimate arguments back. It is true that *Cruising* and other films like it never claimed to be representing the entire gay community, and it is true that one small part of the community *was* indeed like the characters portrayed in the movie. Like any other mainstream feature film, *Cruising* never pretended to be a documentary; it was just a story, set in a very specific place at a very specific time. Mikey and the gay community were upset about this film because, in the grand scheme of things, gays in film were being portrayed only as psycho killers or pathetic suicidal losers. In theory, they didn't object to one film depicting gays that way; they were objecting to *all* films depicting them that way, to there being *no* positive images of gays on film. So to object to *Cruising* by itself, as one film, is a tough stand to defend, but there are bigger issues. It's also true that, just like the many of religious extremists who protest gay-positive films, Mikey has not even *seen* the film he's protesting.

Looking back, it may be hard for us to understand why *Cruising* was such a big deal to the gay activists. And because of that, it's hard to accept Mikey's political awakening coming from such a dull source. *Cruising* isn't even a very good movie to begin with, and there *are* some sympathetic gay characters in it. The leather community depicted did (and still does) exist. But we have to remember how rarely gay characters showed up in movies at that time. For some people out in the middle of the country, the only time they *ever* encountered open homosexuality was in movies like *Cruising*, so with that in mind, it's easier to see why the activists didn't want that rare exposure to be so negative. On the other hand, maybe the *Cruising* protest isn't really that big a deal to Murray and the other activists after all; they can't even agree on *why* they're protesting. Maybe its real significance in *The Ballad of Little Mikey* is that it's Mikey's *first* protest. It's the first time Mikey takes a political stand, the first time he takes a project on and sees it through from beginning to end. Maybe the movie doesn't matter at all; it's the fact that Mikey learns that he has the power to make people think, possibly to change things, that matters. He could be protesting any movie; what matters is that he's doing something. The lyrics in "Pioneer" and the finale both make that point explicitly.

This scene is not really about the politics of *Cruising*. It's about Mikey growing up, learning a big lesson. He has been baptized by fire. He has learned the hard way, maybe the only way to learn in this case, that gay issues are never black-and-white, that some political issues—gay rights, abortion, school prayer, and others—bring with them so much emotion and so much religious baggage that it's nearly impossible to have a rational debate over them. This moment, this debate with the crowd, is Mikey's true birth as an activist. It is the moment when he begins his training. He has learned that to do this, he must be prepared, he must learn the law, he must get comfortable with public speaking, and he must develop a thick skin. Over the years, through law school and the battles he'll fight through his law project, he will become a more sophisticated, more careful, more skillful activist. The subtitle of the show is *The Birth of an Activist*, and there it is.

It's interesting to trace Mikey's growing political awareness. It begins at the meeting in "Blah, Blah, Blah," at which Mikey first realizes that there are gay political issues. He's introduced to the gay community and all its issues, including its history, Harvey Milk, Anita Bryant, and other important figures, in "Coming In." In "Ten Percent," he is a part of a political act: publishing a gay newspaper, which, in 1980, was still a pretty big deal. He takes his first real step by volunteering to organize the protest against the movie *Cruising*. He goes to the meeting of the older, established activists, is utterly intimidated, but doesn't back down. He shows up to picket the movie despite the real possibility of physical harm and the guarantee of verbal abuse. When he does the television interview, he has committed to political activism. He comes out to his parents. His last step is his decision to go to law school and continue the fight. There's an argument to be made that

Mikey has always been a political activist at heart (remember that he was on his high school debate team) and he only needed to find that in himself, which is somewhat analogous to a person figuring out that he's gay.

It's no accident that the flashback scenes in *Mikey* are set in 1979 and 1980. These were important, pivotal years in the gay rights movement, a time when a new era was beginning. Just before the action of the show, in 1978, openly gay San Francisco City Councilman Harvey Milk and Mayor George Moscone were murdered by antigay Councilman Dan White. In 1979, a gay high school senior sued his school for the right to take a boy to the prom. The year 1979 also marked the first national gay and lesbian march on Washington, attended by one hundred thousand protesters. Also that year, the Moral Majority was formed by Jerry Falwell to oppose gay rights, pornography, feminism, and communism; it would later become the Christian Coalition. Just after the scenes in the past, in 1981, AIDS was first reported in the *New York Times,* changing everything. Also that year, California Governor Jerry Brown appointed the first openly lesbian judge, Parents and Friends of Lesbians and Gays (PFLAG) was founded, and the New York City Gay Men's Chorus was the first gay group to perform at Carnegie Hall. The times, they were a-changin'.

Though all the gay references and history throughout the show could be alienating to a straight audience—or to "uninitiated" gay audience members—no one in the audience could possibly know less about gay life, culture, and history than Mikey. So even those in the audience for whom this is a foreign world can make their way through it alongside Mikey. We learn as Mikey learns, although because of the theatrical telescoping of time, he gets a year to learn it while we get an hour and a half. Mikey acts as the audience's surrogate, helping make this heavily gay-informed show very hetero-friendly.

Other Resources

Neither the script nor score of *The Ballad of Little Mikey* has been published, but an original cast album is available commercially from AEI Records. And there are plenty of books and videos to consult on gay life and the cultural backdrop of the show. *A Question of Equality* is an excellent four-part documentary on the gay rights movement in America, first broadcast by PBS but now available commercially on video. *Straight News* is a good book about the history of gay issues and gay journalists in the mainstream media, which will offer some insights into the evolution of gay activism and also Steve's life as a journalist. The *Advocate* has published a comprehensive year-by-year history of the gay movement called *Long Road to Freedom*, which is definitely worth reading. It's also worth watching *Cruising* if you haven't already seen it; it's not a very good movie, and it's pretty tame by today's standards, but it's interesting to see why people protested the film and also why so many gay people really wanted to see it.

8   Songs for a New World

Music and lyrics by Jason Robert Brown
Conceived and originally directed in New York by Daisy Prince
Licensed by Music Theatre International

One of the characters in *Songs for a New World* says, "I don't want to philosophize. I just want to tell a story." And that line describes *Songs for a New World* perfectly; in fact, it tells a whole collection of stories. It's not a book musical; there is no overarching plot and are no consistent characters throughout the evening. In its construction, it owes much to *Jacques Brel Is Alive and Well and Living in Paris* and the theatre experiments of the 1960s. It's a collection of independent scene-songs, but it's also more than that. In a 1998 review in St. Louis' *Riverfront Times*, Mike Isaacson wrote, "*Songs for a New World* is that very rare beast: an abstract musical. There is no specific location other than the natural ambiguity of the human heart and mind." And yet it has a very strong sense of unity about it. Even though some of these songs were actually written for other projects over the span of several years, this show feels like it was planned as a unified whole from the beginning.

It accomplishes this mainly because every song in the show is essentially about the same thing: those moments in life when everything seems perfect and then suddenly disaster strikes, in the form of the loss of a job, an unexpected pregnancy, the death of a loved one, the end of a marriage, imprisonment, even suicide. But it's even more about *surviving* those moments. It's about the way we regroup and figure out how to survive in a new set of circumstances—a new world— even against seemingly overwhelming odds. These are songs about that new world, a world in which the definitions of family, distance, money, technology, the very nature of human contact are changing every day, a world in which the rules *don't* apply just as often as they *do*, a world in which the solutions our parents found don't work for us, and a world in which today's answers probably won't apply tomorrow. For someone who has lost his job or lost a spouse, our everyday world becomes just as frightening, just as dangerous, just as uncharted as the New World was to Columbus.

The other thing that lends unity to this show is composer Jason Robert Brown's musical habits. There are a handful of rhythmic, melodic, and accompaniment patterns that he obviously likes and that he uses frequently throughout the show. And because he wrote the opening number last, most of these patterns are gathered together in the opening to provide a nice musical framework for the evening. Also, the melody and sometimes the lyric of the opening are used throughout the show as transition pieces and even occasionally show up within other songs.

Creating a New World

Composer/lyricist Jason Robert Brown came to New York City at age twenty, determined to write Broadway musicals. Because he had no contacts or connections, he decided to do a cabaret show of songs he had written for various past projects. He had the good fortune to run into Daisy Prince, daughter of the legendary Broadway director-producer Hal Prince, at a piano bar where Brown was working. Out of the blue, Brown asked Daisy Prince to direct this show he was putting together, having no idea if she had ever directed anything before in her life. She agreed immediately. They worked on the material for three years but still had no opening number and no clear idea what the show was about. As they discarded existing songs, Brown wrote new ones. Finally it hit him. In his own words, "It's about one moment. It's about hitting the wall and having to make a choice, or take a stand, or turn around and go back."

They did a workshop of the show in Toronto, and then it was brought to the WPA Theatre in New York, where it played a limited run of twenty-eight performances. The score was recorded in 1996 by RCA and released commercially. In 1998, Brown was given his first Big Time assignment: writing the score for the new musical *Parade*, opening at Lincoln Center in the fall of 1998 with a book by Alfred Uhry (*Driving Miss Daisy*) and directed by Daisy's dad. Up until this point, Brown had done a lot of work writing orchestrations and vocal arrangements for other people's musicals, including William Finn's *A New Brain*, but now it was time for him to get the spotlight. No doubt he will become one of the strongest new musical theatre writers of this generation.

The Opening—The New World

Because the opening number, "The New World," was written last, it functions as an unusually strong opening, more a prologue than a first song, a survey of all that is to come for the rest of the evening. The opening stanza conjures images of frontiers, of brave new worlds waiting to be conquered, of those who crossed oceans to find freedom and land, of those who conquered the skies, first with airplanes, then with rockets and space shuttles (and who knows what next?), and of those who explore the inner terrain, both on the atomic and subatomic level and within the human mind itself.

As the first verse begins, the lyric tells us explicitly what the show is about: "It's about one moment . . . And just when you're on the verge of success, the sky starts to change and the wind starts to blow." In each song we will meet someone who has reached a defining moment in his or her life. It's a moment almost everyone encounters, when you feel like you've finally made it, you've finally crossed the last mountain and there are only good times ahead. But at this particular moment, suddenly everything changes. The environment—whether physical or emotional—transforms, becoming something new and unknown. Things look different and feel different. Forces beyond your control force you off your safe path, making things more difficult, perhaps making it impossible to continue on the road you'd chosen.

When this happens, you find you've become a different person. The woman who just found out she's pregnant redefines who she is. She's no longer a single woman, a person of freedom and opportunity. Now she's an expectant mother, a person of responsibility, of limited choices, of expectations. The man who finds himself fired after a lifetime in one job finds that he can no longer think of himself as an executive; now he's unemployed. Instead of going to his office every day, he now goes to the unemployment office once a month. The rich woman who finds out her husband is having an affair no longer defines herself as a woman of privilege and power but now sees herself as a victim, as a figure of (probable) public ridicule. The song's bridge sums it all up:

> But then the earthquake hits
> Then the bank closes in
> Then you realize you didn't know anything.
> Nobody told you the best way to steer
> When the wind starts to blow.

You are hurled into foreign terrain, a place in which the rules you've learned all your life no longer apply. Parents, school, friends all taught you how to handle yourself and your life when everything's going well, but nobody ever told you how to navigate the bewildering world you find yourself in when genuine disaster strikes, when your life crumbles beneath you. Now you are in a new world and you must learn—quickly—the new rules, the new dangers, the new route to happiness.

In the songs that follow in this show, we meet people who find themselves in new worlds. Some of them triumph in their new landscapes; some of them don't. Some of them see their new worlds as dark and foreboding; others sees them as chances for new beginnings.

Finding God

As the main part of the show opens with the song "On the Deck of a Spanish Sailing Ship, 1492," we meet the captain of a ship in 1492. We might assume it's Columbus, which is interesting because there's a reference to him in "The River Won't Flow," but it's more likely another important group of Spanish sailing ships in 1492, those of the Jews expelled from Spain because of the Spanish Inquisition. Here was a group of outcasts heading for a literal new world, a world of all-new rules, freedom from old dangers, but new dangers to replace them, a new world that will become a metaphor for the emotional and intellectual new worlds the other characters will find. And the many references to God are more powerful if these people are Jews exiled because of their religious beliefs. But despite the very specific title of this song, this man stands for all the explorers in all times who've headed out in search of strange lands—or planets—about which they knew nothing.

Like many of the songs in this show, God and faith figure prominently in this song. This is a song about people for whom nothing is more powerful than their faith. They endure the most profound hardships, putting all their faith in the promise of a better place to which God will lead them. These people are not like most people today who attend church; the people on this ship have placed not only their hopes and dreams in God's hands but also, quite literally, their lives and the lives of their children. They have no idea what they will find in the New World, but they hope it will be better than what they've left.

This song makes real the metaphors that will drive the rest of the show. The other characters in the show find that the journey is a necessary ordeal, one that teaches them and toughens them, one that is often more important than the destination. It puts them through various kinds of hell and in some cases actually kills them. Here on this Spanish ship, some of these people will die before reaching the New World. The others will be put through the most extreme sickness and discomfort. Some will lose their children and some children will arrive as orphans. The message of the show is we *all* go through ordeals, we *all* fail, we *all* find ourselves beaten down by life, but most of us make it through these ordeals. While most of the other characters in the show go through emotional or spiritual ordeals, the people on this ship go through physical ordeals as well. Here, the metaphor becomes concrete.

Though several numbers in the show were written specifically for *Songs for a New World*, some were written for other musicals and some were written for cabaret. Yet they have been assembled and programmed—and, in some cases, revised—so beautifully, so artfully, that they all appear to have been written together as a unified score. After the opening that describes the main themes of the show, this second song gives us a glimpse of the real events that have become merely metaphors to us, metaphors in fact that may have lost some of their potency. So that they will have their full dramatic power for the rest of the show, Brown forces us to look once again—or maybe for the first time—at the real thing.

It's interesting how much God shows up in this musical, throughout all of "Christmas Lullaby" and "I'm Flying Home" and as a major theme in "King of the World" and other songs. Perhaps even more interesting is the line in "The River Won't Flow" in which one of the characters sings, "It's not about God and the master plan." In "River," we meet four characters who believe not in God but in the complete randomness of the world, quite a contrast to the people "On the Deck of a Spanish Sailing Ship."

Mother

Another interesting topic that returns over and over throughout the show is that of parents. With only a few exceptions, mothers are portrayed as nurturing and kind, while fathers are irresponsible and destructive. There's the father who burns the family house down while he deposits the kids on the sidewalk and leaves in "Steam Train." There's the father in "The World Was Dancing," who squanders the family savings on buying his own store and then allows it to be burned to the ground (though we might question the perspective of the singer in this one). There's the father having an affair in "Just One Step." There's the father in "Stars and Moon," who left his wife and kids on a whim. And of course there's the completely absent father of the unborn child in "Christmas Lullaby."

There are two mothers in the show who aren't ideal, but they are the exceptions. In "Just One Step," a woman threatens to jump off the fifty-seventh floor and tells her unresponsive husband that it will be his fault that the mother of his children will be splattered on the pavement. Whether she actually intends to jump is up for debate—perhaps even she doesn't really know—but she is using her own kids as leverage. She wants him to picture having to explain to them why Mommy threw herself off the ledge. She doesn't think about what she'll be doing to the kids, only how to manipulate her husband. She's an exception. The other possible exception is the woman in "I'm Not Afraid of Anything." She may be leaving her husband and her kids. We don't know how old the kids are, but they can't be too old because one is still afraid of the dark. And we don't know the details of the family situation, so perhaps she believes leaving them is what's best for them. But she's certainly not a nurturer. She has shut herself off to both her own mother and apparently her two daughters as well.

But the other mothers in the show are nurturers. The woman on the Spanish sailing ship pleads for God to save her child even though she knows she may not survive herself. The expectant woman in "Christmas Lullaby" finds self-worth, maybe for the first time ever, in the fact of her motherhood. Though her life has meant little, she intends her child to accomplish great things, and we can guess that she will give that child all the love she didn't get. One of the men in "The

River Won't Flow" cites advice from his mother (though it's a bit questionable). The mother in "The Flagmaker" sits at home waiting for news that her husband or her son has been killed in the battle-field, yet she keeps those home fires burning and holds on to hope. And in "Hear My Song," two mothers give their children the greatest advice they can give, that despite it all, through all the pain of life, it's going to be okay.

I'm Not Afraid of Anything

With many of the songs in this show, Brown doesn't explicitly tell us a whole lot about who these people are or exactly what their situations are. There are lots of clues, but they're only sprinkled through-out each song and we have to find them and piece them together. We can't always rely on the characters telling the truth; sometimes they're hiding something, other times they're lying to themselves. That's what makes theses songs so rich and this show so interesting. That's why every one of these songs takes on greater depth and power each time we hear it. Like many of Stephen Sondheim's theatre songs, Brown's songs become richer the more you hear and think about them.

His original intention for the song "I'm Not Afraid of Anything" was to portray a young woman, maybe twenty years old, complain-ing about her parents, her friends Jennie and Katie, and her boyfriend David. She sees herself more ready for adventure than them, more hungry for experiences, less complacent, less scared of the unknown. In the original production, the singer was sitting on a swing; Brown wanted to make clear her youth and keep the song and her emotions simple. It's important to remember that each of the four actors in the show has a kind of overarching character that spans the evening—not a literal character, as the details vary from song to song, but more an emotional journey for each actor that progresses from the begin-ning of the evening to the end. For instance, the woman who sings "I'm Not Afraid of Anything" is also the woman who gets dumped in "The World Was Dancing," who finds herself pregnant in "Christmas Lullaby," and who reconciles with her lover in "I'd Give It All for You." And taken together, these songs chart an emotional journey, show-ing this woman growing over the course of the show from innocence to understanding and self-knowledge.

But though that was how Brown intended "I'm Not Afraid of Anything," is it the only way to play the song? Is there an equally legitimate, arguably more interesting way to approach the character? In every other song in the show, the character's world has crumbled and he or she finds him- or herself in a new world, where the rules have changed and nothing is the same. As described earlier, in "I'm Not Afraid of Anything," the singer's world has not crumbled and there is no new world she must navigate. Every other song in the show deals with complicated people with deeply complex emotions and issues; is this the only one that doesn't? There are lots of questions not answered in this song. Who is this woman, what is the adventure she keeps referring to, why does she keep telling us how brave she is, and why does she keep telling us that every other person in her life is so afraid? Why is fear such a consuming concept for her at this moment? Most interesting, is the singer telling the truth, about herself and about the others? And if she's not telling the truth, does she know that, or is she saying what she believes is true? Might there be fear in her words, hidden truths behind the false bravado?

She talks about Jennie and Katie first, then her parents, and then David. Could she be married? Could Jennie and Katie be her kids and David her husband? That certainly makes sense with regard to Jennie's fear of water and Katie's fear of the dark, not fears you usually find in twenty-somethings. If so, then the song becomes one about family and motherhood, two themes that dominate the show.

The last verse of the song is about trouble between her and David; he's afraid to touch her, to love her, afraid, in fact, *of* her. Perhaps she's decided this relationship is impossible and she has left her husband and children. She's clearly planning a change in her life, as she says to us, "Watch me fly!" She reassures herself that she is strong, that she can do this, that she can survive the choice she's making, that she can make it on her own; and she finds solace in the fact that she is fiercer and stronger than those around her. In fact, maybe she sees herself as having always been one of them, one of those who are afraid, but now she has been transformed by her trials and no longer counts herself among their ranks.

But we have to ask, then, if she really is as fearless as she says. If in fact she is leaving David and the kids, might not that be an act of cowardice? As far as we know, David's greatest—and maybe only—crime is in being afraid to get close to her, and from what she tells us in the song, that may well be her fault. She has built a wall around herself and then complains when nobody can penetrate it. She sings:

> Not a soul alive can get behind this wall.
> So let them call
> And watch them fall.

But if she's so proud that no one can get close, why is she complaining about David? Is it any wonder he's distant? And are her parents just like her and David? If her mother works so hard at hiding her emotions, has the singer learned to build that wall from her mother? The singer tries to focus on the adventure ahead, but her mind keeps returning to David. In the last two verses, the music repeatedly builds as she gets more and more excited about the new life—the new world—toward which she's heading, but the pounding music keeps getting interrupted, musically and textually, by images of David. She doesn't *want* to end it; she feels she *has* to end it.

This is a fascinating, exciting lyric, mostly because it does not tell us explicitly what it's about. It doesn't say "I Ain't Down Yet" or "Climb Ev'ry Mountain." It talks around the subject without directly addressing it, and in that act it becomes so much more real and more compelling than many theatre songs. This character acts like real people act. This woman may not understand her motivations and fears herself, and if she does, she certainly doesn't want to talk about them. So a song cataloging the exact details of her situation would be false. This is a theatre song that speaks completely in the voice of the character who is singing—the way a good theatre song always should—and it never crosses into the writer's voice. It's as if we've just met her in a diner and she's pulled us into a conversation, but she never learned how to express her feelings. Still, we can guess what's wrong. Even though this woman hasn't directly told us all that much about her, we know her by the time the song is over. It's also interesting that in a show that speaks of God so often, here is a character at a crossroads who never even mentions him. She also never mentions the kids after the first verse; that may speak volumes about her. This second, alternate interpretation also sees this woman growing over the course of the show, but from a place of fear, from being scared and judgmental, to a place of balance, peace, and self-acceptance, rather than just from innocence to understanding. Certainly either interpretation works and we should always respect the writer's intentions, but here, his way isn't the only way. And because this song has been so beautifully underwritten, because Jason Robert Brown left so much unsaid, he has generously left the interpretation to the actor and director.

This song is an example of how many numbers in the show deal partly or completely with bad marriages or relationships—"Just One Step," "I'm Not Afraid of Anything," "Stars and the Moon," "Surabaya Santa," and maybe (although we don't have enough details to be sure) "She Cries" and "The World Was Dancing." The relationship in "I'd Give It All for You" was bad but may be better now. Still, that's seven out of sixteen, almost half.

Stars and the Moon

Here's a new twist on the old saying "Be careful what you wish for, or you will surely get it." The singer talks about three men in her life, two dreamers she rejects and one rich man she chooses. All her life she wanted a glamorous, fairy tale life. But this song isn't about bad choices; it's about misinformation. Her whole story is built on the assumption that being rich is always a good thing. At this point in the show, we've already met the rich lady planning to jump off the fifty-seventh floor, and if we didn't know already, we know now that being rich isn't always best. The other misconception is that we always know when we're young what's best for us. Clearly we don't, or the world would be much fuller of astronauts, firemen, and ballerinas. And yet, how many women have done exactly what this woman has done—married for money and security? We can smile knowingly and say, well, maybe that *used* to happen but not anymore. But we'd be wrong. It still happens. Things have changed, but not entirely. Too many people are still today programmed to believe that they can find happiness only in money. And like the woman in the song, they find out the truth too late.

The Steam Train

Like almost every other song in the show, "The Steam Train" operates on several levels at once. The singer, a young man (just how young is unclear) from a poor family, dreams of escaping his poverty by becoming a famous basketball player. He sees himself as a steam train, the traditional image of a powerful, unstoppable force, speeding forward to the future. It's interesting that his main metaphor is that of an outdated kind of train, though. Steam trains have not been the train of choice for a very long time. Still, that's how he sees himself. He has learned from reading the paper, seeing commercials, and watching basketball games that basketball is an instant ticket out of poverty and a world of crime, drugs, violence, and quite possibly death.

So he practices every day, waiting for that day when he will be discovered, offered a contract, taken out of his present circumstances. But early in the song, composer Brown folds into the mixture a hint of cynicism. Though the two women singing backup clearly worship the basketball player, the one man singing backup thinks he's a fake. He negates everything the women have been singing. Suddenly we wonder about the lead singer's boasts. Does the backup singer know more than we do? Is the kid really good enough? Has he really worked hard enough? And, even if he has, what if he doesn't get discovered?

Midway through the song, the kid tells us the story of how his father burned down the family home and then walked away, never to return, when the singer was just five years old—another example of a destructive father figure. Immediately after that story, the backup singers quote a section from the opening number; the kid is instantly living in a new world, with all-new rules. But maybe, like many of the other characters in the show, this kid is a survivor. He got through what was apparently a rotten childhood, and it seems nothing can get him down. We soon see that this is not a song about fame and fortune; quite the opposite, this is a song about surviving, both spiritually and physically.

At the end of the song the singer tells us that of the twelve boys in his fifth-grade class, four are in jail and six are dead. This kid does not intend to join their ranks. It's not about the endorsement deals he talks about; it's about making it to his twenty-first birthday alive. At the end, he says, for the third time in the song, "You don't know me, but you will." The song does not tell us the ending of this boy's story. Will he really make it out? Or will we know him only because he'll become a crime statistic or because we'll read his obituary? Maybe the dream of basketball stardom is beside the point. The question is whether or not this kid has strength, whether or not he is a survivor. Even if he doesn't become the next basketball star, does he have the drive and ambition and intelligence to make it out anyway? If he becomes only a teacher or a lawyer instead, something far less glamorous, the trick is finding his path, his place in the world.

The World Was Dancing

The second act of "Songs for a New World" opens with one of the least direct songs in the show, "The World Was Dancing." A young, adult man tells us two stories in this song. First he tells about his father, who quit his job, bought his own store, and then hired an old army buddy to run it, who then accidentally burned the store to the ground. So the father had to go back to his old job, his dignity sacrificed. The young man also tells us the story of a girl he met at college with whom he began a relationship, eventually got engaged to, and then left at the altar. What's interesting in this song is how the two stories are told at the same time, how the details of the stories parallel each other, and what lesson the young man learns from his father's story. This is a song about risk, or more specifically, the risk of putting your future in someone else's hands. The father takes the risk of quitting his job to open his own store. He takes the risk of hiring an old friend and giving him responsibility for the store. The risks do not pay off. The father's attempt fails. Similarly, the son meets a girl and takes the risk of beginning a relationship with her. But the son does not truly commit himself to this relationship. He meets another girl and has a brief affair. He sees how his father's risk failed, so he decides he will simply not risk. He runs away, without even telling his fiancée good-bye. The son has learned the wrong lesson.

Throughout the song, we see his memory of the girl, Amy, singing of their happy future together. The idea is that taking risks actually makes a person feel free. But the son can never fully risk, cannot give himself over completely to that leap of faith, so he can never really experience that feeling of freedom that his father and Amy both feel. When his father's venture fails, the son refuses to even come home when his parents send him a plane ticket. He can't face his father because he now sees him as a failure. Notice how he tells the story. The father's store is a "piece of shit." The friend the father hires is "some schmuck that he knew from the war." To take his old job back, the son believes the father "hid his pride and shame." Rather than face the possibility of failure, which he believes has turned his father into a loser, the son instead runs away. Rather than have dreams that might get dashed, he chooses not to have dreams at all. Throughout the song, the son has sung that "we were dancing, the world was dancing." But at the end, it's no longer "we"; now it's "I" and "they." He is alone now. There's no one to dance with. Throughout the song,

Amy sings, "We'll never be afraid." But at the end, after he's run away, the son can't finish that line, because now he *will* be afraid. He is alone. He has no dreams. He has no one to risk with.

Here Comes Santa Claus

The second act of the show includes two Christmas-related songs and they couldn't be more different from each other. The title of the first one, "Surabaya Santa," is an insider's joke, a takeoff of the song "Surabaya Johnny" from Kurt Weill and Bertolt Brecht's 1929 German musical *Happy End.* Its only New York production was in 1977 and ran less than three months. Still, the song earned some fame over the years as a vehicle for the German torch singer Lotte Lenya, Weill's wife. Surabaya is a coastal city with a naval base in Indonesia, and the song is about a young girl who falls in love with a charming, sweet-talking heel who loves her, lies to her, cheats on her, and leaves her; but no matter what he does, she can't stop loving him.

In "Surabaya Santa," Brown puts Mrs. Claus in the position of the woman done wrong. It's a brilliant comedy number that takes one of our most entrenched cultural icons and places it in the oddest, most unlikely context possible. How unsettling it is, not only to see Santa placed in a sexual context but also to hear Mrs. Claus' bitter accusations of his deviant sexual behavior, involving both reindeer and young boys. To add to the fun, Brown's music is a delicious pastiche of Kurt Weill's decadent, dissonant German nightclub style (which was also borrowed by John Kander for most of the score of *Cabaret*). Even the song's lyric makes funny references to the lyric of "Surabaya Johnny," and the new song follows the old song's construction to a point. In the original production of *Songs for a New World* and on the cast album, the singer even added a wonderfully funny fake German accent, as Mrs. Claus tries to adopt the tragic Marlene Dietrich torch song posture—and maybe she also thinks jolly old Germanic St. Nicholas might find a German woman more attractive. In the second verse, though, she's just too depressed to hold on to the Dietrich persona and she drops the accent as she gets more and more desperate, making her charade even funnier and more pathetic. How much of all this is lost on an audience, most of whom probably never heard of "Surabaya Johnny," may well be beside the point. Even without advance knowledge of the Weill song, this number is just plain funny.

Brown's other Christmas-related song is deeply emotional. It's called "Christmas Lullaby" but its lyric never mentions Christmas. Here, a young girl has just discovered she is pregnant, and she seems to be alone in the world. In the emotional through-line of the show, this is the woman who was left at the altar in "The World Was Dancing" but who will reunite with her lover later in the song "I'd Give It All for You." Though an unexpected pregnancy might be a devastating predicament for most girls in her position, this girl finds God in it. For the first time, she has worth because she is bringing into the world another person, maybe someone who will change the world the way she never could. She compares herself to the Virgin Mary and by implication, her child to the Christ child. But it's not just her unborn child who is blessed; she believes that heaven has finally smiled down on her as well by bestowing this gift upon her.

Handled differently, this song might have been irreverent or even sacrilegious, but this girl's words are so innocent, so guileless and honest, that we cannot object. She has reached one of those moments in life that this show is all about, and instead of choosing panic, instead of choosing to "erase" her mistake, she has chosen to find grace in it. She does not see it as an interruption or ruination of her life. To her, as an event in her simple, bleak life, it is a miracle.

King of the World

"King of the World" is a song that is hard to figure out on first hearing. It's sung by a man in prison, that much is clear. He is probably a political activist, and the fact that a black man played the role in the original production makes us think perhaps the character is a civil rights activist. But the man also speaks of himself in divine terms, as a kind of god. Perhaps he had a great deal of power—like Martin Luther King Jr. or Malcolm X—the trust of many, and the belief that God was on his side, maybe even that God was acting *through* him. But now, he finds himself in a prison cell, in some ways impotent. Yet his optimism continues. He realizes as he sits in his cell that his work is bigger than just him, that even when he's locked up, even after he's gone, his work and his legacy will live on, and through that he will live on as well. Like a mountain, he will always be here. In fact, maybe his pleas to be set free are pleas to God to take his life and free him from his earthly chains. This makes even more sense, considering that two of the next three songs are about death.

There are references to God throughout the song—at one point, as "Father." There are certainly parallels between the singer and the persecuted Jesus Christ. We have to wonder if the title of the song is a reference to Martin Luther King Jr. But whoever he is and whatever his cause, this is another survivor. Even in jail, even facing death, this is a man who survives. He has his doubts, to be sure, as we see in his faltering sentences at the end of the song, but his cause is a good one and he believes that it will be carried on, either by him or by others. As an instrument of that cause, as long as it survives, so does he.

I'd Give It All for You

Like the musical *Company*, the song "I'd Give It All for You" has a simple message but one not often expressed in musicals or pop songs. The message is that relationships, whether marriage or its equivalents, are difficult and frustrating but they are worth it. Sharing your life with someone else is hard but it's better than being alone. In this song a couple comes back together after having broken up a while ago. We can wonder if maybe this could be the couple from "I'm Not Afraid of Anything." These two people have gone off to create lives on their own, and though their lives were good, they soon realized that they weren't as good as when they were together. The song's bridge articulates one of life's great truths, and one of the show's central themes:

> *God knows it's easy to hide—*
> *Easy to hide from the things that you feel*
> *And harder to blindly trust what you can't understand.*
> *God knows it's easy to run—*
> *Easy to run from the people you love*
> *And harder to stand and fight for the things you believe.*

As characters throughout the show have learned, what is easiest is rarely what makes our life the richest or happiest. They now see that their relationship was far from perfect, but it was still the best they'd ever found. Like the young lovers in *The Fantasticks*, these two went off on adventures and what they discovered was that they'd rather be back home with the one they love. The world is a cold, scary place, one that is much easier to navigate with someone at your side. The last line of the song sums it all up: no matter what happens, no matter how hard it all is, it's about having someone there for you. That's what counts.

War

Even though most of these songs were written for other projects, it is amazing how well they work together, how perfect they seem for one another. In the beginning of the show, "The New World" and "On the Deck of a Spanish Sailing Ship" form a pair of songs about journeys, about their necessity, whether inside or outside of us. "Surabaya Santa" and "Christmas Lullaby" form a wonderful, contrasting pair of meditations on Christmas. It's interesting, and quite in tune with the rest of this very spiritual show, that the secular Christmas song is an unhappy one, and the religious Christmas song is one of hope and joy.

Now almost at the end of the show there is another pair of songs that go together. "The Flagmaker" is about a woman dealing with what war takes from her, and "Flying Home" is about a soldier's death. Once again, the more secular song is a sad one, while the song rooted in spirituality is a song about hope and joy, even though it's about death. Does this tell us something about Jason Robert Brown himself?

The first of these two songs is called "The Flagmaker, 1775," and despite its very specific title, its character transcends time periods. This is a woman whose husband (and son?) is at war. Her house is falling apart, and she cannot sleep at night. To keep her mind occupied, she sews. But this is not just a song about distraction; this woman sews flags. It keeps her mind and her hands busy, but it also allows her to contribute something to the war effort. It is usually agreed that the reason the less trained, less well-fed, smaller American army won the Revolutionary War was because it had something to fight for: freedom. Nothing is more inspiring to a soldier, and the symbol of that freedom is the flag. This woman is helping give the soldiers something to fight for, something to believe in when they are tired and hungry, and most importantly, the inspiration they need to emerge victorious. She knows her contribution is small but it matters. Maybe the flags she makes will help keep morale up, will inspire soldiers to do their best, and maybe the better they fight, the less likely she is to lose her husband (and perhaps, her son). This woman is a survivor.

The second song in this pair, "Flying Home," is sung by a soldier who has died in battle, maybe the husband or son of the woman in the previous song. Not only is he flying home to heaven, into the arms of God; his body is also being flown home into the arms of his mother or wife to be buried. More than that, he reassures her that even though he will be gone from this life, he will live on in her heart and memory ("I'll hear you call me, just like before, and I'll be flying home straight into your arms"). He asks her to carry him on—his memory, his courage, stories of how he fought for his country. As the funeral is of anyone who has died in battle, it is a time of mourning but also a time of pride and a celebration of courage.

Like so much of this score, this is a song about two conflicting emotions coexisting in the same moment. The first two songs in the show describe a mix of excitement and fear. "I'm Not Afraid of Anything" describes a mix of determination and the regret of leaving one's family. "Stars and the Moon" describes a mix of satisfaction at attaining all the singer wanted and regret at not knowing how foolish she was to want that. "The World Was Dancing" describes both relief and regret. "Surabaya Santa" describes both love and anger. As in real life, emotions seldom hit us one at a time. That's what makes life so complicated, and it's what makes good theatre so exciting.

Hear My Song

Just as "The New World" gives us a wonderful introduction to the evening's topic, "Hear My Song" provides the perfect summing up. "The New World" tells us what to expect and "Hear My Song" tells us why we've been through this series of stories. The message of this song—and of the whole show—is that we *all* go through these bad times. In a very real sense, none of us is ever really alone. None of us is ever the only person to have ever gone through a particular crisis. And our salvation comes through community. It is through telling our stories and listening to others' stories that we find the strength to go on. The most important lines in the show appear in this final song:

> Hear my song—
> It was made for the times when you don't know where to go.
> Listen to the song that I sing.
> You'll be fine.

In other words, look at how these ordinary people all survived their extraordinary ordeals, and know that you can, too. We all find ourselves in new worlds from time to time, in situations where the rules we've always lived by no longer apply. We must all know that we can survive and even thrive there. And that's not just the theme of this show. It's the reason for theatre in general. From prehistoric people telling stories around the fire to the biggest technospectacle on Broadway, theatre is about telling stories, stories that unite us, that show us our commonality. It's significant that at the end of the song, the line "You'll be fine" has been changed to "We'll be fine." It's about community. It's about shared experience. And it's about the fact that as humans we are all forced to go on new journeys, into new worlds, over and over again throughout our lives. As Stephen Sondheim wrote in *Into the Woods*, "Into the woods we go again. We have to, every now and then . . . "

Other Resources

The cast album for the original production of *Songs for a New World* is available on CD, and a few of the songs are on other solo CDs as well, but neither the script nor the score has been published. There are plans to publish vocal selections at some point.

9 Floyd Collins

Music and lyrics by Adam Guettel
Book and additional lyrics by Tina Landau
Originally directed in New York by Tina Landau
Licensed by Rodgers and Hammerstein Theatre Library

Raucous comedy, moments of great tenderness, muscular, powerful American music, family, faith, and metaphysics. It's all there in *Floyd Collins*, one of the most impressive first efforts in the history of musical theatre. With this show, composer Adam Guettel (rhymes with *kettle*), established himself as the most likely candidate to lead the next generation into the musical theatre terrain that Stephen Sondheim has been exploring for the last forty years. *Floyd Collins* is a musical full of complexity and sophistication worthy of Sondheim yet also full of the emotional force that the story demands, because, though it is a story about media exploitation, greed, glory, and prejudice, at its core it is even more about family, faith, and God. It is one of those musicals, along with *West Side Story, Company*, and *Ragtime*, that could have been written only by Americans. There is a brashness, an openness, and a muscularity in *Floyd Collins* that is uniquely American.

Though *Floyd Collins* got some mixed reviews and even a few negative ones, many reviewers saw the promise of genius that lay behind this unique and special show. *USA Today* called it "one of the most riveting events of the season." *New York Newsday* called it "one of the three or four truly great musical theatre scores of the decade." *New York Magazine* said, "This is *the* original and daring musical of our day . . . a powerhouse." *Entertainment Weekly* said, "The melodies soar . . . In Adam Guettel a vital new musical theatre writer has emerged." *Variety* said *Floyd Collins* was "easy to admire . . . sometimes ravishing."

The *Los Angeles Times* called it "plaintive, often inspired . . . Adam Guettel is a composer for the new century." The *Cleveland Plain Dealer* called it "a work of exhilarating imagination and humanity . . . daring, intelligent, and almost unbearably poignant."

As these and other reviewers could see, *Floyd Collins* is one of the most interesting, most risk-taking, and most emotional shows written in the 1990s, a show as unconventional in its storytelling and in its musical language as it is in its subject. Stephen Sondheim said during a visit to St. Louis in 1999 that he considered *Floyd Collins* the best musical written in the last twenty-five years. But other critics, including those at the *New York Times* and the *Village Voice*, missed a great deal about *Floyd Collins*, trying to force it into one or another existing category rather than allowing it to exist outside convention, creating its own unique category of musical theatre. The *New York Times* complained about the show's "billboard dialogue," declaring that the show's lyrics "evoke not so much specific characters as abstract sentiments."

A reading of the show was first done in composer Adam Guettel's living room in 1992. After rewrites and further development, the show was then done in a full production at the American Music Theater Festival in Philadelphia in 1994, in a more operatic version. After that, the entire opening sequence was replaced, retaining only the cave echoes. The original opening had been more stream of consciousness, more inside Floyd's head. The new opening did a better job of introducing Floyd to the audience. It was easier to sing and easier for the audience to process, with a clearer structure. The new opening included several musical motifs that would be used throughout the rest of the score to lend the show a sense of musical unity. After these revisions, *Floyd Collins* opened again March 3, 1996, off Broadway at Playwrights Horizon in New York. A cast album was released that created more interest in the show, and it was produced at several regional theatres in 1999.

The story of a man trapped in a cave may not seem like musical material, but it's a story that needs two things only a musical can supply. First, it is said that in a musical a character breaks into song when his emotion becomes too big for spoken words. That's why *West Side Story*, *Carousel*, and *Sweeney Todd* had to be musicals; spoken words cannot contain emotions that large. The same is true of *Floyd*. This is a story of enormous passions, enormous fears, and profound love. This story needs music. Second, musicals are the only contemporary theatre form in which the soliloquy still feels normal. Shakespeare's audiences were used to soliloquies—outward expressions of inner thoughts—but much contemporary theatre has discarded this device. Musicals, on the other hand, still use soliloquies, in songs like "Being Alive" in *Company*, "Johanna" in *Sweeney Todd*, "Now" in *A Little Night Music*, "One Song Glory" in *Rent*, and "I Know Things Now," "Giants in the Sky," "Moments in the Woods," and other songs from *Into the Woods*. In *Floyd Collins*, with the main character stuck in a cave, usually having no contact with the outside world, the only way we can get inside Floyd's head is through soliloquy, in songs like "The Call," "Time to Go," "How Glory Goes," and others.

The Ballad of Floyd Collins

Despite the fact that he was arguably the greatest caver who ever lived, Floyd Collins probably never would have become famous outside of Kentucky if he hadn't been trapped. But on Friday, January 30, 1925, a rock slipped onto his foot, trapping him one hundred fifty-five feet down an impossibly narrow passageway, below the surface of the cold, wet Kentucky ground. That twenty-six-pound rock pinning his foot turned him into one of the most famous men of the 1920s. Floyd's story would appear in newspapers all over the world and he would become the third biggest news story of the decade, after Lindbergh's transatlantic flight and the kidnapping of the Lindbergh baby.

Several books about Floyd were published within six months of the accident. The song "The Ballad of Floyd Collins" (not the one in the musical) became a nationwide hit. Floyd's brother Homer and his father, Lee, both went on the vaudeville circuit telling the story (often inaccurately). Homer was trying raise money to remove Floyd's body, which had been left in the cave once they found him dead. Lee was just looking to make more money off his son's tragedy. In 1951, Billy Wilder's film *Ace in the Hole* was released, based loosely on Floyd's story. All the names and many of the facts were changed and the period was updated, but Floyd was still mentioned by name once. The story of Floyd has become so much a part of our culture that the television sitcom *3rd Rock from the Sun* did a parody episode based on Floyd in 2000, with Dick and Harry getting trapped, a subsequent cave-in, arguments between family members and experts, a media frenzy, press conferences, and family members profiteering. How many people in 2000 knew what *3rd Rock* was parodying is hard to tell, but the source was obvious to those in the know.

The Greatest Caver Ever Known

Floyd came from a poor Kentucky family who lived in Flint Ridge, Kentucky. Lee Collins was born in May 1858 and was sixty-seven when Floyd was trapped. Lee's first wife, Martha, bore him eight children: Elizabeth in 1883 (who died at age three), Jim in 1885, Floyd on April 20, 1887, Annie in 1890, Andy Lee in 1895, Marshall in 1897, Nellie in 1900, and Homer in 1903. Though several of them were present at the site of Floyd's tragedy, the musical's creators combined them into just two siblings—the two youngest and the only two still living at home in 1925, Nellie, who was twenty-five when Floyd was trapped, and Homer, who was twenty-two. Martha died in 1915 of tuberculosis and Lee married Sarilda Jane Buckingham, known simply as Miss Jane, whose first husband had died in a cave.

Floyd loved caves from the time he was a small boy. At age six, he began exploring the Salts Cave near the Collins home. He was often late to or absent from school because he was caving. Everyone remembered him as completely without fear, happily putting himself into physical danger all the time. He saved his money and when he was twenty-three, he bought thirty acres of land next to his family's farm. He found a small cave there, which he named Floyd's Cave, and sold pieces of onyx and stalactites from the cave to area souvenir stands. Floyd worked as a guide for local caves and learned everything he could about caves. In 1917 Floyd discovered a cave that he would later name Crystal Cave because of its gypsum flowers, and he opened it to the public as a commercial venture, with the help of the whole Collins family. It was only occasionally profitable, but Floyd was more interested in finding new passageways and chambers than in making money. Floyd had a theory that all the caves in the area were actually connected in a vast network comprising hundreds of miles of caves. No one believed him, but today we know Floyd was absolutely right. As of 1999, three hundred sixty miles of connected caves, including Floyd's Crystal Cave, had been discovered in the Mammoth Cave system, and the total increases every year. There are also other cave systems nearby that may be connected to the Mammoth system, which could bring the total to well over five hundred miles. And still today, as cavers find "new" passageways and new chambers, they frequently find Floyd's initials carved on the cave walls. No one had any idea how far he had explored.

The Kentucky Cave Wars

The Kentucky Cave Wars had been going on since the late 1800s. Because the land around Mammoth Ridge, Flint Ridge, and Cave City was often rocky and hard to farm, the natives soon found they could make more money by opening the caves to tourists. The Cave Wars really got going in 1915 with the discovery of the Great Onyx Cave and the popularization of the Model T Ford, which made it easier for tourists to drive long distances to visit the caves. The Cave Wars soon got nasty, with people setting up booths and signs on the highway to falsely claim the big caves were closed and to redirect people to their own smaller caves. Sales agents, called cappers, would resort to outright lies to get business, posing as tourists themselves and downplaying the major caves; claiming all the caves were connected, so every entrance was the same; and even hiding and throwing rocks down on tourists entering Mammoth Cave. Lawsuits were filed on a regular basis challenging ownership, disputing profits made from unauthorized connections to other people's caves, and addressing various other conflicts. This was the atmosphere into which the Collins came when they opened Floyd's Crystal Cave.

Trapped

The story of how Floyd got trapped and died in his Great Sand Cave is basically as the musical tells it. Some things are left out, like the court that assembled to decide if Floyd's tragedy was just another publicity stunt perpetrated by the cave owners to get more tourists. Some people are left out of the musical, like Johnnie Gerald, one of Floyd's closest caving friends, who was in early versions of the musical but was later combined with the character of Homer. Andy Lee, Floyd's other brother, was also combined with Homer. Floyd's brother Marshall was cut as well. Lt. Burdon of the Louisville Fire Department and other authority figures were all folded into the character of Henry Carmichael from the Kentucky Rock and Asphalt Company. Ed Bishop is an invented character, loosely based on the famous black cave guide Stephen Bishop. He was created as an amalgamation of all the various friends and rescue volunteers at the site.

The book *Trapped! The Story of Floyd Collins* by Robert K. Murray and Roger W. Brucker is an invaluable help to anyone doing the show or wanting to know more about the real story. It chronicles in great detail the morning Floyd got trapped and every day after that until the end. It goes into detail about Floyd's descent into the cave and how he got trapped, and it even includes diagrams of the tunnel. It's helpful for directors and actors to line up the events in the play with the real-life events, to see exactly when things happened, how long Floyd had been underground at each important moment, and how the telescoped events in the show correspond to the actual events. Landau and Guettel have taken liberties with the musical, to be sure, but they are remarkably faithful to the sequence of events, the major players, and the important moments.

Floyd had been digging in Sand Cave for three weeks at the beginning of 1925 and he had blown a dynamite charge on Monday, January 26, to open up the passageway. It was on Friday morning, January 30, that he went down for the last time and got trapped. It was a full day before anyone realized Floyd was missing. On Friday night, no one could find Floyd, and Ed Estes joked that Floyd was probably still down in his cave. On Saturday morning, Ed Estes, Bee Doyle, and Ed's son, Jewel, went to the cave and found that Floyd was trapped inside. They sent for Homer, who arrived that afternoon and immediately went down, though he couldn't get all the way down to Floyd. After resting, and after others tried, Homer went back down at midnight Saturday night and dug for eight hours, uncovering Floyd only to his waist. At other times, others went down to bring Floyd food, but they were too scared to go all the way down, and they left food and drink in crevices along the way. Sunday afternoon, Homer went down again (which is the "Daybreak" scene in the show), and by Sunday evening, about one hundred people had gathered at the site as news spread.

Louisville reporter Skeets Miller went down for the first time on Monday morning and discovered that he was small enough to get all the way down to Floyd. This made him not only the reporter of record but also part of the rescue effort from then on. The stories he filed from the cave were soon picked up by the Associated Press and distributed to newspapers across the country.

On Monday afternoon, Lt. Burdon decided to pull Floyd out with a harness, despite the fears of the local cavers that it would kill Floyd, as it had done to another trapped caver some years before. They tried to pull Floyd out with the harness but quickly gave up the idea. The first newspaper accounts appeared around the country on Tuesday, February 3, as it became front-page news. Carmichael showed up at the site on Tuesday morning and organized men to shore up the entrance to the cave while others went down and cleared out the rocks in the passageway. He also began looking for a place to dig a shaft down next to where Floyd lay trapped. Homer objected to the shaft on the grounds that the drilling could easily vibrate loose rock in the cave, which could crush or at least further shut off Floyd from the outside.

Skeets went back down Tuesday evening with a crowbar, a jack, and other tools, as well as electric lights to keep Floyd warm. It became a competition between locals and "outlanders" to see who would rescue Floyd first. One newspaper quoted a local who said "It's funny. Fellas that wouldn't have lent Floyd fifty cents are pert near killing themselves going down that hole to pull him out." Early Wednesday morning, the shaft leading down to Floyd began to collapse from all the movement within it. Soon Floyd was completely shut off from the outside world and trapped worse than ever. On Wednesday night, Johnnie Gerald and Lt. Burdon organized a crew to try to remove the cave-in from the passage. Late Wednesday night, Johnnie Gerald got past the first cave-in but found another one. There were now more than two hundred and fifty people at the site.

By Thursday, with nothing new to report, many newspapermen were making up things to write about, including Floyd's fictional girlfriend and dog. General Denhardt and the National Guard arrived Thursday morning and took over. That morning the decision was made to dig a shaft next to the cave to reach Floyd. By Friday night, they had dug only seventeen feet, less than six inches per hour. Miss Jane arrived for the first time on Friday, a week after Floyd had first been trapped. By now, four hundred automobiles were on the road to Sand Cave and more than fifteen hundred onlookers were there, along with several motion picture companies from Hollywood. The films made by twenty-year-old Cliff Roney were being shown nationwide. On Saturday, sound tests were conducted with microphones to see if they could hear Floyd, who was still shut off, but they heard nothing. They had no idea if he were still alive. By Saturday afternoon, two thousand people were watching.

By Sunday afternoon, the rescue shaft was only twenty-three feet deep. Estimates of the crowd on Sunday ranged from ten thousand to fifty thousand. It had become a country fair, with peddlers hawking food and drink, elixirs, balloons, and other souvenirs. Rumors began circulating that this was all a publicity stunt.

On Monday, it was announced that there would be a military inquiry and maybe a grand jury investigation into whether or not Floyd's tragedy was a hoax. On Tuesday morning, the military inquiry convened. The rescuers continued digging the shaft, reaching forty feet by Tuesday evening, and suddenly cave crickets began appearing, indicating that they were getting close. On Wednesday, two phony telegrams were received by authorities, claiming Floyd was not in the cave at all, that he was out and safe. One was supposedly from Floyd himself. On Thursday, the walls of the shaft began to collapse. Floyd had been trapped for thirteen days at this point.

On the morning of Friday the thirteenth, the shaft diggers said they could hear Floyd coughing. Stories immediately began circulating from the press that Floyd had been freed. They kept digging, but that night, more shoring collapsed. On Saturday, February 14, the military inquiry delivered its finding that Floyd was indeed trapped in Sand Cave. The shaft had just six feet to go. On Sunday, the rescuers began digging the lateral shaft over to where Floyd was trapped.

On Monday morning, February 16, they broke through to Floyd. He was dead.

An American Icon

The minute Floyd's story hit the papers, he became an American icon, a symbol for all that is American, for being an entrepreneur and for his good ol' American ingenuity. Floyd was taking what he had—an uncanny understanding and knowledge of caves—and using it to chase the American Dream. He really was the greatest caver ever known. Like all the great Americans throughout history, Floyd was not only ingenious and adventurous, he was also *first*. Floyd was all over the Mammoth Cave system decades before anyone else found those passages. He was a true American explorer and we find out the extent of his exploration early in the show as his friends talk about him, his passion for caves, his willingness to risk, and the frequency with which he got trapped and wriggled his way free.

Floyd's father, Lee, thinks the caves are just get-rich-quick schemes, that Floyd and his friends want success without hard work. But he's wrong; Floyd works very hard. When Floyd opened Crystal Cave, he and his whole family worked hard to get it ready for the public, to advertise it, to staff it, and to make it a success. We see in the first caving sequence in the show that Floyd knows the work ahead of him if Sand Cave is to be opened; he has to find financing through a caving banker, smooth the floors, build stairs, a refreshment stand, a ticket office, a curio shop, erect signs on the highway, and do many other things. He's even thinking about advertising and marketing ideas. He knows all this from his experience with Crystal Cave and he knows there's a lot of work ahead of him again with Sand Cave. It's true Floyd wants to leave behind the backbreaking work of farming on rocky, infertile land, but he doesn't want to abandon hard work; he merely wants to work differently. He wants to use his ingenuity and his instincts, to be a businessman in the American tradition. He's not cut out to be a farmer, but he is cut out to be an adventurer and an entrepreneur.

But Floyd is also another kind of symbol that Americans in 1925 could relate to—he's a symbol of being "stuck" in America, of being trapped, unable to move. Floyd's trap is literal but many Americans were metaphorically trapped, by awful jobs, crippling debt, and horrific living conditions. The American Dream was not available to many Americans and they saw themselves in Floyd, trapped and helpless despite his talents and ambitions. They had an emotional stake in his rescue because they needed rescuing, too.

Homer is a symbol of the American Dream, too. Homer has bought a Model T, a big American status symbol. He says Mrs. Jones has told him he could be a movie star, another big American dream. He has a typically American distrust of outsiders like Carmichael. He believes in self-determination, in community, in family—all American ideals—and Carmichael is a threat to all of that. In fact, some historians speculate that if the local cavers could have run the rescue, they might have saved Floyd, but instead, people who knew nothing about caves were given control of the rescue effort.

Why It Shouldn't Have Worked

Like *Rent, Pal Joey, Oklahoma!, Hair*, and *Jacques Brel*, there are so many reasons that *Floyd Collins* shouldn't have worked. The most obvious is that the main character becomes immobile after the first scene. How do you build a stage musical around a guy who can't move a muscle? Guettel and Landau's answer was simple: make Floyd's family the focus of the show rather than just Floyd himself. The story becomes less about Floyd, the trapped hero, and more about this poor Kentucky family pushed to the breaking point by events beyond their control. It becomes about Homer's battle with the outsiders, Nellie's psychic connection to Floyd and the path toward her rescue of her brother, and about how Lee and Miss Jane handle the attention, the scrutiny, and the responsibility for making life-and-death decisions on behalf of their boy. It becomes, in fact, about the community itself, its character, its history, its strength.

The other thing the creators did was create a rich inner life for Floyd, communicating beautifully to the audience Floyd's deep love for the cave and the world underground. They gave him a healthy fantasy life, so that the actor playing Floyd could move in two scenes, once in "The Riddle Song" and again in the dream in Act II. And in creating the physical world of the play, they found a strong but simple visual representation of the narrow passageway in which Floyd is trapped.

In the original production and most subsequent productions, the minimalism of the set was startling but beautiful. The floor and walls of the set were made of wooden planks that acted as a kind of neutral texture, functioning as the passageways down into the cave in the opening number, as the terrain of Floyd's imagination, and also as the world above ground throughout most of the rest of the show. Over on the left side of the stage was a narrow ramp upon which Floyd got trapped. It kept Floyd upright enough that the audience could see him when he was acting and singing, and it gave him a surface on which to rest, while the passageway above his body was imaginary. An opening in the wall above the Floyd's head was Floyd's way into the passage where he got trapped and the way Homer and Skeets could get down to Floyd. With Floyd on this ramp at the side of the stage, the director could keep Floyd onstage the whole time, even when the action shifted above ground, using only lights to differentiate between the two areas. This underlined the loneliness and boredom Floyd must have felt, being unable to move a muscle for more than two weeks, and it kept Floyd's predicament as a physical presence in every scene above ground. Similarly, lights were what made Floyd's first descent into the cave work, as the entire stage became the cave, and the carefully focused lights delineated the passageways, the twists and turns and chambers along the way. By keeping the set nearly bare, by keeping the inside of the cave and the environment above ground almost wholly within the audience's imagination, the show's creators opened up so many possibilities that a "normal" stage musical could never utilize. Just as Floyd must live only in his mind once he's trapped, so too does the physical world of *Floyd Collins* exist only in the audience members' minds. Guettel says this minimalist style allows audiences to participate more rather than less, by using their imagination, by conjuring not only the cave but also the environment above ground in their minds' eyes. It focuses the audience's attention on the *people* rather than the sets, just as shows like *Hair* and *Rent* do. Tina Landau, who directed several early productions of the show, came from the experimental theatre community, like the directors of *Hair* and *Jacques Brel* did, and she brought that aesthetic with her.

The other problem the show's creators faced was how to write for uneducated, inarticulate characters. Floyd was not a bright guy, even though his instincts for caves were amazing. Most musicals rely on soliloquies in which characters tell us what they're thinking and feeling, as in great songs like "Soliloquy" from *Carousel*, "Now/Later/Soon" from *A Little Night Music*, "Lonely Room" from *Oklahoma!*, "Halloween" from *Rent*, and almost the entire score of *Songs for a New World*. But Floyd doesn't have the vocabulary or self-knowledge to give us that kind of information, and neither do any of the other locals. Again, Guettel and Landau found the perfect answer; they focused the show on the emotional world instead of the intellectual world. This is not a show about people who think too much—that's Sondheim's territory—this is a show about hope ("The Call," "Lucky"), fear ("I Landed on Him"), memory ("Daybreak," "The Riddle Song"), anger ("Git Comfortable"), love ("Heart an' Hand"), and faith ("Going Through the Mountain," "How Glory Goes"). Sondheim has always said that content dictates form, that the style and structure of a show should depend on the story you want to tell, and never has this been more true than with *Floyd Collins*. Guettel and Landau had an unusual story to tell and they found new, unusual methods for telling it, fashioning a very unusual musical in the process. Just like the great writers of the past, Guettel says they didn't set out to break rules or to forge new territory; they just set out to tell Floyd's story the best way they could.

A Stone History Book

The cave is just as major a character in *Floyd Collins* as the title character. Floyd talks to the cave as a person and refers to it more than once as "she." In a way, the cave is the antagonist, both Floyd's lover and his executioner. The cave is Floyd's world, more real to him than the world above ground, the only place where he feels comfortable. He tells Skeets Miller, "It's jes' . . . when I'm under . . . I feel right in my bones." Though Floyd is uneducated and even inarticulate, he becomes a true American poet when he describes the caves he so loves:

> Looks wet,
> Every wall looks wet,
> Meltin' with a snow made a' cream . . .
> Shinin' everywhere with tiny diamonds.
> Shine the lantern an' git
> All the colors of the world comin' back.
>
> . . . .
>
> No tellin' what's on these walls,
> Layerin' on slow
> Like a stone history book
> With a couple of sentences 'bout me.

And more than Floyd could ever know, the caves did indeed tell his story once he was gone, as cave explorers today continue to find Floyd's initials carved on the walls of newly discovered caves, exactly like a stone history book with a couple of sentences about Floyd.

Listen to a Tale . . .

In fact, the real story of *Floyd Collins* is storytelling. Because all the important action takes place a hundred and fifty-five feet below ground, because television doesn't yet exist, there can be no direct, unbiased reporting (if in fact television can be unbiased). And Floyd's lasting fame is the result of storytelling as well, with embellishments and drama imprinted on the actual events leading up to Floyd's death. Composer-lyricist Adam Guettel and bookwriter and original director Tina Landau use storytelling as a major theme throughout *Floyd Collins* to show how Floyd's predicament was communicated to the world, how the players in the drama disgraced themselves, and how the acts of entertaining and passing the time were different in 1925.

Storytelling takes many forms in the show. It figures prominently in many of the songs in the show, such as "The Ballad of Floyd Collins" (obviously), "Tween a Rock and a Hard Place," "Lucky," "Daybreak,"

"The Riddle Song," and "Is That Remarkable?." We see Jewel begin to write "The Ballad of Floyd Collins" midway through Act I, mirroring the actual "Ballad of Floyd Collins," and later in Act II, it blossoms into a full-length song. As we see Jewel's song develop, we also see his understanding of Floyd's situation and his understanding of himself develop.

"Tween a Rock and a Hard Place" is an important song for several reasons. First, after spending twenty minutes alone with Floyd at the top of the show, the audience finally meets the social context from which Floyd comes, in the persons of Floyd's friends and fellow cavers, Ed Bishop, Bee Doyle, and Jewel Estes. Second, after the very sophisticated music of the lengthy opening sequence, music that requires a great deal from the audience, "Rock and a Hard Place" gives the audience some respite. It's a simple song structurally and harmonically, and it establishes the very important musical contrast between the world above ground and the world below ground. Third, and most important, it firmly establishes the theme of storytelling as Doyle, Bishop, and Estes tell one another progressively harrowing—and perhaps fictionalized—stories of bravery, each trying to outdo one another. We see the practice of distorting the truth long before any reporters show up. We see that exaggeration is common here, that storytelling—and embellishment—is in all of us. If these three can distort the truth and we find it charming, why do the reporters become bad guys for doing the same thing? The reporters represent a similarly dishonest form of storytelling—exaggeration, distortion, bald fictions—but it seems a bit more dangerous here, perhaps because it's not just casual bragging. Here, the storytellers' audience doesn't agree to the same rules, that distortion is just good entertainment. A reporter's audience expects the truth (however unlikely that might actually be). The dishonesty is less benign in this case because it's all for the sake of selling papers; it's storytelling *disguised* as objective reporting. Newspapers are frequently used as historical documents decades later; what would we think of Floyd's story today if the papers were our only source of information?

And though reporter Skeets Miller is one of the only people in the show who acts honorably throughout, he is still a reporter, and Landau dramatizes the gap between truth and journalism by having Skeets actually speak the punctuation of his reports, as reporters had to do when dictating a story over the phone. It gives his speeches an artificiality and a distance that reminds us that this is coming through a filter. It reminds us of that eternal question: can a reporter ever truly be objective? More importantly, Skeets breaks one of the primary rules of journalism: he becomes part of the story. Because of his small stature, he's the only one who can get down to Floyd for the first several days, and he joins the rescue effort, which leaves him in an ethically ambiguous position. Is he the storyteller or is he part of the story? Is he being objective or is he manipulating events? Since he's the only one who can get all the way down, he's certainly changing events; and the events change him as well. Skeets starts out being a cub sports reporter and he goes on to become a nationally read news reporter. The real Skeets received a Pulitzer Prize in journalism for his reporting on Floyd's story.

Like the reporters, moviemaker Cliff Roney shows up to tell Floyd's story on film, and he too wants to fictionalize things, to make the story "better" than it is. But is his goal really any different from Guettel and Landau's? More to the point, is it possible to find objective truth? Are there different kinds of truth? Have Guettel and Landau told Floyd's story truthfully even though they've left out incidents and combined characters to give their work structure? Is it possible to get at psychological or emotional truth without adhering strictly to all objective facts? And like the musical *Assassins*, can *Floyd Collins* be truthful without being entirely accurate historically?

Perhaps it all comes down to a question of audience expectations. Bishop, Doyle, and Estes *expect* one another to embellish their stories. They make allowances for this and they know the truth is probably less interesting, less heroic than the storyteller describes it. Cliff Roney's audience is sitting in a movie theatre, watching a film; the question here is whether Roney presented his film as documentary or not, and if he were making the film today, would it become the nebulous "docudrama"? Guettel and Landau's audience does not expect a musical based on a true story to be a documentary, to include every incident and every character. In fact, Guettel says one of the earlier versions of the show was a live "four-hour documentary" and he realized how wrong that was. He realized that as a dramatist it was his job to focus the story, to make his audience *feel* the truth rather than just learn facts. But though Guettel and Landau focused the story, the reporters on the scene *added to* the story facts that did not help get at the truth. They invented a girlfriend and a dog for Floyd, neither of which represented any kind of truth at all. Their audience expected facts, and more often than not, the reporters gave them fiction.

One of the most emotional, most personal examples of storytelling in the show is the song "Daybreak," a beautiful, deeply felt dramatization of the bond between Homer and Floyd. In the show, Homer has gotten down to Floyd for the first time and discovers what Floyd already knows: the situation may be hopeless. Floyd is beginning to lose his calm, beginning to break down, and for the first time, twenty-two-year-old Homer has to take care of thirty-seven-year-old Floyd. It's a moment of passage for both. Homer understands Floyd; he sees Floyd losing his grip and knows exactly what will calm Floyd. Homer knows that Floyd feels safest below ground and he feels most comfortable with Homer and Nellie; these three have a bond that is rare among siblings. So Homer reminds Floyd of a night when the three of them snuck out and went down into the first cave Floyd discovered. They spent the night there, in the pitch blackness, with only the touch of one another's hands to connect them, in the cool silence where nothing could touch them or hurt them, where Floyd was in charge, in Floyd's world. And this story, this memory, is what Floyd needs at this moment of desperation. It calms him enough to fall asleep, perhaps for the first time since he was trapped, in the safety and company of his little brother.

The other parallel example of storytelling also takes place between Floyd and Homer. At the end of Act I, as Homer is once again trying to dig Floyd out, Floyd's spirits are sinking. Again, Homer knows the answer is to take Floyd back to happier times. This time, Homer does this by creating riddles, the answers to which are memories of their shared childhood happiness. To dramatize the impact of these memories on Floyd, Guettel and Landau allow Floyd to rise up off the ramp that stands in for the cave passage. For the first time since Floyd was trapped at the beginning of Act I, he stands up and moves centerstage with Homer as they move back in time to these happy memories. Floyd and Homer go back to the quarry where they swam as kids, a time and place where Floyd felt free and unfettered. It's not only an exciting moment musically but also a stunning visual moment as Floyd stands up for the first time in an hour.

As the verse ends, Floyd and Homer return physically to the cave, but here again, Guettel and Landau surprise us. Floyd and Homer return to the cave but switch places, with Homer now trapped and Floyd digging. It's a physical parallel to the fact that Floyd is now asking the riddle and challenging Homer. They've swapped places verbally and so Guettel and Landau swap them physically as well. We see that Floyd feels in control for the first time since he was trapped. Homer has successfully cheered Floyd up and taken Floyd's mind off his helplessness. Again, it's a stunning visual effect that communicates brilliantly the emotional state of our hero. The structure of the second verse mirrors the first; Floyd asks a riddle and the answer is a memory from their childhood, this time their favorite swing tree. And again, once the answer is guessed, they both move out of the cave and into the middle of the stage as they mentally move back in time into this happy memory. But this time, the flashback leads to an unexpected place. As Floyd remembers the feeling of flying off the swing tree out over the water in the quarry, he sees himself doing a dive they called Jesus on the Cross, but this image reminds Floyd of death, of being trapped by fate, and this image leads to the memory of dropping into the cold, black water, going deep under the surface, down into the rock. And despite Homer's best efforts, Floyd's thoughts return to the cave and being trapped. And as his mind goes back to the cave, he also returns physically to the ramp on which he has spent all of Act I.

Homer makes one more try, this time with a riddle that has an obvious answer, an answer that reminds Floyd how close the brothers are ("kinda like a friend an' kinda like a brother"), how easily Floyd has escaped so many times before from being trapped, and how successful their new enterprise will be. And just as Floyd guesses the answer, Homer breaks through and he and Floyd make physical contact for the first time. Floyd is still trapped, but finally Homer can see him and touch him, rather than just hear him. This is real progress— or so it seems—and Floyd finally has something to be optimistic about, and more than that, a hug from Homer means the world to Floyd. The first act ends on a high note, but one that we've seen throughout this song is very precarious.

Family and God

Two of the strongest themes in *Floyd Collins* are family and God, the two things that sustain Floyd while he's trapped a hundred and fifty feet below ground. Floyd talks about his family a lot and it is clearly very important to him. He wants his father to be proud of him, to approve of him, and Floyd mentions this several times in the opening caving sequence. When he dreams of success, it's not just for him but for the whole family. He wants to set his family up on a valley farm, good, fertile land, rather than the hardscrabble land they now own. He wants to make life easier on Lee and the family.

But Floyd's perspective on family isn't the only one we see. We also see some important moments with Lee and Miss Jane. Miss Jane has one of the funniest and most touching lines: "All of us is a bit touched if you look close. That makes family." We see in the song "Heart and Hand" that Lee and Jane love their family deeply. In fact, it's one of the only times we see beneath Lee's gruff façade. Miss Jane believes in God and family every bit as much as Floyd does. In Act II, she says to the grieving Lee, "When death comes a-partin' a family, you don't know the whole lonesomeness till way long after. I done witnessed the God-fearin' man turn to the devil at such times . . . but I also seen the weak grow stronger in all sorts of love."

It's significant that both Homer and Lee suffer a kind of breakdown when they have to face their impotence, their inability to rescue Floyd. Nellie comes close to a breakdown before "Going Through the Mountain," when she too is feeling impotent, as the men at the camp keep refusing to let her go underground to see Floyd. Family is everything to these people, and facing the impending loss of one of their own is devastating. But Nellie's breakdown is only momentary because she realizes she can get to Floyd without actually going under.

God is another major theme in the show. Though Floyd is not religious ("I know I warn't no Sunday-school Mama's boy"), he is a spiritual man ("But faith is hopin' for somethin', believin' what you cain't see. I had faith all my life"). He tells Skeets he knows his mother is up in heaven. He tells Jewel Estes that when it's his turn to die, he wants to meet Jesus. When Floyd realizes he's dying, he turns to God to ask him what heaven is going to be like. He's not afraid of death because he believes in heaven and he believes he will be reunited with his mother, something he's been waiting for. God and spirituality are a comfort for him, especially now. Like *Les Misérables*, *Floyd Collins* sets up a contrast between two views of God, a merciful God and a vengeful God. In contrast to Floyd, who believes in a benevolent, nontraditional, nonspecific God, Lee believes in an old-fashioned, fire-and-brimstone, vengeful God. Lee believes the devil led Floyd into the cave and that only prayer can get him out. Yet Floyd thinks God let him into the cave, that God gave him the honor of being the first person in Sand Cave's wondrous chambers.

Miss Nellie

Floyd's spirituality is tied to Nellie's mysticism. The show makes it very clear that Nellie possesses some kind of psychic abilities, that she and Floyd have some kind of very real supernatural connection. Nellie is a strong-willed woman, which could easily have been interpreted as crazy among uneducated folk in 1925 rural Kentucky. And she's psychic, which would *definitely* be considered crazy in that time and place. In Act II, she "hears" Floyd during Lee and Homer's argument. Lee hears her singing to Floyd and assumes she's going crazy again. Is this why she was locked up in a mental hospital? Did she hear and talk to her dead mother? And did she tell anyone at the mental hospital that she could hear her brother Floyd back at home?

As we meet Nellie, she has just returned from a lengthy stay in the mental hospital, and we see that she has learned—either in the hospital or maybe before—how to live in her head, how to escape the unpleasantness and restraints of the real world by escaping inward. She sings in Act II:

> *Some people go place to place;*
> *Some people go underground;*
> *Some gotta go crazy like;*
> *I jes' journey in,*
> *An' that is where I've been.*

Nellie has just described her family. Homer has to explore the world, Floyd has to explore underground, Lee is losing his mind, and Nellie travels inward and finds peace in the psychic realm where she can be with her mother and sometimes with Floyd. When Nellie and Floyd connect psychically and musically in Act II, we see that this is where they belong, together in the psychic world. Nellie tells us that she and Floyd were "together" when she was in the hospital, even though they couldn't have been together physically. She carries her mother's life force with her, which she shares with Floyd.

Nellie and Floyd's psychic connection becomes an important dramatic device. When they connect—Floyd from below ground and Nellie from above ground—we hear the same music in Act I and Act II, a kind of psychic musical motif. They are both connected deeply to the natural world. Floyd and Nellie both apparently talk to the crickets. Floyd talks to the cave. Nellie hears things—her mother?—in the wind. When Floyd first hears Nellie in Act I, Skeets hears only the wind. The wind becomes the carrier of their special connection. When Floyd hears her in the wind and asks if she's come to rescue him, the truth is that, in fact, she has come for that purpose, but neither they nor we know that yet. In Act II, she hears the wind blowing and she tells Skeets that it's getting to be time, meaning time for Floyd to cross over, to be with his mother. Has her mother told her this through the wind? She says into the wind, "Cave-in don't matter none. I'm a-come to you, Floyd—no matter what." Floyd has told her that he dreamed of a cave with gold at the end of the rainbow. Is this heaven? Did he dream his own fate and not know it?

Nellie comes to Floyd in his dream, which arguably happens in the blink of an eye, just as Skeets breaks through the cave wall, and she helps Floyd cross over to heaven. In real life, the diggers swore they could hear Floyd coughing just before they broke through, but when they got there he was dead, just as it happens in the show. But in that moment that he lets go of the physical world, Nellie takes him on a journey to help him understand what's happening through the world of the dream. Nellie does finally rescue Floyd by helping him escape his physical tomb and enter heaven. Lee treats Nellie like a cripple, and nobody thinks Nellie can do anything, but ultimately she's the only one who can save Floyd. Early in Act I, Nellie tells Miss Jane that she and Floyd will sing a "cave duet" and in fact they do, in the dream sequence, just before Floyd dies.

Sure Enough, His Fortune Is What He Found

Because of the nature of this story, and because Guettel and Landau had real-life events to follow in their story structure, death looms large in this work. But though the end of the show is objectively depressing, it doesn't feel that way in performance. In the opening number, Skeets sings, "Sure enough, his fortune is what he found." Floyd's fortune—his fate—is to die in his cave. His three friends are introduced with the comic "Rock and a Hard Place," but though it's a very funny, playful song, it's all about near-death experiences and introduces death as a theme. Then we find out Miss Jane's first husband died after being trapped in a cave. We find out Floyd dreamed of being trapped. At the end of Act I, Homer says to Floyd, "You ain't gonna drown or nothin', ya know," and yet he will. The official cause of Floyd's death was drowning, from the water dripping down into his throat. It's a throwaway line that registers as creepy only for the people who know the real story. Death hovers over the entire show.

The Sound of Glory

The music of *Floyd Collins* does so much of the show's dramatic work. As mentioned earlier, content dictates form. Like Stephen Sondheim's *Anyone Can Whistle*, Guettel's music functions as two separate but interrelated scores that describe the two different worlds of the play. The music of the world above ground is a fairly authentic recreation of 1920s Kentucky bluegrass, its rhythms, its forms, and its instrumentation. The music of Floyd's world beneath the ground is in Guettel's own quirky, far more sophisticated musical language, owing much to Sondheim's tradition but also uniquely Guettel's voice. The underground music also hints at the now-familiar Americana style developed by Copland and used by many after him, full of open fifths and broad anthems.

The one exception to these two musical languages is the Act II opener, "Is That Remarkable?," a faux vaudeville number performed by three newspaper reporters. Again, as Sondheim did in *Anyone Can Whistle*, Guettel uses the musical vocabulary of early American musical theatre as the language of falsehood and insincerity. Is this a rejection by Guettel of traditional musical comedy? It's easy to see Sondheim's *Anyone Can Whistle*, the first of his truly groundbreaking scores, as such a rejection. Do Guettel and *Floyd Collins* also share this view? One might argue that "Remarkable," the only song in the show in that style, isn't integrated into the fabric of the score very well, belonging musically to neither the world above ground nor the world below ground. But it works because the very different sound of this song belongs to the very different reporters, the outsiders, the city slickers, the manipulators. They don't belong in this world, so they get music that doesn't belong in the show's musical world. It's a valid musical choice and the show's only old-fashioned showstopper.

In 1999, while the show was running at the Goodman Theatre in Chicago, Guettel added a new song, "Where a Man Belongs," to replace "Rock and a Hard Place." Though the new song is a strong one and better characterizes the community as a whole, it doesn't fit easily into the fabric of the show. First, though it takes place above ground, its music is more like the music of the underground. Second, it's about the community rather than individuals, about ideas rather than people, and it robs the audience of its initial identification with Bee Doyle, Ed Bishop, and Jewel Estes, which is so very important late in Act II. Guettel admits that it's often very difficult for a writer to come back and add material to a piece years after its creation, to get back fully into the world and vocabulary of the show. Just as Sondheim's later additions to his shows ("Make the Most of Your Music" in *Follies*, "Something Just Broke" in *Assassins*) feel grafted on rather than organic to the pieces, so does "Where a Man Belongs." And though Guettel prefers the later song, he acknowledges that others might disagree and prefer to use "Rock and a Hard Place."

The Act II musical sequence, "The Carnival," is mostly dialogue over underscoring, along with cave calls and yodeling from Floyd. At first glance, it seems that this piece also breaks the rule of the two styles; it takes place above ground but sounds like the music of the world underground. But at the end of the piece, we find that Skeets has been narrating this sequence to Floyd while Skeets digs. So in reality, the sequence takes place underground, in Floyd's imagination, as Skeets describes the vendors, the automobiles, the crowds, the balloons and souvenirs. So, strictly speaking, it follows the rule of the two styles, and perhaps it even offers us a clue that what we're seeing is yet another example of storytelling, a view of the world the only way Floyd can now see it—in his mind's eye.

Tying the Score

The use of musical themes and motifs has been a staple of opera for hundreds of years, but since the era of the modern musical in America, since Jerome Kern and Richard Rodgers, these devices have found their way into the more sophisticated American and British musicals. Sondheim has become the master of the practice and the younger generation of composers, including Adam Guettel, Jason Robert Brown, and others, has learned well from him and his scores.

Musical themes and motifs are bits of music (motifs are just shorter themes) that are tied to characters or ideas, to help tell the story, to connect people and ideas, to support textual themes, and to lend a sense of unity to the score. In *Floyd Collins*, almost all the motifs Guettel uses come from the opening caving sequence because Floyd going down and getting trapped is the genesis for everything going on above ground. Just as all the other action comes from his initial action, so too does so much of the other music come from this initial musical sequence. One of the most prevalent motifs is the echo phrase in "The Call," the four-note phrase that jumps way up on the second note, then skips back down (it's the last echo phrase before the lyric "There ain't never been another man in here"). This motif shows up in a lot of places throughout the score, representing Floyd's cave.

Much of the instrumental music that underscores Floyd getting trapped—called "Trapped" in the score—comes back whenever bad things happen in the cave, in Skeets' underscoring for "I Landed on Him," in the Act II cave-in, and in the shaft collapse. The first time Floyd gets trapped, the music also quotes the melody of the song "Lucky" at the end. It's an interesting moment because we haven't heard the song "Lucky" yet, so we can't yet recognize the melody. But this foreshadows Floyd's connection to Nellie, and once we do hear "Lucky," in which Nellie tells Miss Jane the things Floyd has told her, we hear a musical connection back to Floyd—an ironic connection since Nellie's talking about luck and yet the motif connects us back to the cave-in. Also, when we first hear it in the cave-in, it's dissonant, using "wrong" notes that distort the melody. It's not the pretty melody Nellie will soon sing; it shows us that Floyd's luck has gone wrong.

The nonsense syllables Floyd and Homer sing in "The Riddle Song" show up as a "brother" motif a few times in the show, representing the courage Homer brings Floyd. Floyd sings this musical snippet right before the cave-in that shuts him off from Homer and the others in Act II. Floyd senses the cave-in coming and it becomes his version of "Whistle a Happy Tune." This same motif shows up in the dream.

The solo violin at the beginning of Act II, as Homer acts for Cliff Roney's film, is a slow version of one of the main themes in "The Carnival," foreshadowing the craziness that's coming. Roney's movie is only the beginning of the insanity, the music is telling us; it's going to get worse and it's going to get even more out of control. Also, the accompaniment figure that starts "The Carnival" is a faster version of Floyd's cave echo motif from the beginning of the show. This echo motif and a motif from "Lucky" show up all over "The Carnival."

In the middle of Act II, as tempers flare between Homer and Lee, Nellie hears Floyd and starts singing to him music that's based on several of Floyd's echo calls from the beginning of the show, including

Floyd's four-note echo motif. The end of this musical underscoring also quotes other music from the opening caving sequence ("No more plowin' a hardscrabble field"), but this time it's dissonant and harsh, to underline the fact that Floyd was doing all this to impress Lee, to help the family, and now the family is being torn apart by it.

The dream is full of musical motifs. As Nellie prepares Floyd for crossing over, she starts with music that includes Floyd's four-note echo motif, the same music we heard when they connected psychically in Act I. Homer shows up in the dream, representing Floyd's dreams of success, and Homer's music reprises "Time to Go" from the opening sequence. This is the music of Floyd's dreams of success. As the dream crowd sings Floyd's praises, Floyd sings the brother motif from the "The Riddle Song." As the scene focuses on the family, we hear more music from the opening, this time another occurrence of the hardscrabble motif. This is Floyd's hope of making success for his family and finally getting approval from Lee. As the dream music gets busier and more complex, Nellie and Jane join Floyd in singing a melody from the beginning of the dream, a section in which Nellie reassures Floyd that everything's going to be okay. Family is where Floyd finds comfort and strength, and soon Homer adds a melody from "The Riddle Song" in counterpoint. But Lee is noticeably absent from this moment, because he is not a source of comfort or strength for Floyd. Still, later in the dream, as all the melodies come together, Lee does join the mix as he and Miss Jane sing the words *my boy* against the three kids singing the word *papa*. We see and hear that even though Floyd isn't as close to Lee, he still sees Lee as part of the family he loves so much, someone from whom he wants approval, and someone for whom he wants to make life easier through his success.

The dream climaxes as Floyd quiets everyone and demonstrates to them the immensity of his cave by doing his echo call from Act I. But this time, no echo returns. This is not the real world and things don't work the same way here. This is the first big clue that Floyd is dreaming, that he has not really been rescued. Floyd can't understand why no echo returns to him, and it's Lee, the one whose approval means everything to Floyd, who bursts Floyd's bubble, who tells him that it's all a dream, that Floyd is actually still trapped in Sand Cave. The crowd begins chanting Floyd's epitaph, "The Greatest Caver Ever Known" (actually, his real epitaph is "The Greatest Cave Explorer Ever Known"). Floyd is dead and it's time to cross over to the other side.

Ideally, the dream sequence should fool the audience as it fools Floyd. The audience should believe that Skeets broke through, and that like other artificial storytelling devices throughout the show, the way Nellie leads Floyd off the ramp where he was lying is just a stylistic device. But there are clues. Floyd rises easily up off the ramp just as he did in the fantasy sequences in "The Riddle Song." In the real world Floyd can come and go only through the hole over his head; he can just step off the ramp only in his imagination. Also, the lighting is different from the scenes in the real world. Some directors choose not to fully stage the carnival, to keep it as storytelling like the opening "Ballad of Floyd Collins," and like Skeets' various monologues, with the actors standing still onstage, facing the audience. This not only lends the show a degree of visual unity but also helps fool the audience during the dream into thinking that the unreality of the scene is just a stylistic choice.

Glory

The final song, "How Glory Goes," is one of the show's most moving moments and also a fascinating piece of theatre craft. The word *glory* figures prominently in the first and last of Floyd's songs, and we can see in the different ways the word is used in these two songs how Floyd's worldview has changed. In "The Call," Floyd says that the sound of the echoes in the cave is "the sound of glory" calling to him. The echoes, the voice of the cave, the symbiotic relationship Floyd feels with the cave represent to him his future—success, wealth, fame, respect, and comfort for his family. But over the course of the show, Floyd lets go of those dreams. Eventually, his only dreams of the future are surviving, being free, and being above ground. He lets go of his dreams of great success, although as we see in the dream sequence, he does not completely forget them. By the time the show ends, Floyd's idea of glory has changed. Now, glory is heaven, being with his mother and being with God.

What's so wonderful about the way Guettel and Landau wrote this last song is the utter consistency in Floyd's character. He knows he's going to heaven, but he wants to know what he's getting into. He wants to know what to expect. He's never been scared going caving because he always knew what to expect. He knew he was ready for anything. But heaven is a completely foreign place for him and he wants to be prepared. In the song, he asks God questions about what heaven will be like, and in his questions we see what Floyd's own vision of heaven is: being with his mother, trees, wide open spaces, lots of light, the smell of freshly baked bread, friends and family all around. At the very end, Floyd does what he knows best, what he always does when he goes into an unknown cave. He does his cave call out into the great unknown to see how big heaven is. That's what he knows, that's how he explores, and it only makes sense to him to measure the size of heaven the same way he measures the size of a new cave chamber. It's a very touching moment, a little funny, and exactly right.

Though Floyd dies, though we may wonder if he might have been rescued if there had been less chaos above ground, the end of the show is not really sad. After all, Nellie has rescued Floyd. She has shown him the way to heaven, where he will be reunited his mother. Floyd is going from one kind of heaven, his caves, into another kind of heaven. He's a born explorer and he's not afraid. In a very real sense, it's a happy ending.

Other Resources

The original off-Broadway cast album of *Floyd Collins* is available on CD. At press time, neither the script nor score had been published, but Guettel says there are plans to publish the piano vocal score and vocal selections. The most valuable tool in understanding these characters and the events that transpired while Floyd was trapped is the book *Trapped! The Story of Floyd Collins* by Robert K. Murray and Roger W. Bruckner, which was revised and expanded in 1999. This book chronicles the entire ordeal in great detail, day by day, hour by hour. It explores all the major players in detail. It also contains great pictures as well as diagrams of Sand Cave, Floyd's path down, and how and where he was trapped.

Also, it's still possible to visit Sand Cave and Floyd's grave in Cave City, Kentucky, and if you talk to the locals and get the insiders' secrets, you can also find Crystal Cave, down a long, unmarked dirt road, where Floyd's house and refreshment stand, the staircase Floyd built, and the entrance to the cave still stand. Both Crystal Cave and Sand Cave have been closed, but there are other caves in the area where you can take tours to get the feel of being down under. For any fans of the show, it's well worth the trip.

10   Rent

Book, music, and lyrics by Jonathan Larson
Original concept and additional lyrics by Billy Aronson
Originally directed on Broadway by Michael Greif

*In these dangerous times, where it seems the world is
ripping apart at the seams, we can all learn how to
survive from those who stare death squarely in the face
every day and [we] should reach out to each other and
bond as a community, rather than hide from the ter-
rors of life at the end of the millennium.*

Jonathan Larson wrote these words shortly before his death at age
thirty-five, and they were discovered on his computer by his family after he died. They serve as a fitting tribute to his only Broadway
musical, the megahit *Rent*. Larson, a hardworking, long-suffering, not
yet recognized composer-lyricist-bookwriter, had been working for
seven years on the cheerfully transgressive *Rent*, a 1990s rock/pop riff
on Puccini's beloved opera *La Bohème,* this time set in New York City's
East Village.

    Rent is so many things to so many people. It was the first musical
in decades that younger audiences really identified with, that spoke
in their voice, that voiced their concerns, that tackled their issues. It
breathed new commercial life into the Broadway musical, possibly sig-
naling the beginning of the end of the great divide between pop music and theatre music that had existed since the advent of rock and roll
in the 1950s. Even the title means different things to different people.
It represents the financial burden young people feel as they graduate
college full of knowledge but absent any marketable job skills, thrown
into a real world where high ideals don't pay the rent. But the title also
highlights the temporary nature of these characters' lives, the month-
to-month living without permanence or promises. The characters

Collins and Angel sing to each other in the song "I'll Cover You" that though love can't be bought, at least it can be rented. In other words, their happiness won't be forever—both of them have AIDS—but it's theirs for a while.

And the word *rent* also means torn, Larson's favorite meaning of the title, and certainly the characters in this show are torn between conflicting desires—between comfort and idealism, between love and dignity, between anger and pain, between the fear of intimacy and the fear of getting hurt. The word *rent* means shredded in grief or rage. It means split apart when it describes communities, families, or other relationships. And it also means torn open by painful feelings, something nearly every character in the show feels at some point. And all the complexity of that simple, four-letter word parallels the construction of this fascinating musical.

Larson's lifelong goal was to combine the Broadway tradition with contemporary pop music, a very difficult task at which many before him had failed. After seven years of workshops and rewrites, the show was scheduled to open in previews off Broadway at New York Theatre Workshop, on January 25, 1996. But Larson had been feeling ill. He'd been to two hospitals; one diagnosed him with food poisoning, the other with the flu. The night before the first preview, after a great final dress rehearsal, Larson went home, put a pot of water on the stove for tea, collapsed, and died of an aortic aneurysm.

The Phenomenon

In June 1993, New York Theatre Workshop did a reading of *Rent*. The show was a mess but showed real promise. Another reading was done in 1994, this time with director Michael Greif on board. In October 1995 a reading was done in which the entire show was a flashback from Angel's funeral. In December 1995 Larson finished another revision that returned to the earlier structure, and he wrote a one-sentence summary of the show: "*Rent* is about a community celebrating life, in the face of death and AIDS, at the turn of the century." This statement of purpose helped later on. After his death, as previews began, the artistic team found itself trying to figure out what Larson would have changed and what he would have kept working on. They went through his notes to see what he still had been unhappy with, and did their best to make decisions they thought he would have made. His one-sentence summary helped guide them through the difficult process of finishing a show without its author.

After two weeks of previews in early 1996, the show opened to rave reviews and standing ovations. Four months later it moved to Broadway and became the biggest thing to hit the Great White Way since *Phantom of the Opera.* Larson received a posthumous Pulitzer Prize for his work. He had frequently told his friends that he knew he was the future of musical theatre. And he just might have been if he'd had a chance.

The show moved to Broadway and opened at the Nederlander Theatre on April 29, 1996, to both mixed and rave reviews. The *New York Times* called it an "exhilarating, landmark rock opera" and said it "shimmers with hope for the future of the American musical." *Time* magazine called it "the most exuberant and original American musical to come along this decade." The *Wall Street Journal* called it "the best new musical since the 1950s." On opening night, the performance began with Anthony Rapp, who played Mark, dedicating the show to the memory of Jonathan Larson.

Rent was nominated for a staggering ten Tony Awards and won four, including Best Musical, Best Score, and Best Book. It won six Drama Desk Awards, three Obie Awards, the New York Drama Critics Circle Award for Best Musical, an Outer Critics Circle Award, and a Drama League Award.

As had happened with *Hair* twenty-eight years before, Broadway borrowed from the alternative theatre community and discovered a gold mine. In 1992, Larson had written of his show, "*Rent* also exalts Otherness, glorifying artists and counterculture as necessary to a healthy civilization." Larson and later many commentators called the show a *Hair* for the '90s, and indeed it shares much with the 1968 landmark rock musical. Daphne Rubin-Vega, who originated the role of Mimi, said, "We didn't want to go to Broadway to become Broadway stars; we went to kick the motherfuckin' doors of Broadway open, because it's old-school and stodgy. We were invited there and that was cool."

The show became a cultural phenomenon. The cast members soon found themselves in the *New York Times, Newsweek, Vanity Fair, Rolling Stone,* and *Harper's Bazaar.* They appeared on *The Late Show with David Letterman, The Charlie Rose Show,* and *The Tonight Show,* and sang "Seasons of Love" at the 1996 Democratic National Convention. Both *Hard Copy* and *Prime Time Live* did stories on the show.

Frank Rich, *New York Times* political columnist and former senior theatre critic, wrote in a *Times* op-ed piece, "At so divisive a time in our country's culture, *Rent* shows signs of revealing a large, untapped appetite for something better." Both the classical music reviewer and the pop music reviewer for the *Times* weighed in on *Rent*, neither raving but both finding much to admire.

Because the producers were as new to Broadway as the cast was, they did things very differently. They set aside the first two rows at each performance as twenty-dollar seats so that the people the show was about could afford to see it. These special tickets would go on sale at 6:00 P.M. each night and the line usually formed by noon on weekdays and often twenty-four hours in advance on weekends. *Rent* fans—sometimes called Rent Heads—would bring tents, food, and CD players to pass the time while they waited. Some had seen the show dozens of times. But in July 1997 the line was replaced with a lottery system. Still, the actors love having the twenty-dollar seats in front; they say the first two rows are always the most lively, the most passionate, and the most appreciative.

But after the opening, great controversy circled around the mega-hit. Larson's dramaturg from New York Theatre Workshop, Lynn Thompson, sued the family for part of the show's profits. She lost. Sarah Schulman, a playwright and novelist, sued the estate because she claimed Larson stole some of his plot and characters from her novel *People in Trouble*. She also lost. In fact, there is nothing in *Rent* that even comes close to the plot and characters of Schulman's book.

The Birth of *Rent*

Originally, the idea for *Rent* was Billy Aronson's, a young playwright who saw the similarities between *La Bohème*'s artists at the turn of the last century in Paris and the young artists at the turn of this century in America. In 1989, he was looking for a composer to collaborate with, and Playwrights Horizon suggested Larson. When the two met, Aronson said to Larson, "It's time for a new *Hair*."

Though they stuck to the basic plot of *La Bohème*, they exchanged tuberculosis for AIDS, and Paris for New York's East Village. In 1991, after only minimal progress, Larson asked Aronson's permission to go ahead on his own with *Rent* and Aronson bowed out. Larson decided to stray from Puccini's opera, to consult the novel on which the opera was based, *Scenes de la vie de bohème,* and to go his own way. The opera's poet Rodolfo became Roger the songwriter. Marcello the painter became Mark the filmmaker. Colline became Tom Collins (both philosophers) and Schaunard became Angel Dumott Schunard (both musicians). Musetta became Maureen the performance artist. Benoit the landlord became Benny the roommate-turned-landlord. And in Larson's greatest departure, Mimi the embroideress became Mimi the S&M dancer.

When *Rent* opened, everybody made a big deal out of its connection to *La Bohème*. But *Rent* is not an updated *La Bohème* or an adaptation; it's a response to it. The characters are similar, but that's where the comparison ends. While *La Bohème* romanticizes death, which was very trendy in 1896 when it premiered, *Rent* celebrates life with all its might, as evidenced by all the references to life in the show— the Life Café; Angel's group, Life Support; and others. While *Bohème* is tragic, *Rent* is joyous. While *Bohème*'s bohemian world is romantic and poetic, the world of *Rent* is tough, gritty, angry, and *real*. While *Bohème* has "Musetta's Waltz," *Rent* has the cynical "Tango Maureen." While *Bohème* observes the bohemians from a distance, *Rent* is written *by* a bohemian, someone who had trouble paying the rent, whose friends were dying of AIDS, and it fully inhabits that world.

Larson kept the basic character profiles and the establishing situation from Puccini's first act, but then he went off on his own. Like *Rent*, *Bohème* opens on Christmas Eve, while two artist roommates try to keep warm in their apartment. Rodolfo burns his manuscript for heat. Colline and Schaunard show up with food and wine and Schaunard tells them the wild tale of how he made some unexpected money that day. In *Bohème*, he's hired to play piano until he drives a parrot to death; in *Rent*, he's hired to play drums until he drives a dog to suicide. In *Bohème*, Schaunard announces he's taking them all out to eat. Benoit shows up asking for rent. All but Rodolfo leave for their favorite café, and once they're gone, Mimi appears, asking for a light for her candle, whereupon Rodolfo and Mimi fall in love. All that is also in *Rent*.

There's a very funny insider's joke in this scene in *Rent*, in the song "Light My Candle," a joke exclusively for fans of *La Bohème*. In *Bohème*, Mimi comes back the second time because she lost her key on Rodolfo's floor when she fainted. In *Rent*, Mimi comes back the second time also because she lost her key, but it's a different kind of key—a kilo of cocaine. (*Key* is drug users' slang for *kilo*.) So Larson has both remained true to *Bohème*—Mimi came back for her key—and

simultaneously updated it drastically. The other insider's joke in the
show is that *Rent*'s Roger is trying to write his one great song and keeps
coming up with something that sounds like Musetta's waltz from
La Bohème.

Up to this point, the two stories are basically the same. But then
Rent and *La Bohème* part company, as Larson's characters pursue more
'90s story lines. After the setup, only *Rent*'s flea market, the café, and
Mimi's (near) death have counterparts in the opera. However, Larson
takes the operatic Mimi's actual death and transfers it to Angel, while
Rent's Mimi survives. Larson wrote detailed biographies of all his characters and this gave him the freedom to leave the details of *Bohème*
behind and create his own world. In the biographies he wrote, as described in the *Rent* coffee-table book, Mark and Benny were roommates at Brown University; Roger's band was called the Well Hungari-
ans; Mimi left home when she was fifteen; and Maureen dreamed of
being a famous performance artist like Patti Smith or Laurie Anderson.

Rent is Larson's more positive view of the world, with details and
people from his own life mixed in to give the story resonance. In real
life, Larson himself actually had to throw his keys down to the street
for people to get into his apartment, and he had to run orange extension cords all over his apartment to make up for the lack of outlets.
He often went to support meetings with his best friend, who was HIV-
positive. He once lost a girlfriend to another woman. All of this found
its way into *Rent*, along with the names of three of his friends who
had died of AIDS, in the support group scene.

Though Larson strayed greatly from the opera, he used many details from the novel upon which the opera is based, *Scenes de la vie de
bohème* by Henri Murger. The book is unlike the opera in many ways,
particularly in its wonderful, raunchy sense of humor. The book is
funny, first and foremost, and the four friends are much more like the
four friends in *Rent* than they are like the characters in the opera. The
book is chock-full of rampant casual sex and other delightful deca-
dences, a remarkable thing for a book written in the 1840s. Also in
the book, Mimi's great tragic death of tuberculosis really belongs to a
one-chapter character named Francine, who was in love with a man
named Jacques, who died of grief a few days after Francine died. Lots
of details in *Rent* come from the book: the importance of Collins' coat,
their regular restaurant where they often order nothing and don't always pay the bill, the constant burning of manuscripts and letters for

heat, Marcel/Mark's decision to sell out his art, and the structural significance of Christmas Eve. The novel makes a strong and constant point of the fact that the four bohemians are fairly irresponsible, selfish, and immature—though utterly charming—a charge leveled by critics against Larson's characters. Also, in the book, Rudolf is able to write his one great poem only after Mimi has left him, paralleling Roger's song "Your Eyes." And just as the song revives Mimi in the musical, Mimi in the novel sees Rudolf's poem in a magazine and it's (indirectly) what brings them together again. Also, the novel is organized into dozens of short, seemingly randomly ordered and unconnected incidents. When critics complained about *Rent*'s structure, they probably didn't realize it mirrored the original novel.

There are differences, too. In the novel, Rudolf actually marries Mimi, but they separate after eight months because Mimi has champagne tastes and cheats on him repeatedly with rich men (mirroring Mimi and Benny in *Rent*). Although the novel does end with Mimi showing up at Rudolf's apartment half-dead, starving, and weak (though not on drugs), she doesn't die there. They call the doctor and put her in the hospital, from which a false report of her death is delivered to Rudolf. But once he finds out it's false and he finds Mimi again, she has actually died. (And people thought *Rent* could get confusing!)

Why It Shouldn't Have Worked

There are so many reasons that *Rent* should not have worked, that it should not have been a success off Broadway, much less *on* Broadway, much less an international phenomenon. First, rock and roll does not work in the theatre. Admittedly, that's a pretty broad statement, but it's almost always true. Certainly, *Hair* worked, but to this day no one really knows why. Several shows have succeeded that employed a watered-down, Broadway-pop vocabulary, such as *Jesus Christ Superstar, Evita, Cats, Les Misérables, Miss Saigon,* and *Jekyll & Hyde,* but those scores are not real rock. And *Tommy* doesn't really count because it was a hugely successful rock album and movie decades before it ever hit Broadway; it's impossible to know if it would have succeeded without its reputation. And it too was pretty watered-down and sanitized on Broadway. Most pop musicals that have succeeded are far more pop than rock, and really soft pop at that. With the obvious exceptions of *Hair* and *Tommy*, when Broadway tries to speak in the voice of genuine rock and roll, the show is almost always a flop.

The reason is that in rock music the most important element is the beat. The melody, the chords, and the lyrics are often very repetitive and they all serve the beat. Generally, it's the emotion and energy that matter, not the intellectual content. But in theatre music, the lyrics are the most important element. The lyrics not only have to be heard and understood—not always a priority in rock—but they also have to tell the story, to advance plot and character. To do that, they have to convey clearly a lot of information in very few words; repetition is a luxury modern theatre composers and lyricists can't afford.

So it follows that *Rent* shouldn't have worked because its music is genuine rock and roll (though more '70s than '90s). But theatre audiences loved it and so did the pop music audience, though hardcore rockers denounced it as imitation. Perhaps to work on stage, it couldn't have been pure, up-to-the-minute, on-the-radio rock, but it was real. Larson was as tuned in to rock as he was to traditional Broadway musicals, and he did the near impossible by successfully blending the two without emasculating either, creating a kind of Broadway fusion rock that satisfied both audiences. The CD quickly became the best-selling cast album of the decade.

But the question remains: why did it work? Were Broadway audiences ready for *Rent* because the blander Broadway pop of Andrew Lloyd Webber had prepared them to accept a more legitimate rock sound? Did *Tommy* help pave the way? Or was the success of *Rent* due to an audience rebellion against the abundance of elevator pop on Broadway? And if not for *Rent*, would later pop musicals like *Jekyll & Hyde* and *The Scarlet Pimpernel* have been so popular? It's impossible to know for sure.

The second reason *Rent* shouldn't have worked is that it was a big mess. Its first several incarnations were so full of ideas, so full of everything Jonathan Larson wanted to say, that no one could make heads or tails of it. There were so many themes he wanted to explore, so much of his wide-eyed optimism and naïveté that he wanted to inject into his story, so many plot lines. And the specter of *La Bohème* was always getting in the way. It wasn't until director Michael Greif—and dramaturg Lynn Thompson and several others—entered the picture that a coherent story began to emerge.

And there were other issues. Many of the people involved thought his early depiction of homeless people was naïve and borderline offensive. Many people thought too many of his characters were one-dimensional. And Larson could be very defensive, very closed to outside feedback. But luckily, as he began to trust Greif and others, he opened up and listened to what they had to say. He began to trust their criticisms and make changes. But he never finished his show. For many musicals, the preview period is when the most important work gets done, and Larson died before previews began. Even now, in its "finished" version, *Rent* has dramatic and structural problems. Is it better for its roughness and imperfection, more accessible, more loveable for its flaws? Quite possibly.

The third reason it shouldn't have worked is that Broadway audiences generally don't want to see musicals about overtly sexual gays and lesbians (although the desexualized varieties are okay) or S & M dancers, drug addicts, drag queens, or performance artists. And they certainly don't want to see these people have simulated sex onstage. Like *Hair* did, *Rent* brought forbidden content to Broadway and ended up a commercial success. This is even more surprising in an era when Disney is becoming the king of Broadway with its sanitized, family-friendly, substance-free musicals selling out and winning Tony Awards. Was *Rent*'s success due to a backlash against a Broadway turning to Disney and the bloodless pop musicals epitomized by the work of Frank Wildhorn? Were Broadway audiences hungry for more adult fare? Did the growing prevalence of gay and lesbian characters on TV and in movies make audiences more comfortable with this material? Did Larson's innocence and generosity of spirit come through these characters so warmly that audiences couldn't help but care about them? Again, it's impossible to know.

Some critics complained that there was no irony in the material, no cynicism, none of "Sondheim's frosty intellectualism," as one critic put it, that everything in *Rent* was laid bare, right there on the surface. Perhaps that's another reason audiences embraced it.

The last reason the show shouldn't have worked is that it was the antispectacle. It had virtually no set—a couple of tables, folding chairs, a platform for the band, and a junk sculpture on one side of the stage. Its costumes came from the actors' own closets and from thrift stores. The show looked sparser and more low-budget than anything in years. This low-rent show (pun intended) opened at a time when the other hits on Broadway were *Sunset Boulevard*, *Show Boat*, *Beauty and the Beast*, *Les Misérables*, *Miss Saigon*, *Phantom of the Opera*, *Cats*, and a tastelessly overproduced *Grease*, expensive spectacles one and all. Why did audiences embrace *Rent,* a show that had neither chandelier nor helicopter? Then again, though *Les Misérables* had the turntable and barricade, many of its scenes were played on a bare stage. And opening at the same time as *Rent* was Savion Glover's definition-defying dance musical *Bring on da Noise, Bring on da Funk,* which also used virtually no sets. Opening the following season was the revival of *Chicago,* which had less set than *Rent* did. Maybe the time was just right. Maybe audiences were just ready. Maybe they were sick of empty calories.

But aside from all of these problems with the show as a whole, there are also some other problems that may or may not have been fixed had Larson not died. Despite its much-touted diversity—blacks, Latinos, gays and lesbians, cross-dressers, junkies—the two main characters, including the story's narrator, are both straight white guys from suburbia, just like Larson was. Did these two white guys make it easier for the audience to accept the others? Were the others just tokens? People argued both sides of the issue.

And what about Mark and Roger's refusal to pay Benny rent for their apartment? Why is that portrayed as such a gutsy gesture? Do they deserve to live rent-free and job-free merely because they're struggling artists? And let's not forget that they're struggling artists *by choice.* They could get jobs. Larson did; he waited tables for a living. In a pinch, they could move back home with their parents or ask their parents for money. Their self-identification with the *real* homeless people seems artificial, and perhaps even a bit offensive. It's safe to say that most of the homeless people living in the tent city on Benny's lot are not there by choice, some probably suffering from mental illness, addiction, and who knows what else? Then again, this issue was raised over *Hair*—why were these kids panhandling on the streets when they came from middle-class suburban homes, when most of them were college-educated? Is it idealism, naïveté, or just arrogance when Mark and Roger declare they're not going to pay rent this year or even next year?

Back to the Future

Rent didn't really break that much genuinely new ground—one might argue that Greif's staging did more than Larson's material—but like *Oklahoma!* fifty years earlier, its triumph was in bringing together what had gone before it, combining many past innovations all in one new work, and doing it with great skill, and more important, great success. As mentioned before, innovations generally get carried on only if they show up in hit shows. In fact, Larson's great achievement and the reason for *Rent*'s enormous appeal to so many different kinds of people lies precisely in the heady mix of musical theatre traditionalism and innovation.

The show's influences are many. Like the early musicals of Tim Rice and Andrew Lloyd Webber (*Jesus Christ Superstar, Evita*) and the musicals of Schönberg and Boublil (*Les Misérables, Miss Saigon*), *Rent* is through-sung, with almost no spoken dialogue. This is certainly nothing new. Broadway's pop operas have been around since the early 1970s and though their often overblown spectacle has fallen out of vogue for the moment, the pop operas will no doubt continue. (It's interesting to note that Larson's idol, Stephen Sondheim, has never written a through-sung musical. Sondheim enjoys the back-and-forth between spoken dialogue and singing.) Like Lloyd Webber and Schönberg, Larson wrote self-contained songs as well as duets, group numbers (some with beautiful, carefully constructed counterpoint and harmonies), and operatic-style recitative, using the structural vocabulary of classical opera with the harmonic and rhythmic language of rock. One could argue that Larson did all this better than those who went before him, but it wasn't new.

I pause here for some parenthetical comments about one of my greatest pet peeves. Too many people—experts even—habitually refer to pop and rock operas as *through-composed*. This is not correct. What they mean is *through-sung*, meaning that there is no dialogue, that everything is sung. *Through-composed* means something entirely different. It means that the music never repeats itself, that no two verses have the same music, that there are no reprises in Act II, that the composer writes different music for every moment. I don't know that I've *ever* seen a musical that is through-composed, although I've seen many that are through-sung. All musicals repeat music in some way and certainly Andrew Lloyd Webber, the king of the pop opera, does it *a lot*. Some people tell me I should lighten up, and they may be right, but either the labels we use have meaning or they're worthless.

Larson also wasn't the first to adapt classical opera for the musical theatre. Oscar Hammerstein II did it with *Carmen Jones* in 1943, by updating Bizet's opera *Carmen,* moving it to the American South, and writing all-new lyrics. Jim Luigs and Scott Warrender did it in 1995 with *Das Barbecü*, which recast Wagner's operatic *Ring* cycle as a country-and-western musical comedy, but this was more parody than adaptation. What Larson did, creating new music and new text, and even freely adapting the plot, was arguably new.

In a very real way, Larson borrowed from the musicals of the '20s and '30s and the work of the Gershwins, Cole Porter, Rodgers and Hart, and others, by writing in a genuine pop music style, a style that audiences hear in their everyday lives, a style that instantly makes the language of the musical accessible to the untrained ear. Surely today, no one can escape rock/pop music. It's in the movies, in commercials, even in dentists' offices. And like the songwriters of the '20s and '30s did, Larson tells his story in the musical language of the people, something Broadway has rarely done—or at least rarely done well— since the 1950s.

Larson followed the lead of Rodgers and Hammerstein's early musicals (*Oklahoma!, Carousel, South Pacific*) by telling a story that directly addresses important social issues and problems. And as in *Oklahoma!*, Larson's story is about a threat to the community; in *Oklahoma!* it's Jud Fry, in *Rent* it's AIDS. He used long-form musical scenes, which were first developed by Hammerstein in *Show Boat* with Jerome Kern and in *Oklahoma!* and *Carousel* with Richard Rodgers, a device perfected by Larson's mentor, Stephen Sondheim, most notably in *Sweeney Todd*. And like Sondheim did in *Sweeney*, Larson even quoted the dies irae, a musical motif from the mass for the dead, in the song "La Vie Boheme." He also mentioned Sondheim in that song. Larson also learned from Hammerstein's example that the truly great writers always write what they believe. Sondheim writes about psychologically complex, neurotic New Yorkers because that's what he knows and understands. Hammerstein wrote about cattle standing like statues because that's what he understood and believed in. And like Hammerstein, Larson wrote with tremendous optimism, an almost embarrassing naïveté, and a genuine love of life, because that's who he was, despite living in the midst of the AIDS pandemic and watching many of his closest friends die. But like Sondheim, Larson also focused more than anything else on the way people connect (and fail to connect), one of the most important themes in *Rent*, as evidenced by Larson's quote at the beginning of this chapter, and a theme Sondheim returns to in almost every one of his shows.

Larson followed in the footsteps of *West Side Story* in depicting the seamy, gritty side of life on the streets of New York, and in the footsteps of William Finn's *Falsettos* trilogy in his matter-of-fact treatment of gay characters. Like *Grand Hotel* and Sondheim's *Into the Woods,* Larson successfully manipulated numerous story lines, weaving them in and out of one another. He followed *Cabaret* and *Company* in their treatment of social issues and their use of commentary songs. He and Greif followed *The Fantasticks* and *A Chorus Line* by using virtually no set.

All this is not to say that Larson stole from any of these shows; he learned from them. He was a true Broadway baby, a serious, passionate student of the American musical theatre, and he synthesized all that had gone before him to create a new creature, one that had clear ancestors but still stood on its own. He did in 1996 what Rodgers and Hammerstein did in 1943 with *Oklahoma!*—he knocked Broadway on its ass. We can only hope that, like *Oklahoma!*, Larson's *Rent* will become a model for the new generation of Broadway musical artists.

The (Second) Age of Aquarius

Jonathan Larson was born and died under the sign of Aquarius, fitting for the man who wanted to write the *Hair* for the '90s. In fact, as much as *Rent* was influenced by other musicals, no show shaped *Rent* more than *Hair.* The two shows are alike in so many ways. Both originated off Broadway and moved to Broadway. Both intentionally cast some actors who had no stage experience at all. Both used costumes that came from thrift stores and actors' closets to add a sense of realism. Neither show had much set. Both shows were a weird mix of concert and musical (like the subsequent off-Broadway sensation *Hedwig and the Angry Inch*), with both scores relying to some degree on list songs and even sharing some of the same references—sodomy, marijuana, Ginsberg, Antonioni, and others. Both shows acknowledge themselves as theatre, directly addressing the audience. In *Rent,* Mark actually speaks many of the stage directions. In *Hair,* the actors interact with the audience. Both shows are about drugs (marijuana in *Hair,* heroin in *Rent*), death (Vietnam in *Hair,* AIDS in *Rent*), and a strong sense of community as family. Both shows deal seriously with spirituality but reject traditional religious practices.

Both shows also rejected traditional Broadway staging techniques and both borrowed techniques from the experimental theatre movement, because both directors came from the experimental theatre community. In fact, the static, presentational staging of "Seasons of Love" in *Rent* was considered revolutionary by some, but it's taken directly from the staging of "Let the Sun Shine In" in *Hair*. Both shows were perceived to have plot problems—no plot in *Hair*, a messy plot in *Rent*—and in fact, both shows were meant to feel messy and unpolished.

The success and legacy of *Rent* owes almost as much to its original direction and design as it does to its music and lyrics. Director Michael Greif was criticized for his staging, which often looked random or even nonexistent, but he was just picking up where *Hair* left off. Greif was creating a new kind of musical theatre staging, a theatrical equivalent to cinéma vérité, the documentary style of filmmaking in which no directorial control is evident, in which real life is merely recorded without being manipulated. Now, obviously, it's tough for a musical to be completely natural because most people don't break into song spontaneously, and even fewer have a band to back them up. But Greif got as close to cinéma vérité as musical theatre can get, aiming for the impression that these actors are making it up as they go, that they've assembled on this nearly empty stage and are acting out their lives for us. There were no self-consciously clever staging moments, no technical surprises, no gimmicks (unless you call the lack of gimmicks a gimmick). In all these ways, it picked up the central ideas of *Hair*. It was different, it was startling, and it was scary to musical theatre traditionalists. Greif has said that he staged "Seasons of Love" first and the sparse, static staging of that number then determined the look of the rest of the show.

Inside Jonathan

Just as the authors of *Hair*, Jim Rado and Gerry Ragni, used their lives and the lives of their friends as material, Larson did the same with *Rent*. As mentioned earlier, many small details of his life found their way into the show, as did the names of friends lost to AIDS. And Roger and Mark are clearly two sides of Larson, both the artist-observer and the artist determined to leave behind something of value. Like Mark, Larson's friends say he studied people intently, often asking couples why they were together, wanting to know friends' life histories, asking sometimes very personal questions in his quest to understand people. A friend says that on the last night of his short life, Larson told him that he had learned from an HIV-positive friend that it's not how many years a person lives that counts, it's how you fulfill the time you spend here, a philosophy Larson certainly shared with Roger.

Larson also injected his hopelessly sunny disposition and impossible optimism into Angel, the heart of *Rent*. Though Larson died, he lives on in these characters.

Like *Hair*, *Rent* is about the things its creator thought were important. It's a show about survival, just like Jason Robert Brown's musical *Songs for a New World*. Perhaps the message of this generation is that the real heroism is in living, in just making it from one day to the next, against greater odds than a more generous universe would allow. Though many musicals have dealt with death, though some have even killed off their heros, never before has a Broadway musical included four main characters living with AIDS.

Still, the show rarely focuses on death and rarely gets depressing. It's uplifting even as it deals frankly with tragedy. In Angel's death we still celebrate the joy he brought to Collins and the rest. *Rent* deals in spirituality even though it doesn't mention God. The church of *Rent* is Life itself—the Life Café, Angel's group, Life Support, the life teeming through the streets of New York City, the life force that rages through each character as they all struggle to survive. Mark's song "Halloween" asks why this extended family of friends was brought together and the answer is that they are one another's church, one another's reason for celebration and for thanks. Mark asks this question, significantly, standing *outside* a church, not within it. Mainstream religion does not offer this generation what it seeks. Like the generation of *Hair* thirty years earlier, their answers aren't in the Bible; their answers are in the sense of family and community they all share.

And like *Hair*, *Rent* is not just about a community of characters; it's also about the community of artists who created it. Just as each cast of *Hair* takes a tribal name and becomes a family in very real ways, so too does each cast of *Rent* form deep, lasting bonds. It's the nature of the material.

The Legacy of *Rent*

Rent's legacy is tough to estimate just a few years after its opening. Certainly, it will ruin the voices of a generation of singers. Because the producers want actors who don't feel like actors, as Larson wanted, many of them are untrained and don't know how to warm up their voices and bodies before a show, how to rest their voices on days off, how to prepare their bodies for a kind of abuse few people ever experience. Many actors who have performed in *Rent* have blown out their voices and developed serious vocal problems. This was less of a problem with *Hair* because no single actor had all that much music to sing, but in *Rent*, several characters sing a great deal of music each night. In August 1997, the *New York Times* did an article on absenteeism in *Rent* and in Savion Glover's *Noise/Funk*. At some performances of *Rent*, as many as nine out of fifteen cast members would be missing. This had also been a problem with *Hair*, but due more to drugs than to sore throats.

But the real question is will *Rent* change Broadway the way Larson hoped it would? So far it hasn't. Would it have been different if Larson had lived? Maybe. Who knows what his next show would have been like? Then again, maybe Larson's other shows wouldn't have made it to Broadway. Maybe they wouldn't have been the near masterpiece that *Rent* was. The other young composers making their marks on Broadway are more often following in the tradition of Sondheim's sophisticated, complex musicals than following Larson's populist lead. Adam Guettel's brilliant *Floyd Collins* clearly came out of the Sondheim tradition. Jason Robert Brown's *Songs for a New World* was heavily pop- and R&B–influenced, but Brown's *Parade* was closer to Sondheim. Frank Wildhorn's musicals *Jekyll & Hyde*, *The Scarlet Pimpernel*, and others came directly out of the Top 40s sound, but they don't succeed as theatre, really amounting to nothing more than *Star Search* with a slight story, so he won't be the heir to Larson's legacy. Maybe the only hope resides in a new voice we haven't heard yet that will appear on the scene as suddenly as Larson's did, who will finish the work of putting musical theatre and pop music back together again, without sacrificing the integrity of either, the way Larson did so brilliantly and so lovingly.

Other Resources

The original Broadway cast album has been released on CD and several songs have been published in vocal selections. The script has been published in a handsome coffee-table book, along with lots of photos and interviews with Larson's family and friends. Several versions of *La Bohème* are on video. Murger's novel, *Scenes de la vie de bohème*, on which the opera is based, is out of print, but it's terribly funny and worth hunting for.